H. L. Eads.

SHAKER SERMONS:

SCRIPTO-RATIONAL.

CONTAINING THE SUBSTANCE OF

SHAKER THEOL...

TOGETHER WITH

REPLIES ... CRITICISM ...

LOGICALLY ...

H. L. EADS,

Bishop of South Union, Ky.

"The Supreme Good of the mind is the knowledge of God ..."—*Spinoza.*

"There is no science in the world but ... the highest position ..."—*Herbert Spencer.*

"And this is life eternal, that they might know Thee ... and Jesus Christ, whom Thou hast sent."—*John.*

SHAKER SERMONS:

SCRIPTO-RATIONAL.

CONTAINING THE SUBSTANCE OF

SHAKER THEOLOGY.

TOGETHER WITH

REPLIES AND CRITICISMS

LOGICALLY AND CLEARLY SET FORTH.

BY

H. L. EADS,

BISHOP OF SOUTH UNION, KY.

"The Supreme good in the mind is the knowledge of God, and the highest virtue of the mind is to know God." — SPINOZA.

"There is no soul so feeble but that, well directed, it may attain to absolute control over the [animal] passions." — DESCARTES.

"And this is life eternal, that they might know Thee the only true God and Jesus Christ whom Thou hast sent." — CHRIST.

NEW EDITION
REVISED AND ENLARGED.

...

SHAKERS, N. Y.
THE SHAKER MANIFESTO.
1884.

CONTENTS.

iv   TABLE OF CONTENTS.

PREFACE BY THE EDITOR.

This BOOK OF SERMONS scarcely needs a preface The author and orator began life among the Shakers when less than one year old, and may therefore be supposed to be excellent authority upon Shaker theology He was born in North Logan county, on the south side of Gasper river, on the 28th day of April, 1807. For fifteen years his home was in a log cabin, in which also, from four to thirteen years of age, during the winter months only, he received his entire instruction in letters. This is the first book ever written for publication, by an individual whose whole life has been consecratedly devoted to and guided by the principles of Shakerism , and the tenor of the discourses denotes "words fitly spoken, like apples of gold in pictures of silver " The sermons embrace nearly or quite every feature of Shaker polity, and will be highly appreciated by very many as a book of reference upon the subject of Shakerism. That the author is a most excellent representation of what Shaker principles can do for a man, we are only proud to vouch therefor ; and we feel a certainty that in the perusal of the following pages by the seeker after truth, the reader will feel the hallowed influences of one who has been with the Christ, and who walks and lives with the Christ ; and will also realize that he is one of the " *Saviours to come upon mount Zion, to judge the mount of Esau.*" To the rearing of such individuals as Saviours is Shakerism devoted. That it is successful, as evidenced in the author of these Sermons, gives a renewed confidence that *Virgin Purity, Non-resistance, Peace, Equality of Inheritance and Unspottedness from the world — the fundamental principles of Shakerism —* have not been, nor are they preached and practiced in vain.

☆

HARMONY OF TRUTH.

I begin my discourse with the enunciation of two or three aphorisms; neither of which, I presume, any honest, unbiased mind, of ordinary comprehension, will have an inclination to gainsay; for they consist of a simple declaration of the *harmony* of *truth*.

FIRST. — All truths, both spiritual and natural, harmonize. One truth cannot be opposed to another truth; hence, any two statements or propositions that antagonize or conflict, one or the other, or both, must be false.

SECONDLY. — In the end, nothing but truth will have been or can be advantageous to any soul; hence, it would be wisdom in us to cast off all prejudice and prepossession, and make any required sacrifice to obtain the "knowledge of the truth," especially that sacred truth by which we expect to obtain our redemption and the salvation of the soul. It is necessary that some of our discourses should be mainly argumentative or theological, from the fact that mere declaration of truth, scriptural or otherwise, does not in this day seem to satisfy the inquisitive mind, and people must learn to *think* correctly before they can either *speak* or *act* correctly.

Well nigh two centuries ago a certain philosopher penned the following:

FIRST. — That a man use no words but such as he makes the sign of a certain determined object in his mind in thinking, which he can make known to another.

SECONDLY. — That he use the same word steadily for the sign of the same immediate object of his mind in thinking

THIRDLY. — That he join those words together in propositions, according to the grammatical rules of the language he speaks in.

FOURTHLY. — That he unite those sentences into a coherent discourse. Thus, and thus only, I humbly conceive, can any one preserve himself from the confines and suspicions of jargon

Were all men to observe these rules, which I most sincerely approve, there would be but little difference among men on any subject. With their terms clearly defined, strictly applied and adhered to, no two really honest men can very widely differ; each would yield in turn in theology and ethics, just as they are compelled to do in mathematics.

Every rational creature will admit that the salvation of the soul is, or should be, paramount to every earthly consideration whatever, and he who fails in the attainment of this fails in all, and he who is fortunate enough to secure this lacks in nothing that is worth contending for. "For what is a man profited if he shall gain the whole world and lose his own soul?" or "what shall a man give in exchange for his soul." Matt. xvi, 26. Since then, from these words of our Saviour, a man's soul is of more value to him than all worlds beside, he ought to be willing to forsake the world, with all its habits, customs, maxims and practices, for his soul's sake.

It appears that this globe now contains over 1,100,000,000 souls, and there are eleven hundred different religions — one creed, if I may so speak, for every hundred millions, differing from all the rest; and, as there can be but *one* right way, a hollow cry comes up from the "vasty deep" asking which one of the eleven hundred is right. Any line diverging in the minutest degree from the *right* one *must be wrong*, and the further it is traveled the more distant the traveler will be from the right way; hence it becomes a matter of the utmost importance for each one to *know he is right* — not to *guess* at it, but KNOW it. You will ask me, then, if there is any possibility of acquiring this knowledge; and in response I give an affirmative answer. In the words of the Saviour, as to the doctrine, he says: "My doctrine is not mine, but His that sent me. If any man will *do His will* he shall *know* of the doctrine whether it be of God," etc. Matt iii, 8. Not *guess* at it, but *know*. As to His true disciples and followers, He has given us one criterion or mark — and one only — by which they are to be known: "Ye shall know them by their *fruits* Do men gather grapes of thorns or figs of thistles?" But after all this, and without troubling yourselves to look into the different sects for the good fruits, which are the only real evidence, you rest in your easy chair, simply saying you know

"The good must merit God's peculiar care,
But who but God can tell us who they are?"

thus giving evidence of one of two conditions, viz.: Your own lukewarmness and lack of interest in your soul's salvation, or your infidelity respecting the existence of any religious body where those fruits can be found; and some of you, when you have found the fruits and acknowledge them, then find *fault* with the *doctrine* — at the same time acknowledging you do not keep the commandments of God ; and it is only such that should know of the doctrines or should presume to judge them.

Nearly all men agree that among the thousand forms of religious belief some *one* must be right, and, as before said, the consequence is, that every other one that essentially differs with it must be wrong and inadequate to the purposes of salvation. Every religious system has for its foundation or formation some reference to a Supreme Being or Beings, who is, or are able to reward its followers for well doing, and punish them for evil doing, and, as this seems to be the beginning of religion itself, I purpose offering a few remarks on this subject I shall try to remember what I said in the beginning respecting the necessity of having distinct ideas in the mind, defining terms, etc., for I by no means wish to leave the thoughtful part of the audience, especially, in the dark respecting my own position. Laying aside all others for the present, I bring myself to the ground called Christian, whose religious systems have been taken from this Book — the old and new Testaments; and so multifarious are the forms derived from the same reading that it seems to almost justify the remark, that,

> " Faith, gospel, all seemed made to be disputed,
> And none had sense enough to be confuted "

I am not so uncharitable as to conclude that this state of things has arisen entirely from the dishonesty of the race, but rather more from education, prepossession, and a want of distinct ideas, clear definitions of terms, and their consistent application.

GOD, UNITY AND DUALITY RECONCILED.

No critical Bible student can fail to have taken cognizance of this truth · that throughout sacred writ *God* is spoken of in two senses, the *infinite* and the *finite*, or subordinate sense. Thus, whenever God is spoken of as coming, going, traveling personally from one place to another, it then must be understood in the *finite* or *subordinate* sense ; because in this sense He is considered as being *less* than something else If He travel, there must be some place where He is not, to which He is going; hence, He must be circumscribed. We cannot help associating with such being the idea of extension, figure, size, etc.,— such as angel or man. Also, when God is represented as having forgotten something, not knowing, or changing His mind or purpose, it is understood as speaking of God *subordinate*, not *infinite*. Of the Infinite, or Supreme Being, it is truly said, " *His* purposes alter not — HE *is without* change or shadow of turning." The same holy writ makes the distinction clear by the saying of Christ. When accused by the Jews of making himself God, He showed them that they were " called gods unto whom the word of God came." Moses was God to the children of Israel in this subordinate sense : " And the Lord said unto Moses, see, I have made thee a god' to Pharaoh ; and Aaron, thy brother, shall be thy prophet," etc. Exodus, vii, 1. Joshua was called Jehovah. Elijah, God the Lord, etc. To the careful reader the distinction is clear. But God, when spoken of as " the All and in all," " in whom we live and move and have our being," is understood to be the " Eternal Unity," the " Infinite " Jehovah, and He it is whom we have assembled here to worship, and Him only. Almost without exception every intelligent, unbiased mind, with whom I have come in contact, acknowledges that God in the supreme sense, is Infinite spirit-indivisible, immutable, uncaused, self-existent, omniscient, and omnipresent, filling immensity — the creator and arbiter of the Universe, permeating all worlds and all existences at all times, which remove the necessity of His going and coming. But, strange as it must appear, many good-meaning persons, after this admission, stultify themselves by admitting a plurality of supremes, or divisibility in the Supreme, to favor some theological dogma or scheme of redemption, that they have fixed in their own minds, or others have fixed there for them. The merest tyro, having taken but his first lesson in inductive philosophy, cannot help realizing the fact that an infinite existence is indivisible. *Truth never conflicts.* The term infinite signifies " *without bounds.*" This seems to be either forgotten or ignored. We say of space that it is *infinite*, but draw a line through it ; we then have *two finite spaces*, when infinite space disappears. I know it may be argued that a line beginning at a given point and extending in any direction without end may be called an infinite line, and that this idea might, by parity of reasoning, be applied to dividing space ; and even should this be conceded as sound reasoning, which I deny, the same cannot be applied to an infinite being or existence. Thus, I think it clearly demonstrated that such a thing as an infinite plurality, or *plurality of infinites*, is impossible. I am aware that *we* are believed to hold to the dogma of duality in Deity, male and female, which may seem repugnant to reason. But I will try to clear this point. It is admitted by all that of the attributes ascribed to Deity some are considered masculine, others feminine; and hence comes the idea of Father and Mother of the universe. We admit the revelation of these attributes of the *Eternal Unity* by son and daughter; that is to say, *God as father*, or the *fatherly character of God*, was *revealed by the Son, Christ Jesus;* and *God* as *mother*, or the *motherly character of God*, was *revealed by the daughter* (Ann Lee). Thus, " God manifest in the flesh," not of *man only* but also of *woman, male and female*, constitutes the duality of God, and dual only in this subordinate sense being equally manifest in and through finite human beings, who are dual, male and female Thus the apparently conflicting ideas of unity and duality are reconciled. In this I can perceive nothing irrational, nothing but what any dispassionate, reasonable mind would readily admit. I will, however, very frankly allow, that, any man who should declare that God in the highest sense was the *Eternal Unity*, and afterward declare he was the *Eternal Duality*, or *Eternal Trinity*, (*Eternal Three*) would stultify himself, because either of the latter would negative the former, and we should not know at last what the man did believe I fully concur in the remarks of John Locke on this subject. " Every deity " that men own above *one* is an infallible evidence of their ignorance of Him, and a proof that they have no true notion of God (in the highest sense) where unity, infinity, and eternity are excluded " But if, as Christ says, "they were called gods, unto whom the word of God came, that the scriptures might not be broken," I have no difficulty in applying this high term in the subordinate sense to the Son of God. Nor would I exclude Jeremiah from among the number of the " prophets of the Lord," for applying the same high title to the daughter. " This is the name whereby *she* shall be called : The Lord our righteousness." Jer. xxxiii, 16. Perhaps I have drawn too largely on your patience, but I wished to make a fair beginning, so as to leave no one in the dark, to carp at our doctrines without understanding them. We claim that the son and daughter already named now stand at the head of the new creation of

God, and we, their children, in the " unity of their spirit and the
bond of peace," are striving to follow their example, by obeying
their teaching and walking as they walked, and by so doing have
found that peace which this world can neither give nor take away,
and may become " heirs and joint heirs with Christ," who has
said : " Be of good cheer, for I have overcome the world ; " the
"prince of this world cometh and hath nothing in me," "and to
him that overcometh will I grant to sit with me in my throne,
as I also overcame and am sit down with my Father in His throne."
Rev iii, 21.　　These are the great and glorious promises to all
who will take up a daily cross and follow Christ in the *regeneration* — not *generation*, but *re-*generation ; not to those who have
a blind faith in his atoning blood and still lead a worldly life;
but to those who " walk even as He walked," and " have followed
Him in the regeneration "　And the invitation is now extended
to every sin-sick soul.　To every one who " panteth after righteousness as the hart for the water-brook," we " say come, without
money or without price " and " partake of the waters of life freely,"
for now has come salvation and strength, and the kingdom of our
God and the power of Christ.　Rev. xiv, 10.

GOD INDIVISIBLE.

There are three things I know, and the fourth I strongly believe These are: First, I must convince you that you are in error, and building on a sandy foundation, instead of the rock of truth ; and, secondly, must convince you that we are right and building on the true foundation ; and, thirdly, must convince you that by entering the fold, adopting our life, and submitting to the law of Christ, as you can be made to understand it, you will thereby be rendered more happy in this life, and be assured of eternal life and heaven in the world to come. And additionally, I am strongly impressed with the belief, that, after having been fully convinced of the facts as we see them, few of you will forsake the world for Christ ; for truly He hath said : " For wide is the gate and broad is the way that leadeth to destruction, and many there be which go in thereat ; and straight is the gate and narrow is the way which leadeth unto life, and *few* there be that find it." Matt. vii, 13, 14. " Strive, therefore, to enter in at the straight gate, for many will *seek* and shall not be able." When once the master of the house is risen up, and hath shut the door, and ye begin to stand without and to knock at the door, saying, "Lord, Lord, open unto us, He shall answer and say unto you, I know you not whence ye are." Luke xiii, 24, 5. Sorrowful as it is, I feel a strong degree of certitude that this will be the condition of the most of you unless you take warning, turn from the world, and *strive — yea, agonize —* to " enter in at the straight gate " That the nominal professors of Christianity are in error, both in faith and practice, and that none of their schemes of salvation will insure to them either happiness or heaven, here or hereafter, I do most conscientiously believe. They being under the " veil of the flesh," imbued with its lusts, are in spiritual darkness; hence all, or nearly all of their ideas concerning God and Christ — their true character and their demands upon them — must necessarily be imperfect.

After admitting, as I presumed you to do, what was said in a former discourse, that the Supreme Being was *infinite* in His existence, in order to maintain your consistency, you cannot attach to His being plurality in any sense, and His *indivisibility* precludes the possibility of making either two, three, or more of the same being. His *immutability* also debars you from any change in Him, either in thought, word, state, character or deed. His omniscience being acknowledged, there is nothing but what He knows. His *omnipresence* admitted, there is then no point of space where He is not.

Can you not then see the inconsistency and impertinence of those sonorous invocations, vehement utterances, loud vociferations and demands upon, as well as instructions, given to God, which we so frequently hear from your pulpits and in your public assemblies, as though God were deaf or " had gone on a journey," or at least was not nearer than the lower strata of clouds? I am glad, however, to admit that some are honestly sincere, occupying, as best they can with their present light, the talent God has given them ; such will be accepted of him. For saith the apostle : " Of a truth, I perceive that God is no respecter of persons. But in every nation he that feareth Him and *worketh righteousness* is accepted with Him." Acts x, 35. But *acceptance* merely is not *salvation*, as Jew, Gentile, Pagan, Mahomedan or heathen, are all alike accepted of God, who live up to the best light that He has vouchsafed to them ; but there is only *one* way to be saved, that is, to " walk as Christ walked," and " overcome the world within as He overcame " Even though some may be sincere, I have little faith in the efficacy of the word from the mouth of a hireling preacher. Every servant of God should be a producer. Should put his " hands to work and his heart to God," who will give him words to speak as occasion demands. But (I wish not to offend), there are many who say they are the called ministers of God who barter their God-given faculties for gold. What observing person has not discovered that where the largest pile of money is offered there is the greatest call of God? For instance. Should the people of Logan offer a priest a salary of five hundred dollars a year for preaching to them, and the people of Warren should raise the pile to a thousand, who does not know that the call of God would be in Warren? To such one I would say: " Paid hypocrite," God is within thee, making up the record which thou shalt be obliged to face, even the very motives that actuate thee, and by these shalt thou be judged   But whilst the omnipresent is within thee, the tribunal and focal power by which thou wilt be tried may, at present, be at some distance from thee. "Know ye not the saints shall judge the world?" 1 Cor vi, 2   Paul still goes further: "Know ye not that *we* shall judge angels. How much more the things that pertain to this life?"   This. is doubtless God's order of judgment, who first gave all power to the Son, and He in like manner delegated the same to His true followers; hence, to come to judgment is to come to the *order* of God, to repent of, confess and forsake all known sin, and henceforward lead a godly life, "walk righteously, soberly, and godly in this present evil world"   This is the first link to connect the sinner with his maker: "For as I live," saith the Lord, "every knee shall bow, and every tongue shall confess to God." Rom xiv, 11.   To confess to God, then, is to confess to the agents of his appointing, or to God through them, and by these agents to be judged, received or rejected.   The meaning I here attach to the term *confess* is to reveal and acknowledge your faults and bring your hidden deeds to the light.   In this sense it is impossible for any one to confess to the Supreme, who knows your motive to sin before your action, and who was remonstrating with you through your conscience at the time of its commission. Joshua says to Achan: "Achan, my son, give, I pray thee, glory to the Lord God of Israel, and make confession unto Him ; and tell me now what thou hast done; hide it not from me" Joshua vii, 19.   This is the way and the only acceptable way to confess to God — the only way any soul can find forgiveness and gain the victory over his sinful propensities, and rise into newness of life, and become a branch of the "living vine."   The first thing that Christ did after His resurrection, was to commission His disciples to preach.   He said to them: "As my Father hath sent me, even so send I you. " " Whosoever sins ye remit are remitted unto them; and whosoever sins ye retain, they are retained." John xxii, 23.   But previously He said to Peter, when He prospectively appointed him head of the church: " I will give unto thee the keys of the Kingdom of Heaven, and whatsoever thou shalt bind on earth shall be bound in heaven, and whatsoever thou shalt loose on earth shall be loosed in heaven." Matt. xvi, 19.   Thus you cannot fail to see clearly what God's order of confession is , and that the power to loose and bind, remit and retain, was committed to earthen vessels, and very justly and ra-

2

tionally so, because every sin that man commits is against him-self and his fellow-man. But the thief who steals your horse or your gold is the very first one to cry out and say he does not be-lieve in confessing sin to man; he would much rather confess to the horse he had stolen, or go back in the dark hour of midnight and confess to God while he was bitting another. Not very dis-similar to this is the man who religiously retires to his closet once a week and confesses to God, with no calculation of forsaking, and perhaps, with the certain calculations that he will violate God's law of nature before another day shall have expired.

Such as these expect to get to heaven by faith in God's mercy and in the atoning blood of our Saviour, and not by obedience to his commands. But the priest, you say, confesses in public to God, acknowledges himself a sinner, and pleads for God's mercy for himself and his flock. According to my understanding of the term, it is no confession at all; for he tells you nothing but what God and the flock already know. He, like you, confesses that he is a sinner, and might have added, O, Lord! I expect to remain a sinner, entirely forgetting the injunction, "Cleanse your hands, ye sinners, and purify your hearts, ye double-minded." James iv, 8, and the unalterable decree, "The soul that sinneth it shall die," and "He that committeth sin is of the devil" 1st. John iii, 8. And so it goes, sinners first, teaching a sinning people and encouraging them to live in sin by telling them they cannot help it; thus "The blind lead the blind," and the conse-quence is they both "fall into the ditch together." I say not these things out of ill will to any mortal, nor do I wish to hurt nor offend any soul, but to encourage you, to enlighten you, and to so strengthen you that you may be able to take the apostle's advice and find your way out of sin now, in this world, so that it may be said to you, "Well done, good and faithful servant" — not well done, *weak* and *sinning* servant, but *faithful servant* — "enter thou into the joy of thy Lord." "If we say we have no sin, we deceive ourselves, and the truth is not in us; but if we confess our sins, he is faithful and just to forgive us our sins, and to cleanse us from all unrighteousness." 1 John i, 8, 9. Again, some apparently honest minds will say they do not believe any man on earth has power to forgive sin. Simple creatures! They do not know this is "rank infidelity," and equal to saying they do not believe Christ has any Church on earth. If He has not, then no man has the power; if He has, the power still remains in his Church It follows then that the Church that has not this power is not the Church of Christ at all, but some spurious concern, gotten up by hypocritical or ignorant men. This may serve you as a clew in your search for the true Church You, my friends, may rest assured of *one* thing — that is, Christ's Church is not *governed* by *sinners*, *led* by *sinners*, *filled* by *sinners*, nor worked throughout by *sinners*. This kind of a Church, one would think, would please the devil a little too well. I only use this term Devil in condescension to the general sense

I would have you understand, and bear it in mind, that when you have confessed your sins in God's order, and, as the apostle says, have been "*cleansed* from all *unrighteousness*", you are then *righteous*, and need not sin any more, and consequently not be a sinner any more. The wise man said · "He that covereth his sins shall not prosper, but who so confesseth and forsaketh them shall find mercy." Prov. xxviii, 13 Cover from whom? We cannot cover from the Supreme, who "knoweth the thoughts and intents of the heart." If there is any meaning in the text, it is covering from, or confessing to the order of God. Then it is he who *forsaketh* them, not he that goes on *committing* them, that is to find mercy. Much more might be quoted from the Bible, on this subject, which is replete with evidence of its high authenticity. But, besides this, there is a deep philosophy in it, aside from the spiritual cleansing and peace of mind occasioned thereby For how could the physician certainly determine what remedies to prescribe for *internal maladies* without a statement from the patient of his internal condition? If a person comes to the church for assistance, how could it be known what guards were necessary to be thrown around him without knowing his weak points? If he had been addicted to the intoxicating bowl, we should be careful not to expose him to the temptation of liquor : and just the same with regard to other habits by which people may have been enslaved.

I have now, as I set out to do, endeavored to show you : First — That you who profess to be Christians were in error in a very essential point of doctrine, and consequently the practice under it must be inefficacious to a given extent. Secondly — I have endeavored to show you from scripture and reason that we were right in the first and most essential step into the fold of Christ; and now, Thirdly — I would wish to convince you that you would increase your happiness by taking this step and becoming peaceable lambs in Christ's Kingdom ; but I must say but few words on this subject at present, as I have detained you quite long enough, but must recur to it hereafter. I hope you will continue to give me your attention, as I shall, from time to time, endeavor to answer the many objections urged against us, both by friends and enemies. The one most often repeated is : " What would become of the world were all to turn Shakers? That our whole system of religion is repugnant to scripture, reason, and the common sense of mankind, and therefore cannot exist but a short time at farthest ; " and secondly, "the very fact that God made woman and gave her to man to be a help-meet for him shows that it is by this means the world is to be perpetuated. It is therefore fighting against God to abrogate the relation which he instituted, " etc. These, with many others of like character, will be answered by and by, if you will continue to give me audience ; and any objections that I should fail to think of may be noted by you and handed or sent to me, and they shall be respectfully considered, as truth, and truth only is what we want. If we find we have it not, it will be to our interest to be corrected, and certainly we shall be in duty bound to thank any of you for its unfoldment. As said in a former discourse, error can be of no advantage to any soul, and, seeing an error, we shall not strive to uphold it, for

> " Truth crushed to earth will rise again ;
> The eternal years of God are hers ,
> While error wounded writhes in pain,
> And dies amid her worshipers. "

It is sad, yet true, that the minister in the pulpit generally dares not divulge to the audience all the truths in his possession, because they would be unpopular. He *must please his audience,* and hence cannot be the real minister of truth. His bread and meat depend upon it, and this seems to have been the case in years long past, as expressed by the poet :

> " Pulpits their sacred satire learned to spare,
> And vice admired to find a flatterer there."

Happiness is of three kinds — spiritual, intellectual, and sensual, or animal. The first is found only on the Christ plane, and only attainable by the true followers of Christ. The second is found by the philosopher, the learned, the astronomer, mathematician, etc The third is found on the natural plane. The second may combine either with the first or last, but the three cannot combine, for " he that findeth his (worldly) life shall lose it (the spiritual), and he that loseth his (worldly) life for my sake shall find it (the spiritual), and he that receiveth you receiveth me; and he that receiveth me receiveth him that sent me " Matt , x, 39, 40. This clearly shows that the worldly or sensual life is incompatible with the spiritual life of Christ. It is clear that the Saviour could not mean that they could both find and lose the same life, but the finding and enjoying of one excluded the other; so let the miser and sensualist, and those who are engrossed in the things of this world, beware, that whilst they are watching and shunning the " Scylla " of what they are pleased to term " Shakerism," they fall not into " Charybdis," the deep, dark, and " bottomless pit," where their course may be one eternal descent, and thus lose their souls forever.

GOD IMMUTABLE.

It is written that " the reproof of a friend is better than the kiss of an enemy." If any one should feel wounded or become offended at my remarks, let the rising thought be assuaged by the reflection that it is a friend that speaks, as most certainly I have no cause to be any thing else but a friend to every one of you. It is again written, " ye adulterers and adultresses, know ye not that the friendship of the world is enmity with God? Whosoever therefore will be a friend of the world is the *enemy* of God." James, iv, 4. And again, " God so loved the world that He gave His only begotten Son, that whosoever believeth in Him should not perish, but have everlasting life." John, iii, 16. The apparent conflict here of God loving what He requires us to hate is ideal, and explained by the apostle; " Love not the world, neither the things that are in the world. If any love the world, the love of the Father is not in him; for all that is in the world, the lust of the flesh, the lust of the eyes, and the pride of life, is not of the Father, but is of the world, and the world passeth away and the lusts thereof, but he that doeth the will of God abideth forever." 1st John, xv, 16, 17. It is clear, then, that those who choose these worldly elements, and live in them, are God's enemies. This is a good criterion to judge ourselves by. Do any of us love the lust of the flesh? Do any of us love the pride of life? According to the apostle, all whom truth compels to answer affirmatively may know they are enemies to God; and all such cannot forsake the world and turn to God any too soon, for without Him all is lost, but if He be " on our side who can be against us ? "

From what I have already said, in respect to Deity, it would seem superfluous to add any thing; yet I feel compelled to say a few words more I am well aware that your divines (?) when closely pressed, acknowledge the Unity of the Supreme Being; but for want of clear ideas, and a consistent application of their terms, whenever we question the Supreme Deity of the Son, the

oscillation commences; and by adroit manœuvring, and a very
licentious use of language to sustain a preconceived notion, they
seem to lose sight of what they have conceded, and so interpret
words as to make you believe that the terms *unity* and *trinity*
are synonyms — that at least there was a harmonious oneness in
them — their chief illustration being this : " Water is one substance, but the same substance may be either snow or ice without
changing the *substance*, there being no change except in the condition." But God's immutability, already acknowledged, denies
you even this, but He is ever the same, without change The
illustration is, therefore, inapplicable. If, however, we admit
that the office of water, snow and ice is different, the *substance*
is the *same*, and to make the comparison at all available we
could only say : God was at one time *pleased*, another time
angry, and another time *indifferent*. We could neither divide
Him, nor make three beings of Him. According to the illustration, God must be all the time God, or all the time the Son, or
all the time the Holy Ghost, but never at any time all three, each
with a different office to perform at the same time , hence the
comparison fails to answer the purpose intended. Illustrations
badly chosen always serve to darken rather than to enlighten the
understanding.

But these divine reasoners, whilst they declare that the *Son is
the Father* still hold that *there is a Father aside from the Son*,
because they are unwilling to admit that the universe was without an Infinite Being, during his sojourn on, with especial attention to this mundane sphere. So, when their ideas clash, their
reasonings clash also Who can gainsay the words of the poet :

> " All are but parts of one stupendous whole,
> Whose *body Nature is*, and *God* the soul ? "

Some of you little know the disastrous consequences that
would follow a denial of this. When this is denied His Omnipresence is denied. His *Omnipresence* being denied, His *Infinity*
is denied ; and this being denied, makes Him a circumscribed,
limited, Finite Being. Thence follow the " gross conceptions of
corporeity." figure, size, shape, etc. And how should He get
from world to world ? A universe without a God, only as it
pleased Him to visit its parts ! This is Atheism — equal to saying there is no God ! Nay, my friends, if there is any part of

space where He is not, He is *finite*, and there can be no compari_son between the finite and the infinite.

> "Jove's satellites are less than Jove"

If He is finite in his existence, He is finite in all his attributes; but the reverse of this is true. There is no atom in the wide universe without the presence of the *divine energy.* He,

> " Warms in the sun, refreshes in the breeze,
> Glows in the stars, and blossoms in the trees —
> Lives through all life, extends thro' all extent·
> Spreads *undivided* and operates unspent "

But the defenders of the triple-God doctrine say the three are combined in a " mysterious yet all harmonious union ; " that this is a matter of revelation, out of the reach of and above the cold philosophy of this world, must be believed or the soul be damned! while if terms mean any thing, we have no choice in the matter. No rational mind can believe a statement that contradicts itself. But there is another difficulty —difficulties beset us on every hand. If it is mysterious, how do we know it to be harmonious? This conclusion is clearly hypothetical. It is impossible for any man to really believe a mystery, according to my sense of definition of the term. Yet mystery seems to be the great whale that swallows all the modern Jonahs. A mystery is something hidden from the human understanding and beyond human comprehension ; consequently something of which the sense cannot take cognizance. A man, therefore, cannot believe a mystery. Still it is affirmed that we are believing mysteries every day. I admit there are some things which persons sometimes carelessly take upon trust, without investigation ; but nothing can be really believed but what the senses can take cognizance of. If the geometrician tells you that the three angles of a plain triangle are equal to two right ones, you may take it upon trust, as your senses take cognizance of angles. Still, he should demonstrate the problem before demanding your entire credence.

The first argument in the mouth of a man who asks you to believe a mystery is something like this : The grass grows; this is a mystery, and we believe it. But this, as well as all of the kind, is shallow reasoning, so shallow that it is not reasoning at all. That the grass grows is palpable to the senses, but *how* it grows we know not, it is incomprehensible ; we, therefore, do not know *how* to believe *how* it grows, we cannot believe how it grows, because this is a mystery. When the *how* is revealed to the understanding the mystery ceases; we then shall be able to believe how it grows, and not before. No man, therefore, can believe any thing entirely hidden from the senses or understanding. A thing thus hidden is the same to us as though we had not the senses necessary to belief. This, with the rational mind, will answer for any mysterious proposition that may be given you from man, relative to God, or the Son of God, including all the mysteries of animal and vegetable life. Yet we are thrown back to the bible, and told that it is revealed there, from God in heaven, that such and such things are mysteries not to be comprehended, but believed on pain of hell's torments if we do not, for "great is the mystery of Godliness" Godliness is mysterious only to the sinner; it is not at all mysterious to the men and women whose lives are lives of godliness. God is no mystery to those to whom He is revealed. Paul, when he arrived at Athens, said: "I perceive that in all things ye are too superstitious; for as I passed by and beheld your devotions, I found an altar, with this inscription: To THE UNKNOWN GOD. Whom, therefore, ye ignorantly worship, Him declare I unto you." Acts xvii, 23 God to him was no mystery, else he could not have declared Him.

Some sinning priests, going their rounds through the country, are making mysteries of many things—especially things sacred— which they urge you to believe, on pain of damnation. If they succeed in satisfying you, they well know the good matron of the house will have the fatted pullet ready by the time they come round again. This is understandable. The only mystery about this is, that so many are "taken in." I would here give this little piece of advice: If any man should come to your domicile to instruct you and your family how to be saved, and is not saved himself, you should quote to him the pungent proverb, "Physician, heal thyself." It may be confessing too many of their sins for them, but such persons generally have quite as much interest in the pullet as they have in your salvation. Miracles are next urged upon you, especially the great, grand miracle of miracles, "revealed in God's word," that the Infinite Jehovah, the Creator of worlds, beyond thought, focalized himself in a woman, became a baby, a boy, a man, then permitted His fellow man to kill Him that He might reconcile it with His sense of justice

3

to admit the sinner into Heaven, especially all who were simple
enough to believe the story! But this story is not as palpable to
the senses as that grass grows. It so happens that this so-called
word of God reveals precisely the negative of all this. It is a
perfect neutralizer. Then, which shall we believe—the reasonable or unreasonable? This Supreme (?) that walked the earth
says He was the Son of Man. Is He to be believed? He says
also He has a Heavenly Father. Is this true? Now, that He
can be the supreme God and son of the supreme God, the father
of himself, and the father of the father, and father of the son,
and the son of the son, and son of himself, is not plain to the
senses, it not only "admits of a reasonable doubt," but is entirely
beyond the power of belief to any educated and unbiased mind.
The proposition utterly annihilates itself before it is half told.
All this is the result of a wrong education—a biased mind and
morbid intellect, and can work nothing but injury to the human
race.

Having taken the Son from the triple God, it is necessary that
I should now place Him right in your minds, the son—the "Man,
Christ Jesus" "For there is one God, and one mediator betwixt
God and man, the *man* Christ Jesus"—1st Tim. ii, 5 No text
in the Scriptures shows the truth, and the distinction between
God and Christ, more clearly than this: First, one God;
secondly, one Mediator betwixt God and man; and thirdly, that
man is this *mediator*—not that the *Supreme* is the mediator, but
the man, Christ Jesus How very dull must be the perception of
the person who cannot see this truth!

The subject of the Christ is not an intricate one when divested
of the far-fetched and extraneous verbiage with which it seems
to be surrounded and intertwined. It only needs to have the
smoke and fog that have been accumulating around it dispelled,
and the cobwebs brushed away, to enable the most common capacity to comprehend it I have no sympathy with, nor affinity for,
a mysterious godliness, nor a theology, nor philosophy, that no
two can agree upon nor comprehend; and in order that I may
proceed understandingly I will begin at the beginning, and give
you the signification of the term Christ, and its origin and use
If I am right it is important that you should know it. If wrong,
it is also necessary that you should know how much I am wrong,
and wherein, I shall quote authority that you will acknowledge,
taking pains to keep clear and distinct ideas before you.

Webster defines the term Christ thus. "Greek, Christos Anointed, from chrio, to anoint. The Anointed, an appellation given to the Saviour of the world, and synonymous with the Hebrew Messiah. It was the custom of antiquity to consecrate persons to the sacerdotal and regal offices by anointing with oil." Thus we see the verb *chrio*, from which the noun *Christos* is derived, signifies to anoint, the act of anointing. This act, therefore, cannot be called Christos; neither can the unction—Hebrew *Semen Meshe*, or Greek *Chrisma*, anointing—be called Christ None but the person anointed, according to Webster, can be called or ever was called Christ in past history Alexander Cruden agrees with Webster, and says the Evangelists took care to put the people in mind of the prophecies concerning him to prove thereby that *Jesus* was the *Christ* whom they expected. Buck, in his Theological Dictionary, agrees with both Webster and Cruden. He says: "He is called *Christ* because he is *anointed;*" for this reason, not on account of a miraculous birth, but because he was anointed. The learned Richard Watson agrees also with what has been said, that the term " as used singly by way of *autonomasis* to denote a person sent from God as anointed prophet, priest, or King." "Christ," says Lactantious, " is no proper personal name, but one denoting power; for the Jews used to give this appellation to their Kings, calling them Christ or anointed by reason of their sacred unction." But he adds. "The names of Messiah and Christ were originally derived from the ceremony of anointing, by which the Kings and priests of God's people were consecrated and admitted to the exercise of their functions; for all these functions were counted holy among the Israelites But the most eminent application of the word is to that illustrious personage, typified and predicted from the beginning, who is described under the character of God's anointed, the Messiah, or Christ." One mistake our translators have made is by too seldom prefixing the article *the* before Christ. The word Christ was at first as much an appellative as the word Baptist, and one was as regularly accompanied with the article as the other, yet our translators who would always say, " *the Baptist,*" have, it would seem, studiously avoided saying " the Christ." The article in such expressions as occur in Acts, xvii, 3—xviii, 5, 25, adds considerable light to them, and yet no more than the words of the historian manifestly convey to every reader who understands his language. It should therefore be, as

Paul testified to the Jews: " Jesus was *the* Christ," or *the* Messiah, etc. Watson further adds (p. 522): " Jesus of Nazareth was the Christ," or Messiah promised. That *He* professed himself to be that Messiah to whom all the prophets gave witness, and who was in fact, at the time of *His* appearance, expected by the Jews, and that *He* was received under that character by *His* disciples and all Christians ever since, is certain. All lexicographers agree with this; in fact there is no standard work extant but what acknowledges that the term *Christ* signifies the anointed *person*, and is confined to that signification and use. From all that I have said and the evidence adduced you cannot fail to perceive that the term Christ is but an appellative noun—an official title of the man Jesus, the same as Baptist was of the man John, or the same as " Jones, the Sheriff," or " Smith, the Auditor." This is all plain; easily fathomed by the common capacity. What some would veil in mystery, is clear as day when plainly stated. It will be perceived, also, that to come from God is nothing more than to be commissioned or appointed by Him. This coming has no reference to altitude, longitude, nor latitude, as many are made to believe. I know this kind of discourse is prosy and irksome to many, but I could not, if I would

> " Round the period and the pause,
> And form the rhetoric, clause on clause,"

so as to be very attractive; but to those who are in quest of simple truth, I propose to be of no disadvantage. I beg you not to be alarmed, fearing that I may derogate from the character of Christ; for it adds a thousand fold more lustre to His character to know that, notwithstanding " He was made in all respects like unto His brethren "— Heb. ii, 17 — " tempted in all points as we are," He yet gained the victory, than it would be to think He was not made in all respects like unto us, but overcame by virtue of a higher creation. So, my friends, cheer up, you have an example. " He left us an example that we should follow His steps " — 1 Peter, ii, 21 — not the steps of the supreme God, but those of a good man, godly man, or God-man, if you please, and if you have the moral courage to " come out from the world," and undertake the good work, you will find that salvation is not unsusceptible of attainment in this life. Is not this good news ? Come, then, to Christ; He will receive you, if you will confess and forsake all sin. " For in a little wrath, I hid my face from thee for a moment; but with everlasting kindness will I have mercy on thee, saith the Lord, the Redeemer." Isa liv, 7, 8 Then, oh! my friends, "seek ye the Lord while He may be found; call ye upon Him while He is near." " Let the wicked forsake his way, and the unrighteous man his thoughts, and let him return unto the Lord, who will have mercy upon him, and to our God, for He will abundantly pardon"

RETROSPECTION.

Before proceeding with this discourse I propose to take a very short retrospect of the essential points thus far made. It is not a difficult matter to forget acknowledged truths when new ideas are brought before the mind, and side issues introduce themselves; it is therefore necessary to proceed cautiously, with a kind of retro-action, to insure harmony of thought, so that the past, the present and the future may agree. I have declared to you the *harmony of all truth*. I have endeavored to impress upon your minds the necessity of having distinct and clear ideas, and of using well-defined terms, in order to preserve consistency of thought and speech; and also of the necessity of divesting your minds of all bias, prepossession or prejudice, and to look at things as they are. Locke says, " No man is suitable to investigate for truth who has an object in his mind which he *wishes to find true.*" Such person is apt to see truth only on one side. But truth alone should be the object, regardless of our desires. This I think is my condition. I am not before you to defend any dogma, particular theory, nor *ism*, not even what you are pleased to term *Shakerism*, but to aid in removing error, and to unfold to you the simple truth as I perceive it. Truth is usually simple, while error is complex.

> " For *modes* of faith let graceless zealots fight ;
> His *can't be wrong, whose life* is in the right "

I have endeavored to impress upon your minds a truth, which we are apt to forget, respecting our Creator, and that is that no atom of the boundless universe is or ever was without the eternal presence; that " the hairs of our head are all numbered ; " that this has ever been the case, before as well as since the advent of our Saviour ; that all is right, save only man and what man has done, and especially have I endeavored to impress you with the great and important truth that the ever present God commissioned the man, Christ Jesus, to represent Him and to make known His will to the race, and made him "judge of the quick and the dead ," and that the power thus delegated to Him He delegated to his successors, and said : "They shall do greater works than I, because I go to my Father." John xvi, 12. And at the bar of this tribunal, the head of Christ's church, shall all souls be tried in time or eternity, and the first step any soul can take to bring him or herself into harmony with the Creator, whose laws have been violated, was by auricular confession of sin to the order of his appointing, and thenceforward leading a godly life. Thus, and thus only hath a merciful God opened the way for our return to Him. But how discouraging it is when the most irrefragable proof is set before the mind, that many will not heed it, and would rather put their trust in something unproved and unprovable than to abide by known and acknowledged truth A lawyer of some note, lately said that, while he could not dispute the truth of the indivisibility of the Infinite, yet he believed in the Infinite Three! because, forsooth, it was Bible doctrine, which assertion I deny. It seemed impossible for him to fix his eyes or sense on any thing else but a *judge*, two attorneys and a criminal ; believing that there is such a court somewhere above the clouds, to attend to his case when he gets ready for trial; if he expects to get to heaven, he must of course think the practice there is somewhat similar to what he is accustomed to here. A large enough fee, adroit pleading, etc , will somehow clear the culprit, and thus, in common parlance, "cheat the devil out of his dues" A certain preacher also said : "deprive me of the imputed righteousness of Christ, and I am damned, sure" Not so, friend. Your damnation will be in the precise ratio of your willful violation of God's laws, and your justification in exact proportion to your obedience to them. Be not fearful, for God is just, and will do as he has promised — "reward you according as your works shall be." It matters little what people profess to believe The truth is, no man can believe the affirmative and negative of a proposition. When he thus affirms, it is evident that he is either dishonest or remarkably weak. Such a person might receive instruction from some who are called pagan. In his Phædo of the soul, Plato says : " It appears to me that, to know them clearly in the present life, is either impossible or very difficult On the other hand, not to test what has been said of them in every possible way — not to investigate the whole matter, and exhaust upon it every effort is the part of a *very weak man.* For we ought in respect of these things either to learn from others how they stand or to discover them for ourselves, or if both of these are impossible then, taking the best of human reasonings, that which appears the best supported, and embark on that, as one who risks himself on a raft to sail through life "

Such a man, let him be either Pagan, Mohamedan or Christian, is head and shoulders above any one who professes to believe the contrary sides of a proposition, such as the existence of an *infinite indivisible one*, and of the same being as an *infinite divisible three!* And moreover, I feel quite sure that an honest, truthful pagan is much nearer the Kingdom of God, than a dishonest, equivocating, falsifying professor of Christianity How many there are who accept the mere "letter of the Bible that killeth, and reject the spirit (of truth) that giveth life." 2 Cor. iii, 6. I have always, not only been taught a due veneration for the Bible, but also the greatest veneration for *truth*, as I became able to perceive it. Nothing either in or out of the Bible can be believed to be true unless its truth can be perceived, and a truth unperceived can be binding on no one The Bible makes no such declaration as that of a three-fold God, nor of a first, second and third person in one God Such terms as trinity, triune God, etc., are not to be found in the good book They have been coined in the jumble of thoughts of inconsistent sectarians, as a foundation on which to build or to bolster up some particular creed I have further endeavored to show, producing evidence that could not be disputed, that *Christ* signified *anointed;* that the term cannot by any rational construction be applied to any human being. nor angel, without such being anointed or appointed to consummate some special work, or perform some new mission for God — that is to say *Christ* is a *God-appointed agent* The term means this, nothing more, nothing less.

I have further striven to impress the truth, that the Bible speaks of three worlds or creations. The Biblicist will acknowledge that Moses and those after him, till Christ, spoke of two worlds, viz · First, the visible creation, heavens and earth, moon, stars, etc ; and secondly, the "old heavens and earth" that were to "pass away with a great noise," at the ushering in of the "new heavens and earth," some time, called *world* or *worlds;* and that the Evangelists wrote only of the "*New* Heavens and Earth." Should we forget these truths, Alps on Alps arise before us; but keeping them in view, all obstacles vanish. and our way is plain.

With some, it matters not what amount of evidence is brought
forward, if it does not accord with their understanding of certain
texts of scripture, it is all coolly set aside, and the Bible text relied
on   Hence, it becomes my next duty to examine some of the
principal texts supposed and believed to declare the existence of
Christ, in and with the Creator before the formation of man, or
even the creation of the visible universe   It will at once be seen,
that, after admitting the authority I have introduced as true and
reliable, we cannot consistently admit the pre-existent theory.   If
we admit the latter, the former must be rejected.

The text usually first introduced on the side of the pre-existent
theory is found in John's gospel, 1st and 14th verses, as follows .
" In the beginning was the Word, and the Word was with God,
and the Word was God ; "   *   *   *   " And the Word became
flesh and dwelt amongst us."   The first thing to be considered in
the text is the term *beginning*.   What *beginning ?*   According
to what we have said, it must be the beginning of God's new creation   Christ was there   The whole, however, is metaphorical ;
but metaphors have need to be understood.   This metaphor,
then, consists in calling God's word, or the medium through and
by whom the word was conveyed, God Himself.   When I say the
word is God, I mean it conveys His will and mind to me, which if I
obey then, I obey God ; if I disobey, I disobey God ; and in this
sense, is the same as God   The word became Jesus Christ in the
same way and by the same rule that it became God.   He received
the word, mind, or will of God ; that mind or will became His
mind and will ; His mind and will was then Himself.   Then it
was Jesus Christ, who was flesh and blood, that " dwelt amongst
us "   To obey that man, therefore, was to obey God.   Other
metaphors. exemplify this.   We say we read Moses when we read
his laws ; we preach Christ, when we preach His doctrine.   The
apostle fully sustains the view here taken with respect to the beginning.   In his first epistle he says : " That which was from the
beginning, which we heard, which we have seen with our eyes,
and our hands have handled "   It is clear that his hands had not
handled any thing in the beginning of the old creation ; but with
the new he had been conversant from the very start.   This same
John records the words of Jesus : " And ye also shall bear
witness, because ye have been with me from the beginning "
That is, the beginning of the new creation   This is proof positive of the truth of the exegesis here given — unless both Jesus

4

and His apostles all pre-existed with God, which none are simple
enough to affirm. But let us look at it as explained and held by
the blind guides of this world. In the beginning was God, and God
was with God, and God was God, and God became flesh; and God
says " all flesh is as grass " Then God became as grass; and what
is grass? I hope my friends will take a common-sense view of the
subject and not allow themselves to be led away from the truth,
" which alone can make you free." I know how difficult it will be to
yield long-cherished opinions, even when their falsity and absurdity are shown, and more especially will it be hard for learned
divines to acknowledge light from a quarter so obscure, and esteemed so ignorant, as we are; but error has nearly had its day,
and it is a happy thought that truth will finally triumph. Secondly : " He (Jesus Christ) was the true light that lighteth
every man that cometh into the world. He was in the world
and the world was made by Him and the world knew Him not."
John 1, 10 Notwithstanding Jesus was "the true light," it
must be evident to even the most superficial mind that this true
light did not, does not enlighten every man that cometh into the
old, or natural world. This being the case, which none will dispute, it follows that some other world was meant. It must have
been the new world which he made, whose inhabitants were enlightened by this "true light" This relieves the text from mystery, and every feature of pre-existence is removed. It is admitted that the new world was made by Him, but not the old;
and although those who came into the new world were enlightened by Him, yet it is evident they knew Him not — that is, they
did not fully comprehend His mission and His doctrine — for He
said : " Have I been so long with you, Peter, and you have not
known me?" Thirdly. "God, in these last days, hath spoke
unto us by his Son, whom He hath appointed heir of all things:
by whom also He made the (new) worlds" Heb i, 2. Fourthly;
Christ Jesus "who is the image of the invisible God, the first-
born of every creature For by Him are all things created that
are in heaven, and that are in earth, visible and invisible, whether
they be thrones, or dominions, or principalities, or powers; all
things were created by Him and for Him : and He is before all
things, and by Him all things consist, and He (Jesus Christ) is the
head of the body, the church; who is the beginning (of the new
creation and church), the first born from the dead." Col. xv, 16,
17, 18. I quote these texts entire, because they are supposed by

divines to be proof positive not only of the pre-existence of Christ, but that *Christ was God Himself;* but, when fairly considered, they fail to do either. They fail in the former, because reference is had to the *new,* not the *old* world; and fail in the latter because Christ, the head of the church, was the image of another. It would hardly do to say He was the image of himself! It is true that " by Him were all things created that are in the (new) heavens, and that are in the (new) earth; and all things therein were created by Him and for Him." But this could not be truly said of Him in relation to the old heavens and earth that were to pass away, which existed before Christ, who is called the second Adam, nor of the visible universe, which existed before the *first* Adam was created And he (Christ), the text says, *is* before all things (in excellence), which is true Should we give the text any other construction it would clash with what the good apostle elsewhere affirms of the Son of God He says: " Concerning His Son, Jesus Christ our Lord, which was made of the seed of David according to the flesh (and that is the way we were all made), and declared to be the Son of God with power, according to the spirit of holiness, by the resurrection from the dead " Rom i, 3, 4.

According to the general construction given by the sectarian world to the first quoted text, one would be led to conclude that the apostle was not speaking of the same Son of God in the latter text, and, with *their* exegesis, reconciliation and agreement -between them are impossible. But to proceed with Collosians, the 18th verse. It will be evident that the first-born of the new creation is meant. He was called the first-born of the whole creation, because He was the "first-begotten from the dead;" consequently the "first-born of every creature" from the dead. The text does not say He was before all things, but He *is* before — stands before, or is foremost, in the new creation; and "by Him all things (appertaining thereto) consist." This is no forced construction, and leaves the apostle in harmony with himself and in harmony with truth, and divests the reading of all obscurity and mystery. " He that hath ears to hear let him hear;" for in all I say, I hope to be so plain that the most common capacity can understand and comprehend me. We claim to be denizens of this new world made by Christ — "the new heavens and new earth which He created, wherein dwelleth righteousness," *where* all " old things pass away, and all things become new, and all things of God" This is the place and this is the feast to which we all are invited. Who would not have "old things pass away" "and all things become new?" Who is there that would not this day, before God, give all his worldly possessions to have his past sins, in the acts of his life, wiped out, and be restored to the innocence of a child? I hear a response from the deep chambers of the heart, saying: "I would, I would." Then let me assure all, even the chiefest of sinners, that a compliance with God's requirement in His Order will bring to you this happy result.

"O ye Corinthians, our mouth is open unto you, our heart is enlarged What fellowship hath righteousness with unrighteousness? What communion hath light with darkness? What concord hath Christ with Belial? What agreement hath the temple of God with idols? For ye are the temple of the living God; as God hath said: I will dwell in them and walk in them, and I will be their God, and they shall be my people. Wherefore come yet out from among them; be ye separate and touch not the unclean thing, and I will receive you, and I will be a Father unto you, and ye shall be my sons and daughters, saith the Lord Almighty."

TRUE HAPPINESS.

Before people will forsake the world and come to Christ, they will have to feel a strong assurance that by so doing they will be rendered more happy here and hereafter. Happiness is of three kinds, viz.: celestial or spiritual; intellectual; and sensual, or animal; and the latter is unworthy the name, yet the multitude seek it and are thereby ruined. "He only can be esteemed really happy who enjoys peace of mind in the favor of God;" and this can only be attained through Jesus Christ, by obeying His teaching, and walking as He walked. The second is attainable by the good and the bad, according to their capacity and application. The third is enjoyed by animals, and by animal, sensual man. "Every gratification," says Dr. Beattie, "of which human nature is capable, may be comprehended under the one or the other of these three classes, viz.: The pleasures of the outward sense, the pleasures of imagination and intellect, and the pleasures that result from the right exercise of our moral powers. The delights that arise from the latter source, and from the approbation of conscience, are, of all gratification, the most dignified. The more a man attaches himself to them the more respectable he becomes; and it is not possible for him to carry such attachment to excess. With disgust or with pain, they are never attended * * To virtue, therefore, which is the right exercise of our moral powers, the character of chief good does belong, which will appear still more evident, when we consider that the hope of future felicity is the chief consolation of the present life, and that the virtuous alone can reasonably entertain that hope. As, on the other hand, vice, in the most prosperous condition, is subject to the pangs of a guilty conscience and to the dreadful anticipation of future punishment, which are sufficient to destroy all earthly happiness."

This corroborates what I have said, and, coming, as it does, from one of your own number and class, can be the more readily and easily received; but I shall endeavor to make it still more evident   I love to collate, compare and draw evidence for truth from any quarter   "The prudent man foreseeth the evil and hideth himself, but the simple go on and are punished."

Every reflecting mind will admit that the combination of the spiritual and intellectual forms the only happiness worthy the name, which I call true happiness. This being in the possession of any soul, he may be said to have obtained "the pearl of great price." But none ever reached this goal till Jesus Christ came, and, by the sacrifice and crucifixion of all the sensual and merely animal appetites, obtained and then declared the truth to the world: "This is the way, walk ye in it" Since then, philosophers and pious men, on the natural plane of life, could only approximate the truth, we should learn of those, if such can be found, "who have purified their souls in obeying the truth through the spirit," — (1 Pet. i, 22) — by obedience to Him who first found the whole truth and brought "life and immortality to light" For, "if any of you err from the truth, and any one convert him — he who converteth the sinner from the error of his way shall save a soul from death." James v, 20. Then, in accordance with the testimony and life of the Saviour, I affirm this great truth, which was hidden from the world till Christ, viz : that all the miseries that are in the world, and afflict the human family, or ever will afflict them, are, and will be the consequence of the indulgence of the lower passional nature of man. On the other hand, all true happiness that was ever gained by any soul, was the consequence of self-abnegation, that is the denial of the selfish, sensual, and lower propensities; that is to say, in brief, self-denial bringeth happiness — self-indulgence bringeth misery. None can gainsay this truth. It comes to the home experience of every man   Take any twenty-four hours of your life, and before God and your own conscience compare notes, and see if I am not sustained in this declaration.   Then write it in your minute-books and in your albums, and above all, write it in your hearts ; and if you practice it in your daily conduct through life, "your soul shall be saved from death."   All men — great and good men — anterior and subsequent to the advent of Christ, who are living on the Adamic or natural plane, have believed, and still believe, that a moderate indulgence of the selfish and sensual appetites was compatible with the celestial or higher, Christ life, and the best of them think some such gratification cannot be avoided   Hear Plato : "The nature of mankind is greatly degen-

erated and depraved All manner of disorders infest human
nature, and men, being impotent, are torn in pieces by their
lusts as by so many wild horses." So it was; man was impotent.
Until Christ, there was none to set the example or lead the way,
but He comes with a light eclipsing all former lights; with this
great truth inscribed on His unfurled banner, floating before the
eyes of the world: *Self-indulgence bringeth misery ; self-denial
bringeth happiness.* He does not admit of even a moderate
indulgence of the selfish and sensual, but gives His whole soul
and body to God, and then says to the world, "FOLLOW ME."
Christ does not admit impotence in his true followers, and Paul
says he " can do all things (necessary to salvation) through Christ
strengthening him " And how does Christ strengthen His followers? He strengthens them by His teaching, but more by His
example. Although Locke admits the impotency of man, he tells
us some good things: "If any extreme disturbance (as sometimes
it happens) possesses our whole mind — as when the pain of the
rack, love, anger, or any other violent passion running away with
us, allows us not the liberty of thought — God, who knows our
frailty, pities our weakness, and requires of us no more than we
are able to do, and will judge us as a kind and merciful father.
But the forbearance of a too hasty compliance with our desires,
the moderation and restraint of our passions, so that our understanding may be free to examine, and reason, unbiased, gives its
judgment, being that whereon a right direction of our conduct to
true happiness depends — it is in this we should employ our chief
care and endeavors In this we should take pains to suit the
relish of our minds to the *true, intrinsic good* or *ill that is in
things.* How much this is in every one's power, by making
resolutions to himself, such as he may keep, is easy for every one
to try. Nor let any one say he *cannot govern his passions ; nor
hinder them from breaking out and carrying him into action ;
for what he can do before a prince or a great man he can do
alone, or in the presence of God, if he will."* This is certainly
commendable advice and sound reasoning, but I am of the
opinion that none will be able to fully keep themselves without
the facilities afforded in God's Zion, or the order He has established on earth for the protection and redemption of man We
must put on the "whole armor of God," and follow Christ in
the regeneration. "If thou will be perfect, go sell that thou
hast, and give to the poor, and thou shalt have treasure in heaven,

and come and take up the cross and follow me" Mark x, 21. But some complain of the tempter: "Watch and pray, lest you enter into temptation." The vigilance which saves from the tempter for one hour will save for two, and the vigilance that saved for two hours will save for a week, and that which saved for a week, if continued, will save throughout life. But of him that yieldeth, it is written: "He goeth straightway as an ox goeth to the slaughter, or as a fool to the correction of the stocks, till a dart strike through his liver; as a bird hasteneth to the snare and knoweth not it is for his life. Hearken unto me now, therefore, O ye children, and attend to the words of my mouth: Her house is the way to hell, going down to the chambers of death." Prov. vii, 22, 23, 27. But let no man say another tempts him, for the motor is within, the tempter is there, and the power of resistance is there. "Let no man say, when he is tempted, I am tempted of God. But every man is tempted when he is drawn away of his own lust and enticed (not the lust of somebody else, but his own). Then when lust hath conceived, it bringeth forth sin, and sin, when it is finished, bringeth forth death." James i, 13. This is the consequence. Now, then, the life of Jesus Christ — what was it? A life of self-denial or of indulgence? Was His life a worldly life or something else?

Let me ask you, who profess to be Christians, was the Christ life a higher life than any of you now live, or was it lower? Or was it the same? One thing is very certain — His life, which He commends us to copy, was either a higher life than yours, or it was lower, or it was the same. Can any one lay his hand upon his heart and say his life was the same as that of the professing world? If not, all are bound to acknowledge that His is the higher life, which we are bound to copy, or not call ourselves Christians. When Christ came, he found the natural order in as much perfection, the marriage relation as sacred and as much respected as it is to-day, and all the old heaven system, with its pillars and corner-stones as erect and perfect as now. Did He come to make no change? Was He satisfied with the old? or did He set about the creation of new heavens and earth? If so, how comes it that His professed followers are satisfied with, and to be in, the old heavens, on the lower floor, and this in a very dilapidated condition? How is this? Did He only come to get up the most fallacious story, and then say to the world: "Only believe this story, and you can remain in the old heavens, and live the life of generation, copying the old life of Adam and Eve, and I will receive you, and you shall be my children?" How is this? Does this appear reasonable? Let us not be longer deceived, "for God is not mocked. Whatsoever a man soweth that shall he also reap. If we sow to the flesh, we shall of the flesh reap corruption; but if we sow to the spirit, we shall of the spirit reap life everlasting." Gal. vi, 8. What do any suppose is meant by "sowing to the flesh?" "Let us have clear ideas, and understand each other. What did old Adam do? Did he sow to the flesh or sow to the spirit? Whatsoever is born of the flesh is flesh, and whatsoever is born of the spirit is spirit." You will doubtless acknowledge that Adam, Noah, and the Patriarchs, and all the pillars of the old heaven sowed to the flesh, and so they all did till the coming of the "Son of Man," and so do the professors of to-day — they all go on sowing to the flesh, and the promise of God is sure to them, and that is, "they shall reap corruption." What difference do any suppose God will make between a professed minister of the gospel and his slave, when both of them are sowing to the flesh? Will he give corruption to the slave and life everlasting to the minister? By no means. God is just, and no respecter of persons; and where the works and motives are the same, the reward, rest assured, will be the same.

Again, how cruelly mistaken, and what an egregious blunder the Son of God made, if He came to "create new heavens and earth wherein *righteousness* should dwell," if the *old* would still answer the purpose of salvation, wherein all manner of *unright-eousness*, and hardly any thing else, exists! Christ was not the *supreme*, but the *Son of God* — a godly man — who was "tempted in all points (not some points) as we are." But what did He do? Why He denied himself to all ungodliness, and every worldly lust, even in its most refined and modified forms, and required the same of all His followers. Then I put to all the pertinent question: Is not the man, who, for purity's sake, likewise denies himself as did Jesus, nearer like the pattern than any one who does not thus deny himself? The honest answer must be that he is. Hence, after denying himself, Christ says: "If *any man* (black, white, bond or free), will come after me, let him *deny himself* (not gratify himself), and take up the cross and follow me;" not follow somebody else, neither John the Baptist, Moses, nor some

5

of the patriarchs, but FOLLOW ME. But how do the people act?
They act as if Christ had said: "If any man will come after me,
let him gratify himself." People by their actions imply all this
and more. But the apostle says: "They that are Christ's have
crucified the flesh with the affections and lusts." "And if we
live in the spirit, let us walk in the spirit." Gal. 5 : 24. If Paul
had only said: "They that are Christ's have gratified the flesh
with the affections and lusts," I would at once bow to the professors of Christianity, black and white, "blue spirits and gray;"
for nothing more true could be said of them. But it so happens
that the terms *crucified* and *gratified* are not synonyms. And I
would ask where is the professor of Christianity among all the
worldly sects — I mean outside of this fold — who can, with this
single test of Paul's before him, stand up, with his hand on his
heart, and his eyes turned toward heaven, and say: "I am a
Christian?" I venture the assertion that not one can be found.
And why? Because they all go on gratifying the flesh instead
of crucifying it. They also live in the flesh and walk in the
flesh; all in direct opposition to the test here given by Paul.
This is a sweeping charge, and oh! that it were only false! In
heaven's name, and the name of Christianity, I fervently wish it
were. There is but *one* right way, and I cannot say any are right
when the good fruits are not manifest.

I have endeavored to convince all that by coming into the "new
world" — by taking up the cross and leading the Christian life of
self-denial — all would thereby be rendered more happy here and
hereafter, than by remaining in the "old heavens" and continu-
ing in the worldly life. If this is not true, the Son of God failed
in His mission, and came into the world in vain. All will admit,
however, that moments of pleasure attend you:

> "There is, I grant, a triumph of the pulse,
> A dance of spirits, *a mere froth of joy,*
> That mantles high, that sparkles and expires,
> Leaving the soul more vapid than before."

But if there are still those who contend that true and perfect
happiness is to be found in the outer world, let them produce
their evidence. Statistics have shown that in at least one locality,
out of about one hundred thousand families, only thirteen were
considered perfectly happy! But the condition of even the best

of these, the confessional might disclose the part of Popes Placebo
and Justin :

> "In spite of all his praises must declare,
> All I can find is bondage, cost and care,
> Heaven knows, I shed full many a private tear,
> And sigh in silence, lest the world might hear!"

If this, then, is the case with those considered most happy,
what must be that of the most miserable?

And what the condition of the *libertine*, whose sole enjoyment is —

> "——————— A transient gust,
> Spent in a sudden storm of lust—
> A vapor fed from wild desire—
> A wandering, self-consuming fire?"

THE CAUSE OF TRUE HAPPINESS.

It would be a heinous crime in any person to use his endeavors to render any human being unhappy; but the surgeon who amputates a limb, although he produces momentary suffering, does a benevolent act, as the pain thus inflicted is for the salvation of the body. So it is with individuals, who many times inflict on themselves temporary pain for the sake of future comfort

There is scarcely any thought within the mind that does not either produce happiness or misery, and this happiness or misery depends mainly on our previous action. If we have governed the passions, and acted honorably, our reflections produce happiness; if we have not, we have misery.

" The infinitely wise author of our being has given us power over the several parts of our bodies, to move them or to keep them at rest, as we see fit; and the same over our minds, to choose among its ideas which it will think on." " And He will show us the path of life; in whose presence is fullness of joy, and at whose right hand are pleasures evermore." Psa. xvi, 11. Then, " let the unrighteous man forsake his *thoughts*." Here is where self-denial should begin. If the thoughts are directed aright, right actions will follow as a consequence, and happiness be the result. Of this I feel certain, that any one who will avail himself or herself of the facilities afforded by the gospel of Christ, even though he or she may have been weakened by malpractice, can, by the choice of his or her mind, in preferring subjects to think on, or actions to perform, or motion or rest for any part of the body, cause the existence or non-existence of such action or motion, " they shall have power to become the Sons and daughters of God " Hence, says Christ· " If thine eye offend thee, pluck it out and cast it from thee, for it is profitable that one of thy members should perish, and not that thy whole body should be cast into hell; and if thy right hand offend thee, cut it off, and cast it from thee," etc. Matt v, 29. Christ would not have thus instructed us, unless we had the power to do. What I would show in this connection, is that, notwithstanding

I have said that we could secure greater happiness here and hereafter by entering Christ's fold, and practicing the work of self-denial, than by following the course of this world, yet I would deceive none If any suppose he can pluck out and cut off the members, which are dear to him, without suffering pain, he is laboring under a delusion. What I would have all understand from these words of Christ is, that in order to secure *true happiness*, a painful operation must first be endured. The adulterous eye must be plucked out, and the hand that worketh iniquity must be amputated, and each must do it for himself; but he cannot do it to any good purpose until they offend his higher impulses and aspirations. Whenever we become so far enlightened by the truth as to discover that those organs are obstructions to our spiritual progress, we will then be prepared for the operation, and not before Think not that this can be effected without tribulation. "And one of the elders said unto me, what are these arrayed in white robes, and whence come they?" "These are they which came out of great tribulation, and have washed their robes and made them white in the blood (life) of the Lamb For the Lamb which is in the midst of the throne shall feed them, and shall lead them into living fountains of waters; and God shall wipe away all tears from their eyes." Rev. vi, 13, 14, 17. Thus, we may perceive, that, after amputation, the washing, cleansing, and healing processes are to be endured, and, without faithful endurance in self-denial, the true happiness sought for is unattainable But I would not, on the other hand, have any one to be the least discouraged on account of anticipated tribulation; but whenever any of the works of the flesh become offensive, then is the call of God to commence the plucking, amputating and cleansing to be healed ; and, if we are faithful, God will give the necessary power of execution and endurance When this period arrives, we should not stop to consult first, second nor third cousins, nor nearer relatives about it; but like Paul, come right up to the good work, and stop not to " confer with flesh and blood ; " and when once we have put our hand to the gospel plough, look not back, lest we " fall away," when our misery will be augmented in proportion to the light, gifts and blessing of God we have abused.

> " Ere such a soul regains its peaceful state,
> How often must it love, how often hate—
> How often hope, despair, resent, regret,
> Conceal, disdain, do all things but forget "

None will now say that I have tried to deceive them. But it cannot be portrayed so plainly, but what it will " come as a snare on all them that dwell on the face of the whole earth." Luke, xxi, 35. " Think not," says Christ, " I am come to send peace on earth: I came not to send peace, but a sword. For I am come to set a man at variance against his father, and the daughter against her mother, and the daughter-in-law against her mother-in-law, and a man's foes shall be they of his own household. And he that taketh not his cross and followeth after me, is not worthy of me." Matt. x, 34, 38. The whole nature of the mission of Christ may be herein discovered : The call is from the rudimental to a higher state of existence. Every one who has taken time to reflect will agree that the generative is the rudimental condition of man ; promiscuity, the first and lowest ; marriage and orderly generation, the second and best condition of the rudimental state, which still leaves man on the same plane with the orderly part of the animal creation. To progress at all from the animal, is to rise with Christ to the celestial, for we " cannot serve two masters "—the flesh and the spirit—nor live on the animal and celestial plane at the same time. If we attain to the latter, the former must be rejected. " Choose then this day whom you will serve: if the Lord be God follow him; if Baal, then follow him. For know ye not that to whom ye yield yourselves servants to obey, his servants ye are to whom ye obey, whether of sin unto death, or of obedience unto righteousness." Rom. vi, 16.

It is very clear, then, that all who choose the rudimental life must remain on a level with the animal part of God's creation— on the plane of self-love. The very quintessence of this state is a contracted selfishness. The love of God, which is universal, cannot reign in the soul ; for any contracted love is not the love of God. It is in the very nature and fitness of things, in the highest rudimental condition, that their loves be partial, animal, selfish ; it is, and must be so with man and beast, with fish and fowl ; and cannot be otherwise. Men may be willing for, and even wish others to be blest—still it is self first ; and the very best prayer that any such can offer from the heart is :

" Yet, O Lord, bless me and mine,
With graces temporal and divine,
That I for gear and grace may shine,
Excelled—by none;
And all the glory shall be thine—
Amen, Amen ! "

Men may and do repeat verbal orisons of higher import, but
sounds are nothing when the acts of their lives are at variance
with them.   Their loves being partial, their happiness is partial;
their desires contracted, their happiness is contracted, being contracted, it has its beginning; having its beginning, it has its
ending.   The quaint Thackeray, thus well describes it: " Who
does not know of eyes lighted by love once, where the flame
shines no more?   Of lamps extinguished, once properly trimmed
and tended?   Every man has such in his house; such mementoes
make our most splendid chambers look sad, such faces in a day
cast a gloom on our sunshine.   To oaths, mutually sworn, and
invocations of heaven, and priestly ceremonies, and fond belief,
and love so fond and faithful that it never doubted that it should
live forever, are all of no avail toward making it eternal.   It dies
in spite of the banns of the priest.   It has its course like all mortal things—its beginning, its progress, and decay.   It buds and
blooms into sunshine, and it withers and dies."   The love of God
alone is eternal

The Saviour's command is: "Love your enemies.   If you
love them that love you, what reward have ye?   Do not publi-
cans the same?   If ye salute the brethren only, what do ye more
than others?"   Matt. v, 46.   This is the love of God that you
keep his commandments   1 John, v, 3.   Hence we see the love
of God is universal, and must extend not only to neutrals, but to
enemies.   How many of us can say we are in possession of God's
love?   One thing is certain: His love is either contracted and
partial or it is not; and if any partial love can be God's love, it
only then remains for us to know how much it may be contracted
and still continue to be God's love in the soul.   Can it be contracted to one nation? or one tongue? or one color? or one profession?   If so, why not to one family, or to one person, or even
to one's self?   Can any one of these be God's love?   By no
means.   It follows, then, that any one thus circumscribed has not
God's love in the soul.   Oh! how weak short-sighted mortals
sometimes are!   What folly, what miserable folly it is in any
one to base his happiness on such a fleeting shadow.   Of its disastrous consequences, evidence is nowhere wanting.   Such ones
generally expect the loved one to afford them much pleasure; but
failing in this expectation, their love oozes out in proportion to
their disappointment.   It wanes, withers, fades, and dies.   The
loss of the realization of their fond hopes, either before or after

trial, not unfrequently destroys the functions of the body, and occasions pining, melancholy, insanity and death. Of one such, who took to the Dismal Swamp, in Virginia, the poet Moore sang:

> " He built him a boat of the birchen bark,
> Which carried him off from the shore—
> Far, far he followed the meteor spark—
> The winds were high and the clouds were dark;
> But the boat returned no more!"

Not so with God's love. In this, there are no mistakes, no blunders; it brings no disappointments; it brings no tears, no sorrow, no pining, no repining, no melancholy, no insanity, no death, but is like a " well of water springing up to everlasting life." In the picture given by Thackeray, we see the condition of rudimental man, with his perishing hopes, loves and joys. But it is said " truth is stranger than fiction;" and certainly it is passing strange that enlightened, human beings, who know the truth of these statements, and with the life and teachings of the Saviour before them, still continue to " chase a phantom through the fire, o'er bog and brake, and precipice, till death, all for contaminating trash or one thrill of sensual delight ' even at the expense of their union with God, their hope of heaven; they stoop down and worship mere filthiness! And thus are they goaded through every slough, from the cradle to the grave!" forging their own manacles, and loading themselves down with fetters and ponderous chains, coil after coil, each more difficult to sunder than the first; locking their own prison doors, and darkening the windows, that no light may possibly reach them, to expose them even to themselves!

> "Oh' where the slave so lowly,
> Condemned to chains unholy,
> Who, could he burst
> His bands at first,
> Would pine beneath them slowly? "

But it is one of the easiest things in the world for men to find reasons for what they desire. I venture the assertion that there never was a soul that experienced hell, but could furnish you a reason how he came to get there, just as though he ought not to suffer because he could furnish a reasonable excuse for doing the acts that brought him there! Thus people go the road to ruin, pleading excuse to themselves all the way, and flattering God with his goodness and mercy, but forgetting that he is just. The dram-drinker pleads the stomach's necessities; the tobacco-chewer, the inactivity of the salival glands; the gambler, "if we're agreed whose business is it?" the publisher of light literature, the demands of the public; the lawyer must defend his client, innocent or guilty; the doctor had better take money for a dough pill than for one that would injure the patient; the merchant and broker must accommodate the public; the harlot pleases the demands of libertines as a means of subsistence; the libertines plead the harlot's necessities and the demands of their God-given natures (?), and the orderly generative man cannot follow Christ because he has the higher (!) duty to perform of peopling the world, that God may have more souls to worship Him. This latter I propose to examine, as it carries on its face a degree of plausibility which entitles it to some consideration — all the rest sufficiently exposing themselves.

First, Are these generating men sincere, who at the same time acknowledge it more than probable that nine-tenths of the souls thus propagated will be candidates for, and denizens of the lower regions? Thus nine-tenths of their work is for the devil, and only one-tenth for God — nine-tenths for misery, one-tenth for happiness — nine-tenths for hell and one-tenth for heaven. While this is the belief, and facts appear to demonstrate its truth, the excuse for propagation seems utterly void of justifiable or reasonable foundation, and only exposes the hypocrisy of him who urges it

Secondly, the argument further runs: Whether one or all of my offspring get to heaven or hell is a matter between them and their God But it is right for all men to do right; a right cannot be wrong, and what is right for *one* man is right for *all* men, and what is right for all men is wrong to be neglected by any man; for to neglect a right thing is a sin of omission. It is further urged, if we are not to be saved until we cease propagation, then all ought to cease; for certainly all ought to be saved. If this cessation is necessary to salvation, it is then right for it to cease. Hence it follows if all do right the earth will inevitably become a howling wilderness in less than two hundred years, and thus God would be made to defeat His own purposes.

I will examine the sincerity of these generating saints. They assert that it is right for men to propagate, and according to their

6

mode of reasoning it is right for all men, and being right for all men, it is wrong, and consequently a sin, for any one to omit or neglect this right thing. This would make Jesus Christ and Paul, and in fact all of Christ's immediate followers and the apostolic church at Jerusalem sinners! Again, these sophistical reasoners say it is right to fight, and go themselves as chaplains for the army, urging mad men on to carnage, blood and slaughter,

> " Who, foe to nature hears the general groan,
> Murders their species, and betrays his own."

Then, according to their logic, it is right to kill men, and if it is right for one, it is right for all, and being right for all, it is wrong in any to omit it; and what would be the consequence? The world would be depopulated in less than one decade, instead of two hundred years. Thus do those sophists outreason themselves. But candor compels me to admit the reasoning to be good from the premises assumed ; and were the postulate true, it could not be faulty ; but, unluckily for them, their postulate is false ; for, what is right for one man is not right for all men. There is only one thing in my knowledge which is right for all men, and that is : It is right for all men to think, speak, and act in conformity with the highest light God has vouchsafed to them—the highest they are capacitated to receive. In so doing they obey God, and to obey God is to do right. This I think cannot successfully be resisted It is either right for a man to do what he conscientiously believes to be right, or else he must do the contrary—what he believes to be wrong If it is right for a man to do what he believes to be wrong, then I grant the whole world is doing right ; for the number is small, indeed, who do not do what they think is wrong under the shining sun of every day

But I am pressed further, and told that a principle is wrong in the abstract, which, if carried out, would militate against the plans of the Creator. I beg leave to say that abstract evil is only a creature of the imagination ; instead of wrong existing abstractly, it exists concretely, nowhere only in persons. We make ideal abstractions of goodness, whiteness, blackness, etc., when such abstractions have no existence only in our minds ; for goodness can have no existence only as it inheres in some being or substance capable of being, or doing good, and just so of all other abstractions. But the same argument comes against the principle of propagation that does against non-propagation The earth, we know, is of a given size—just so many roods and perches. The best calculation makes it to contain thirty-two billions of acres. It is ascertained that there are now about eleven hundred millions souls on the earth's surface, and this population doubles itself in less than sixty years, with all the deaths by disease, wars, famines and celibates that have ever existed. According to this, five hundred years will see the end of the world if propagation goes on at the former rates of increase ! The professing evangelical churches believe that at some time God will burn up the earth—men, women, children, beasts, fish and fowl. This grand conflagration must take place inside of five hundred years, else people will die of starvation, if propagation goes on as formerly But professors who depend so very much on God's mercy, seem not to be alarmed, neither at the shortness of the time nor at the inhumanity of the act ; but profess to believe that God, with a lucifer match, will touch off this earthly ball when they have propagated and filled it with human beings to its utmost capacity ; and that this awful day may soon come is the prayer of all Christendom ; and when the trump sounds, they suppose that a select few will mount the skies in the upper air, the majority left to be consumed in the fire—these to groan, those to rejoice. And all this because the chosen few stuck to their faith without wavering; not that their lives had been better than others, but because they never ceased to believe they should see

> " The wide earth to heaps of ashes turned
> When heaven itself the wandering chariot burned "

This has been the theme and the song of the poet and the orator, and the fervent prayer of the sinning Christian for the past thousand years and more. Oh how devoutly is it prayed for by those who consider themselves the select few , who on that auspicious day will rise in their ascension robes! Holy families' Men and their wives and their children shall ascend up out of harm's way :—

> " Far in the bright recesses of the skies,
> High o'er the rolling heavens, a mansion lies,"

there to wait and shout themselves hoarse, until God, for their special convenience, shall have created a new earth out of the ashes of the old one, when they will descend and take " peaceable possession," and then propagate a new race, which, of course, will not fall again as old Adam did, for all the Adams and Eves of this country will be holy !

Although Pope, in the lines quoted, might seem to favor the general belief, yet he forcibly corrects it :

> " O Sons of earth ! attempt ye still to rise,
> By mountain piled on mountains to the skies ?
> Heaven still with laughter the vain toil surveys,
> And buries madmen in the heaps they raise "

But Dr Young, the pious believer, most sublimely portrays the (anti) Christian idea.

> "   *   *   *   At the destined hour,
> By the loud trumpet summoned to the charge,
> See all the formidable sons of fire—
> Eruptions, earthquakes, comets, and lightnings play
> Their various engines; all at once disgorge
> Their blazing magazines, and take by storm
> This poor citadel of man   *   *   *
> *   Hell bursting forth her blazing seas
> And storms sulphurous, her voracious jaws
> Expanding wide, and roaring for her prey;
> Above, around, beneath, amazement all !
> Terror and glory joined in their extremes,
> Our God in grandeur, and our world on fire ! "

But the professing world are mistaken in this, as they seem to be in most other things They are, first, mistaken in Deity ; secondly, in Christ; thirdly, in the Judgment; fourthly, in the world that God has promised to burn up ; fifthly, in the qualities requisite to constitute a true Christian , and sixthly, in God's plan for the redemption and salvation of man.

I do not doubt the honesty and sincerity of the professing world in the matter here set forth ; but their ideas are as simple, ill-founded, and not more sublime than those of the little girl, who, being asked by her mother what the stars were, replied: " They were holes God made in the sky to let the glory down."

It is very evident to me that God's plan for burning up the world is quite different from that entertained by the nominal professors of Christianity. *His* plan is wise, just, merciful, and good. *Theirs*, contracted, partial, selfish, diabolical, and unjust ; doing the utmost violence to all the attributes they ascribe to Him The " arch-fiend " himself whom they suppose presides over the " infernal regions," could invent nothing more at war with the attributes of God than this plan for the consummation of all things. To fill the earth to its utmost capacity, then on a given day burn it up with literal fire — men, women, boys, girls, babies, born and unborn; and then give his "infernal majesty nine-tenths of the proceeds" Not so, friends. The wisdom of God is displayed in this, that, while He burns up the world, He checks propagation — elevates and happifies the man by calling him out from, and above, the rudiments of a sinful world

At the risk of being thought tedious, I will notice the principal text of scripture relied on to sustain the old heaven theory "But the day of the Lord will come as a thief in the night, in which the (old) heavens shall pass away with a great noise, and the elements (of the old or Adamic world) shall melt with fervent heat; the earth also (the old earth and earthly works of the earthly man in contradistinction to the spiritual) and the works (carnal) that are therein shall be burned up" (by the fire of the gospel of Christ). "Seeing, then, that these (old, earthly, carnal) things shall be dissolved, what manner of persons ought ye to be in all holy conversation and godliness (so as to be worthy occupants of the new earth and heavens in which ye now reside'" II Pet. x, 11.

The careful student need not have any, nor but little difficulty, if he will correctly apply the terms *earth*, *world*, and *heaven*, as well as *fire* and *burning*, etc. Reference being nearly always had to *man* and man's condition in the different dispensations, and rarely to our globe and the visible, literal heavens, as thought by many. I would cite a few texts: "They shall be burnt with hunger," etc. Deu xxxii, 24. "A *fire* goeth before him His lightning enlightened the world (the people of the world). The earth saw (earthly men) and trembled. The *hills* melted (high, exalted men) at the Lord's presence" Psalms iii, 4, 5. Then, says Paul: "That wicked world (or spirit of iniquity in man) shall be revealed, which the Lord shall consume with the spirit of his mouth (whose tongue is a devouring fire (Isaiah xxvi, 27), and shall destroy by the brightness of his coming (with a light eclipsing all other lights)." Thess ii, 8

"Give ear, O heavens (people of the old heavens), and I will speak; and hear, O earth (earthly man), the words of my mouth: My doctrine shall drop as the rain; my spirit shall distil as the dew, as the small rain upon the tender herb, and as the showers upon the grass" Deut. xxxii, 1, 2.

ABSTRACT EVIL.

A minister of note, and of much more erudition than I can claim for myself, insists upon the fact of abstract evil, saying — first, a principle, which, if acted upon, would produce evil, is an evil principle, therefore evil in the abstract; secondly, a being that is evil in and of himself, such as the devil, is abstract evil; thirdly, the disposition in man to do evil is an evil disposition, and therefore is abstract evil; fourthly, the fire that burns, and the floods and hurricanes that destroy are natural, abstract evils. I will examine these positions, and, if I find them true, it will be my pleasure to yield. In order to be clear, terms must be well defined. First,—" Principle in a general sense is the cause, source, or origin of any thing." Secondly, Evil — " having bad qualities — deviation from good by a moral agent." Thirdly, — In the abstract, "a state of separation," etc. First — If, upon examination, it be found that the cause of evil is evil itself, or has bad qualities, we shall then have abstract evil. The numbers 6, 8, etc, are of themselves abstract numbers, but when we say 6 feet, 10 men, they become concrete. They are nothing more than an idea until linked with some substance. So it is with principles.

When God had finished His works, including man, He not only pronounced them good, but *very* good; so that we find the evil all the while resulting from the misapplication or wrong use of some good thing — so, *evil* is *concrete;* for instance, the principle of hunger in man causes him to eat to sustain life, but a wrong use of the faculties that satisfy hunger produces evil and death. It is just so with all the faculties and dispositions pertaining to our existence. When we see a man disposed to do wrong, we say he is yielding to the evil principle, when it is nothing more than a wrong use of a good faculty or principle. The same may be said of all natural evil — the wrong use of a good thing. It is therefore unphilosophical to suppose that good and evil exist abstractly. If we speak of whiteness or roundness, the *terms* are abstract, but we must have reference to some substance, either white or round, as white flour, round table, etc, which renders them concrete and not abstract. All the mental abstractions which we make of good and evil are but the dispositions of the mind with regard to pleasure and pain. Whatever results in happiness we call good; and whatever results in misery we call evil; and although the ideas of good and evil are distinct and opposite, as much as pleasure and pain, yet nothing is more obvious than that these two sensations can be and constantly are produced by the same agent. How pleasant, good, and agreeable is fire in a cold day at a proper distance; but if brought too near, what evil and pain it produces. How terrible the calamity when this *good thing* devours cities and multitudes of human beings, and destroys, as it does sometimes, the labors of a century in a day! The same may be said of water, air, and other substances As to his "Satanic Majesty" — if he is a ball of evil and nothing else, rolling through God's universe, throwing off his scintillations wherever he can find a receptacle, I would be compelled to admit that there was such a thing as abstract evil; but as this is not palpable and admits of a reasonable doubt, I feel obliged to maintain the position that evil is concrete. I shall, by and by, pay my *devoir* to the supposed important being called Devil, that has claimed so great a share of public notice for many years. But I am informed that, since I have agreed that God gave us *all* of our faculties, and that they are not only good, but *very good*, in their right use, where is the reason for singling out and condemning the faculties of procreation? Please do not forget, that while they are *very good* in their *right* use, they are very evil in their *wrong* use. And where is the man who is able to use the faculties of propagation and confine them to the right use? If there is none, then they become very evil instead of very good, and who will say it is right to persist in very evil?

I am further told that I affirm it to be right for a man to do what he conceives to be right, and in doing this he is obeying God, and in obeying God " he is accepted with Him ;" hence if a man believes it is right to propagate, he is justified and accepted in it. I still affirm the same; and that no man does his whole duty short of obeying the highest light God has given him. He must obey the higher or lower light The man who feels it a duty he owes to God to propagate, and will confine himself strictly within the bounds of God's law of nature, this man will be an honor to the race and will be "accepted with God," but he will not be removed from the natural plane of being to the higher Christ plane, until he becomes further enlightened. He will still be on the lower floor. But if he continues honest, he will leave the earthly works of Adam and come to Christ. Nor can he be a full Christian and denizen of the new heavens until this last move is made. We must remember that people's consciences need to be enlightened as well as the understanding, and if this is not done, as it was to Paul, by an especial afflux from Christ himself, may it not be done, as Paul says, by our preaching? Let me again impress it upon you that the very best condition of a man who lives on the natural, Adamic plane is *below* the Christ plane and below the condition and state of His followers. You are kindly invited, then, to come up stairs, away from the rudimental, and leave the less enlightened to propagate until they shall have become enlightened by "the true light that enlighteneth every one that cometh into the (new) world."

But if your unfoldment or spiritual development is not yet sufficient to enable you to see the necessity of this, then it is neither proper nor right for you to come. The best thing for you is to remain on the lower floor and obey the Adamic gospel: Multiply, replenish and subdue the earth — devoting earthly propensities to the uses of propagation and to nothing else.

What would any of you think of the husbandman who, after sowing his field in wheat, would go on sowing the same field until harvest? thus not only losing his wheat, but blasting every expectation of realizing a good crop. Would you not call him insane. Most certainly. Just as insane is the man who is continually violating God's law of nature for the sake of pleasure; deadening his conscience, injuring his health, shortening his natural life, and blasting every prospect for sound and healthy offspring! Where is the man so stupidly blind as not to see the degeneracy of the race under such action! Ye men of nature, let your *consciences*, and not your *desire for pleasure*, guide your action.

Hear Dr. Beattie: "Conscience is the highest faculty in the human soul—the commanding, the authoritative portion of our nature—that which we are constituted to feel it our obligation, as well as interest, to obey. When we disobey its monitions we feel blame-worthy and are so. Since conscience prompts to virtue, it is a just inference that man was made for virtuous action ; and he

does not act according to the dictates of his nature as a whole,
when he gratifies his other faculties and propensities disapproved
by the supreme faculty—that which the Creator evidently designed to control our actions. The conclusion is, that to allow no
more to this part than to other parts of our nature—to let it
guide and govern only occasionally, in common with the rest, as
its turn happens to come—this is not to act conformably to the
constitution of man. * * ⌐ How foolishly those men argue
who give way to all their passions without reserve, and excuse
themselves by saying that every passion is natural, and that they
cannot be blamed for doing what nature prompts them to do. It
is only a part, and that confessedly inferior part of their nature
that prompts them to such indulgence. Their nature as a whole
remonstrates against such indulgence. It is, therefore, unnatural
in the proper sense of that word, and, therefore, to be condemned
and abandoned." Dr. Beattie was doubtless a good, natural
man, on the natural plane, and it would be well for the world
were there more such. He was under the law, and, perhaps,
obedient to the law, and as such an honor to mankind ; but salvation is not to be had under the law. " For what the law could
not do, in that it was weak through the flesh, God sending His
own Son, in the likeness of sinful flesh, condemned sin in the
flesh that the righteousness of the law might be fulfilled in us,
who walk not after the flesh but after the spirit. For they that
are after the flesh do mind the things of the flesh." And where
is the man of the world, married or single, who is not after the
flesh, and minding the things of the flesh? " But they that are
after the spirit do mind the things of the spirit. For to be car-
nally-minded is death (to the spirit), but to be spiritually-minded
is life and peace. Because the carnal mind is enmity against
God, for it is not subject to the law of God, neither, indeed, can
be ; so, then, they that are in the flesh cannot please God."
Rom. iii, 4, 5, 6, 7, 8.

I would have you particularly notice the last quoted sentence.
" *They that are in the flesh cannot please God.*" Show me then
the married man who is not emphatically in the flesh, and continually minding the things of the flesh. The man that thinks he
is not, and lives in nature's works, must be blind indeed.

> "Oh ! blind to truth and all God's works below,
> Who fancy bliss to vice, to virtue woe "

It only remains for us to examine ourselves. Ask yourselves

7

the question: Am I in the spirit (of Christ), walking in the spirit? or am I in the flesh and minding the things of the flesh? If we decide we are in the latter, then we must know we are weak through the flesh and under this law, and cannot please God. This is reason sufficient to justify any one in rejecting and coming out from the rudimental condition. But as before stated, if any one having no higher light than the Adamic gospel can and does rule and regulate his passions in the natural order, take a separate chamber, and give his soul to God on retiring to rest, never indulging his passions only as a duty for the sake of propagation, I would say of such a man as Jesus once said: "He is not far from the kingdom of God." He only wants one more step on the rounds of "Jacob's ladder" to enter the "new heavens," and be counted among the redeemed. But if this cannot be done, the only chance for the inebriate is "total abstinence." I think, my friends, that legal prostitution (pardon my plainness of speech) is almost, if not quite, as odious in the sight of God as the illegal, for he will take the motive for every act in the final balance. Let me illustrate: Two men are in the habit of drinking to excess; one rolls a barrel of brandy into his cellar and takes his excesses at home in a legal and orderly way; the other visits grog-shops and takes his by the glass. I wish to know, now, first, if both do not drink brandy? and, secondly, if it has not the same effect to demoralize and destroy both body and soul of each of them? If it does, where is the essential difference between them? Just so it is with perverted amativeness in the married state. Do not misunderstand me. I mean they are the same if they are both actuated from precisely the same motive, as motive must constitute the crime.

But I am told I might as well, and for the very same reason, condemn the faculties of the body that are given to satisfy hunger and thirst, as most men and women "now-a-days" use these faculties merely for the pleasure arising from mastication and deglutition, and not for use nor health. My response to this is: "Christ, our head and lead, has left us no such example; nor such teaching as total abstinence from eating and drinking. He has left us the example of total abstinence from sexual intercourse; He and His disciples denied themselves on this point, and taught all who would rise into newness of life to do the same, and the abuse of the faculties that satisfy hunger and thirst does not produce the one-thousandth part of the ills that "flesh is heir to,"

that the abuse of amativeness does This latter ramifies all nations, kindreds, tongues, colors, sexes and ages, from children to
the hoary head, dealing out desolation, misery, destruction and
death to soul and body, in the whole depth and breadth of its
wide track around the world. This is reason enough for its entire abandonment. Dr Dwight, in an essay on this subject, says :
" I shall devote a little space to the *mental* effects from the abuse
of amativeness (the sexual faculty).

> " I waive the quantum of the sin,
> The hazard of concealing
> But oh' it *hardens* all within,
> And *petrifies* the feeling "

It produces individual peevishness, fretfulness, irritability, and
irascibility, family jars and discords, conjugal quarrels, spite
vented upon innocent children, domestics, and slaves, social
animosities, sectarian strife, religious controversies, political
traduction, civil commotion, legal revenge, professional abuse,
academical conflicts, national wars ; all these will be coeval with
our present dynasty of lust and concupiscence. All the propensities and appetites are excited and inflamed beyond the natural
antagonistical control of the moral powers. But I cannot merely
glance at these. Philoprogenitiveness loses the moral balance of
conscientiousness and benevolence ; becomes detached from
reflection, vacillating between excessive indulgence to children,
and unjust repulsion. Adhesiveness, causing indifference and
contempt for friends, taciturnity, seclusion, and hermitage
Inhabitiveness, causing indifference to home — loaferism. Con-
centrativeness inducing fickleness, inapplication, unperserverance,
ennui, a social blank. Acquisitiveness, leading to improvidence
for one's self, household or the world, or the opposite ; exciting
unjust unlawful means to obtain money for the gratification of
lust, pride, vanity, etc. Alimentiveness, giving irregularity and
depravity of appetite ; all manner of cravings, gnawings, and
perversions, paving the way for flesh, grease, narcotics, stimu-
lants, excitants, irritants, etc ; by connection with perverted
taste one of the principal foundations for chewing tobacco, betel,
opium, etc But among all the fountains of the brain, vitativeness is the most supremely affected by perverted amativeness,
especially artificial indulgence. But in the wonderfully incomprehensible result, by which mankind can be the authors of life,
the vitality is suspended for a time. The spirit flies to the portal

for its exit. It returns to stay, but not to live under criminal repetitions of similar acts. The source of life is dried up. In this sin, and still more in self-abuse, we are " dead while we live " — a living death at the core of life! Existence becomes a shame, a burden, then a curse. The organ of vitativeness so injured by this abuse has the same relation to life that the heart has to the blood or the lungs to the atmosphere. Life perverted to lust is an outrage as positive as to turn the blood from the heart to the stomach, or the air from the lungs to the heart. Excited amativeness, then, is a *mountain of darkness and death* between our very existence and its fountain, and you might as well expect the sun to warm and enlighten the earth behind an eclipse of the moon. Lust is an iceberg between the mind and its fountain of life. But here we make the fundamental error when we consider these faculties were created for the insane paroxysms of gratification! * * Amativeness in repose results in health, sanity and felicity; in excitement, in disease, imbecility, impotency, fatuity, dementation, idiocy, insanity and death. * * The pores of the skin ooze out their fœtid odors; then perfumes must disguise the stench. Through the same channel come all artificials, gewgaws, ribbons, flaunting colors, pouting manners, sickly sentimentalism, etc. But the moral powers suffer the most deadly ruin in self-abuse. It terminates not upon the body, but lights upon the moral powers, which have their antagonisms of sin, death, hell, and devils in the perverted animal propensities — amativeness, the foundation pillar. Under this pollution and conscious shame, hope of happiness here and hereafter is forfeited, and as hope departs religious gloom and melancholy are the natural successors. Despondency and despair people the imagination with phantoms, ghosts, demons, and gorgons dire. Shut out from communion with light, purity, and holiness, they are in "fellowship with darkness," haunted visions, and mysteries. With truth and faith perverted, a disordered marvelousness gluts every sense. The vacant soul roams in midnight darkness, awaiting a still darker realm and more horrid gloom beyond the valley of death. In the progress of this vice veneration suffers, too shameful and impure to face man, how can he face God? If he worships the divinity at all, it is in his own temperature of icebergs and tartarian agues. That inextinguishable divinity in the efflux of his moral nature flickers in its socket. He seeks escape from his misery in some artificial

device of theological divination of man's devising; hides his face
upon some anxious seat, or under the curtain of some revival.
He has no eyes to see that morality which saves him *from* his
sins He gropes into the lap of some of the children of the
mother of mysteries (harlots) to be saved *in* his sins. We
should have the most clear convictions that such abuse of ourselves is the blackest cloud that intervenes between our souls and
the temple of goodness ; that while in this sin prayers and
churches will not save us. * * * Talk about educating ourselves for happiness under our present institutions ! As well
plant the vegetable before the sun at the focus of a burning lens.
Our carnal legislation and social systems of inhumanity and lust
are galling every muscle, sinew, and nerve to the bone. Humanity is reeking in gore ; groans, tears, blood, weeping, wail-
ing and gnashing of teeth are food to the mind * * *

Marriage nearly always originates in lust; and the prevalent
idea that it gives license to indulgence is a bane to health and
morality. One upas of the age; and until the mistaken idea of
happiness by animal gratification is cast from us, as an obsolete
dream, we cannot understand Christ's adultery of the heart ' Oh '
how long will society live under the destructive, putrefying theory
that lust may be conceived without sin !'' Echo answers, Oh '
how long ? Here, again, we have evidence piled on evidence from
among yourselves, corroborative of what I have said, and, notwithstanding I will agree, and even affirm, that marriage and
orderly generation are the true and best conditions for the natural
man on the animal plane of life, yet it can form no part of
Christ's kingdom It belongs exclusively to the " children of
this world," but not to Christ's followers and children, who are
not of this world; for " the children of this world marry and are
given in marriage. Those (of us) who shall be accounted worthy
to obtain that world and the resurrection from the dead neither
marry nor are given in marriage, but are as the angels in heaven ''
(who do not marry).—Luke xx, 34 It follows, then, that all
true Christians, in order that they " shall be accounted worthy,"
must not marry. We should be more consistent than Doctor
Dwight, who, after telling us that marriage nearly always originates in lust (he might have omitted the adverb *nearly*), turns
and tries to make it a holy institution, and thinks that under it
true happiness may be found. Delusive idea ' Has it not been
tried for more than five thousand years ? Where on the wide

earth is the man or the woman who has found it? What said
the wise man? "I made me great works; I builded me houses;
I planted me vineyards; I made me gardens and orchards, and
I planted trees in them of all kinds of fruit. I made me pools to
water therewith the wood that bringeth forth trees; I got me
servants and maidens, and had servants born in my house; also
I had great possessions, of great and small cattle, above all that
were in Jerusalem before me; I had gathered me also silver and
gold, and peculiar treasure of the kings of the provinces; I got
me men-singers and women-singers, and the delights of the sons
of men, as musical instruments and that of all sorts. I was great,
and increased more than all that were before me; * * and
whatsoever mine eyes desired I kept not from them; I withheld
not my heart from any joy. * * Then I looked on all the
works my hands had wrought, and on the labor that I had labored
to do; and behold, all was vanity, and a vexation of spirit. * *
Therefore, I hated life, because the work that is wrought under
the sun is grievous unto me."—Ecclesiastes i, 4 to 12, 18. Who,
after this, can have courage to try the experiment again? So far
it has proved an utter failure. "Why cumbereth it the ground?"
Doctor Dwight seems not to understand Christ's adultery of the
heart himself. Let me explain: The worldly elements are:—
"The lust of the flesh; the lust of the eye; and the pride of life."
The conception of these worldly lusts, or any of them, in the mind,
is sin. The individual *chooses* to think on them, instead of his
duty to God; this is the first step in the wrong direction. Then,
when the mind becomes fixed on them, this is sin or adultery in
the heart; then the very highest part of our nature has yielded.
Next, the mind directs the eye to look out for the object of its
carnal desires. All, then, that is wanting is the opportunity for
its consummation, which, of course, is effected at the earliest convenience. The man then is confessedly a "poor sinner in thought,
word, and deed!" But he stands accountable, because he *chose*
to think upon it; he *chose* to fix it in his mind; he *chose* to look
out for an object; he *chose* to consummate it; and he chooses
not to be damned for it! but would have Christ suffer in his
stead — the innocent for the guilty! But in this last, the culprit
cannot have his choice. God will attend to this in due time.
He cannot shift the sin he chose to commit on the shoulders of
another. This being true of *one* sin, it is true with regard to all

the sins of a man's life, either of thought, word, or of deed   Is
not this plain ?

If, as the doctor has said, marriage originates in lust (he was a
married man and ought to know), then the first thought to obtain a wife is sinful   The man commits the heart's adultery before he obtains the means for its manifestation   And here is
where the doctor loses sight of himself—the sight of duty—the
sight of Christ—the sight of heaven—the sight of God.   And
just so it is with all who may choose to fix their minds on pleasures instead of their duty to Him to whom they must " render
an account for the deeds done in the body, whether they be good
or whether they be evil "   But the doctor is to be pitied   Being
married, he was in a dilemma, and had to take one of the two
horns, either to come out and lead an entirely pure life, after the
example of Christ, and hence become a *Shaker*, or else gloss over
the marriage state and stick to his wife.   The difficulty, it seems,
was ·   " He had married a wife, and, therefore, he could not
come "   Luke xiv, 20   That woman in the valley of Sorek
was too hard for him   After slaying his thousands, and carrying
off the gates of Gaza, he was shorn of his locks, and is now
grinding in the prison-house of the Philistines.   Nay, ever since
" the sons of God saw the daughters of men, that they were fair,
and began to choose for themselves " (Gen. vi, 2), lust and nothing
else has been directing this matter.   Those sons of God took it
out of the hands of God, and their vile progeny " ———— whose
ignoble blood has crept through scoundrels ever since the flood,"
have kept it out, and so man stands accountable for all the evils
that follow in its train

Thus, I have answered the query why we do not deny the demands of hunger and thirst as well as that of propagation, still
admitting the abuse of the former   Let us all retire to our
homes, to our closets, and to our knees, and ask God for strength
to enable us to do His will.

If we find it impossible to do it there, then return to our
Father's house, where strength can be found, " for in our Father's
house are many mansions."

GOD'S LOVE.

In my remarks concerning the love of God in the soul, I did not think whether it would be understood that the love of the individual should be co-extensive with that of the Creator, or not. It may very rationally be affirmed that nothing which is finite can be co-extensive with the infinite—the creature with the Creator. It does seem to me that there must be a point where the wearied thought in its flight must stop to rest and return home. But this partakes too much of the speculative. I dislike to get into water so deep that my line cannot take the sounding. It has been well written that "the great occasion of disputes is that of men extending their inquiries, and letting their thoughts go beyond their capacity, to wander into those depths where they can find no sure footing." This position I wish to avoid.

The admission of limited thought implies limited love, and seems disastrous, as the advocates of this claim the right to set the limits of their love, most of whom would incline to make the circle very narrow.

The good Apostle John says: "God is love, and he that dwelleth in love dwelleth in God and God in him." 1 John iv, 16. This, at least, leaves no room for hate. This declaration of the good apostle needs some explanation. God is *infinite spirit*. *Love* is an essential attribute, as well as *power*, *wisdom*, etc. We speak as correctly when we say God is power, God is wisdom, God is truth, as when we say God is love. But it will not do to apply any of the negatives of these attributes to God—such as God is hate, God is weakness, God is folly, falsehood, etc. So it may be seen that all the apostle meant was, that if we live in God's attributes, or the attribute of love, we live in Him and He in us. In fact love is an attribute so prominent, that if we are in its possession, we can do no violence to any of God's attributes; hence the apostle said truly: "If we dwell in love (hate having no part in us), we dwell in God, and God in us. " We will emulate God's love, if we have His love in the soul;

that is, extend our love to all mankind, as far as we have capacity, and, if our capacity is unlimited, then we should equal God in loving; but if it is limited, then love to the extent of that limit —

> "Grasp the whole world of reason, life, and sense,
> In one close system of benevolence ;
> Happiness is kinder, in whate'er degree,
> And height of bliss, but height of charity
> God loves from whole to parts — but human soul
> Must rise from individual to the whole
>
> *   *   *   *   *   *   *   *
>
> Friend, parent, neighbor, first it will embrace,
> His country next, and next the human race
> Wide and more wide, the o'erflowings of the mind
> Take every creature in of every kind "

Such are the souls " who dwell in God and God in them "

Those professing Christians, who contend for, and strive to justify themselves in partial love, argue in this wise: They say "self-preservation is the first law of nature," and this includes self-sustenance in every sense — to kill rather than be killed, and to cheat rather than be cheated ; and seem not to know that all this is contrary to the teaching and life of Christ, whom they pretend to follow ; saying also, "who can love a mean man ? Besides, they say, it is impossible to love any thing that is not lovely ; that love begets love, hate begets hate, and every thing begets its like, and the Apostle Paul gives this piece of sensible and good advice, viz : "If any provide not for his own, and especially for those of his own house, he has denied the faith, and is worse than an infidel " 1 Tim v, 8. This was sensible enough for the kind of people Paul was addressing — those who had not left the rudimental life — who were babes in Christ, who had only made a beginning in the gospel work.

I admit, that while men continue in the private, worldly relations, they are yet on the animal plane, and their loves must be necessarily partial and selfish, the same as with bird and beast, consequently theirs is not God's love, but animal love. But all partiality must cease when we come out of that condition to Christ, and enter " the new heavens and earth wherein dwelleth righteousness "

Paul gave different counsel to the more advanced : " Let every one please his neighbor" (instead of himself), "for Christ did not please himself." Rom. xv, 2 Again : " Let no man seek his

8

own, but his neighbor's good." 1 Cor. x, 24. Thus we have
another standard by which to test our Christianity. If we cannot come on this ground, we may know we are not of that number who are one with Christ, one with God, with His love dwelling in us. "Thou Father in me and I in Thee that they may
also be one in us, that the world may believe that Thou has sent
me." John xvii, 21.

But, I am asked: "Why may I not be a Christian outside of
the Shakers as well as among them? Why cannot I cease from
propagation and live above the rudiments of the world, lead a
Christian's life, and be numbered with the redeemed, as well
as to come and submit to your discipline?" I will answer:
Why cannot a man get a good education without going to school
and submitting to school discipline? Why cannot a man learn a
trade without binding himself to service and obedience for a
term of years? Why cannot a man learn the art of war without
going to West Point and first becoming a mere automaton —
without being obedient to the letter to his superiors, and without
question of why or wherefore? Why cannot he learn it just as
well at home with his wife and family? All would say at once,
a man entertaining such ideas was a brainless idiot. Just as brainless is the man who supposes he can gain his salvation and the
treasures of eternal life without going to the God-appointed
place, and submitting himself in child-like obedience to the God-
appointed agents, and be instructed in that which, as yet, he
knows but little about.

God has said, He has placed his "fire in Zion and furnace in
Jerusalem" for the trial and purification of His people. We
then can be tried and purified only where the fire and furnace are.
Here is where "the Lion and the Lamb shall lie down together
and a *little child* shall lead them" — (the great and meek ones of
the earth) — Isa. ii, 6. '"Suffer little children (says Christ) to
come unto me and forbid them not, for of such is the Kingdom
of God. Verily I say unto you whosoever shall not receive the
Kingdom of God as a little child, he shall not enter therein."
Mark xi, 14, 15. By this we are made to perceive that the sacrifice to obtain the Kingdom is as great or greater, than to obtain any thing earthly, and must of necessity be so, as that which
is to be obtained is worth more to the soul than all worlds and all
therein. We here see that men must become as little children.
What are the condition and qualities of little children? Are

they not devoid of concupiscence, sexual and worldly lusts? Are they not dependent on their parents, father and mother? Obedient, simple, pure? Then, if the Saviour tells the truth, we may all know just how we have to become, or utterly fail to enter the Kingdom of God. "By their *fruits* shall ye know them." And Christ says, "an evil or corrupt tree cannot bring forth good fruit." Others may take issue with me, and ask, what are the fruits of the marriage tree? And answer that *children* are the fruits of marriage; and Christ says, of such are the Kingdom of Heaven; and what constitutes the heavenly Kingdom must be good, and the declaration of the Son of God that the fruit is good, and this fruit is the production of the marriage tree, is proof positive that the marriage tree is good, or else it could not produce this good fruit. With triumph you say, here - a "gordion knot" for you! Let us apply the sword of truth, and see whether or not it can be severed.

The sophistry in this reasoning consists in not only perverting the meaning of the Saviour, but wrongly placing the fruits of marriage. It should not be on the child, but on the individuals who form the marriage relation. What kind of *fruits* does it produce in *them?* Does it produce good fruits in them? Does it produce purity, chastity, holiness, godliness, and love for one's neighbor? Does it produce in them the state of the little child that knows no lust? If not, how are we to become as the little child, in order to be saved? But does it not produce the reverse of all this? Does it not produce impurity, unholiness, ungodliness, and selfishness? These are vital questions. I affirm that under it no man can possibly "love his neighbor as himself, and do unto all mankind as he would have them do unto him," in similar circumstances, without himself becoming a town or county charge That relation must be selfish. But, thanks to God, it *can* be done in Christ's Kingdom But further: If innocent children prove marriage to be an incorrupt tree. they also prove the same of whoredoms and the vilest incest; thus the gordion knot is severed.

It seems that there is nothing on the broad earth that man will not do to save his worldly lusts To him heaven would be hell without them He will argue for them; swear for them: toil for them; sweat for them; rise up early, sit up late; lie for them; steal for them; smile for them; weep for them; suffer for them; fight, bleed and die for them They are the life of

the world, and " what will not a man give for life?" And
although clouds of witnesses affirm that Christ has re-appeared
and established His church upon earth, and is the head thereof,
from which the worldly lusts are excluded, yet the whole world
wanders after the beast, "both professor and profane, and will
not be persuaded to renounce them for happiness and heaven,
although hundreds have arisen from the dead, and now declare to
a perishing world that such renunciation is the only possible way
to obtain it. How well the scriptures are verified which say :
" In the latter times there shall be scoffers and mockers walking
after their own lusts, saying, where is the promise of His coming?
For since the fathers fell asleep, all things continue as they were
from the beginning of the creation." II Pet. iii, 4. It has been
and still is the nature of man, to take his own way, and follow
his own inclinations ; and hence the whole world, in a moral
point of view, lies prostrate, mangled and bleeding at every pore.
And all this the consequence of each acting from his own selfish
impulses. I venture to affirm that there is no man, from the
king on his throne to the beggar in the street, who would not be
better, spiritually, if he were willing to be advised in all moral
action by another, although the latter might be intellectually his
inferior ; because all men are liable, when acting from their own
desires, to be led astray by them, instead of being ruled by conscience, judgment, and reason. Whereas, they should coincide
with the poet —

> " What *conscience* dictates to be done,
> Or warns me not to do,
> This, teach me more than hell to shun,
> That, more than heaven pursue."

Our friend would always advise us from his conscience and
judgment ; and hence would doubtless cross our desires, which
would be a benefit to us. The great wisdom of God is displayed
in Christ's church, where this counsel can always be had. Happy
indeed is the individual who avails himself or herself of it, and
surrenders entirely to its control. In no other way can we sur-
render ourselves to Christ, and those who do so are truly the ones
who can lead a sinless life. For the moment our own will, or
the will of any individual, usurps the place of this judgment,
Christ is denied, and passion, inclination and private feeling
warp the understanding and lead the soul astray.

Jesus Christ himself could not have been saved in doing His own will; but as the unfolding spirit of God within Him made known the Father's will, He had to deny himself, yield His own, and obey the Father or else be lost Can we be saved any cheaper? Not at all God, through this faithful agent, and His sub-agents, has established His kingdom or church on earth. To receive these agents is to receive Christ, and God. To deny them is to deny Christ and God, and cut off our prospect of salvation. Hence in doing his own will no soul can enter the kingdom of heaven

Still, with a modest show of reason I may be asked: What would be the consequence of an error in judgment of the governing power? We may as well ask, what would be the consequence of an error in the judgment of Christ himself If God has an agent, and we receive the agent, we then do what God requires of us — certainly He cannot condemn us for doing what He requires of us! But I will answer the question. It is impossible for them to lead you into moral evil; because it is always their conscience and judgment — God in the soul — that directs, and not their natural desires and passional nature. The greatest and only danger is, that of their yielding to *our* desires, through sympathy, and fearing we could not yet bear the whole truth Any one could direct a neighbor to his advantage morally, even though his inferior in goodness; but no sinner could tell him how to be saved, because of such not being saved from sin. How much more reliable, then, is the advice from one who gives it as Christ did.— by example more than by words. Coming to Zion, then, we cannot, with any reason or consistency, set up our own will in contradistinction to the judgment there established; but must become as little children, and learn how to be saved from all sin But how often have people fallen under conviction for their sins and gone to their minister for relief, and found none; because the minister himself was their co-sinner, and himself bound to say with the poet Burns —

> " Yet, O Lord, confess I must,
> At times *I'm* fash'd wi' fleshly lust,
> And sometimes, too, wi' worldly trust
>   Vile self gets in
> But thou remembers we are dust
>   Defil'd in sin."

This is all the priest can do for the poor sinner, acknowledge himself in the same category; but, being pressed by the convicted applicant, some such consolation as this is given by the blind guide: "My dear brother, you must throw yourself in confidence on God's mercy, which endureth forever. He well knows our weaknesses, temptations, and trials. Lean on the blessed Jesus; He is our only hope. There is no man liveth and sinneth not.' Believe His holy word. He is the Almighty God, who took upon Him our sinful nature and satisfied His Father — that is, satisfied Himself. God, by this very means, found out our precise condition. The great God became man for this very purpose. He was God and He was man. He died for us, and 'bore our sins in His body on the tree.' In the agonies of death He asked His heavenly Father to forgive the wicked Jews, and you know the Father would do whatever the Son would ask, because the Son was the Father Himself!" etc. The applicant, perceiving some inconsistency, begins to waver, but is told emphatically not to yield to doubts, for "he that doubteth is damned already." "Great is the mystery of godliness." The poor sinner, fearing worse consequences, brings himself to the sticking point, and exclaims, "Lord, I believe!"

When Christ came into the world and was commissioned to make known the way of eternal life to man, we are told that "when He was gone forth into the way, there came one running and kneeling to Him, saying: "Good master, what shall I do that I may inherit eternal life?" Jesus answered him: "Thou knowest the commandments, Do not commit adultery," etc. The young man, it seems from the statement, was a moral man; for he had kept these commandments from his youth up, and, supposing he was about right, he wished to know what he still lacked. Ah, how we hate to be told of our shortcomings! Jesus said: "If thou wilt be perfect, go sell that thou hast and give to the poor, and thou shalt have treasure in heaven; come, take up the cross and follow me."— Mark x, 17, 21. This was startling! The young man had no idea of meeting with such a rebuff; had no doubt but what he should receive "faint praise" for his moral honesty; but, instead, what a disappointment! The sword of truth penetrated his heart, and all at once he discovered he had done little or nothing toward his soul's salvation. Shocked by the startling idea of giving up all, he was filled with sorrow, and slowly arose from his knees, and turned his back upon the Saviour and walked off, as many of us would to-day were Jesus here in person to make us the same offer. Here the treasures of heaven and treasures of earth were placed before the young Jew, and we see which he chose, and will doubtless say he was foolish thus to reject the only means of his redemption for an earthly treasure which must so soon perish, and think we would not have done so. Christ this very day makes the same overtures to every one of us which He did to that young man, and He will receive nothing short of a strict compliance with the same requisition   Now let us see how many will do as the young man then did   If we do as he did, and we call him foolish, what should we call ourselves?

When Christ showed that all had to be forsaken that belongs to this world, Peter said to Him, "Lo, we have foresaken all, and have followed thee, what shall *we* have therefore?"   Jesus answered and said: "Verily, I say unto you, there is no man that hath left house, or brethren, or sisters, or father, or mother, or wife, or children, or lands for my sake and the gospel's, but he shall receive an hundred fold now in this time, houses and brethren and sisters, and mothers and children, and lands, with *persecution*, and in the world to come eternal life." Mark, x, 30.   Here, now, every one has the opportunity given him to "show his faith"   Christ plainly tells us what has to be forsaken and *left* and lost to us, and what is to be gained by the exchange   Who would not rather have a hundred houses than one?   An hundred brothers and sisters than half a dozen?   An hundred fathers and mothers than one? An hundred children, with a hundred acres of land than one child and one acre?   These are all easily answered, but here comes the difficulty, who will exchange his wife for persecution   Who will exchange the whole, wife included, for *eternal life in the world to come?*   Mind, we cannot get it without.   It is a fair offer.   Who will come to Christ and close in with the terms?   We will never get it any cheaper if we wait till doomsday.   Can we expect to get it cheaper bye- and- bye, persuading Christ to take back the persecution and let us keep the wife?   This is all that creates any difficulty on our part — all that makes us unwilling to exchange earth for heaven — the old heavens for the new.   The exchange is all on the side of the new heavens till we come to the wife.   It seems that a little persecution "is not adequate payment for the wife"   So men act, and they might as well at once confess, that they had much rather have one cabin, one acre of land, and one wife, than to become heir to all the heavenly promises, the wife being excluded! Such is the madness and folly of men and the power of lust over them.

The priest is as deep in this mire as the people, the surpliced minister as the layman; and they strive to mislead their congregations by telling them that Christ by using the term "*left*" did not mean to *leave* the partial relation for the hundredfold. He only meant to leave them in the affections, or out of the affections, and love Him more than these other things; as though Christ would be well satisfied if He could get only a little the larger portion of the love and affections, allowing the balance to go to the wife and children. But Christ shows that a divided love will not answer. He requires us to "love the Lord with *all* the heart, with *all* the mind, with *all* the might, and *all* the strength." If we do this, how much is left for wife or children, or other partial objects. Absolutely none But let any one undertake to divide it, and see if he does not find the poet's words true:

> "I waste the matin lamp in sighs for thee;
> Thy image steals between my God and me."

The buffoon in the street only portrays what is in the minister's heart, when he jocundly sings:

> "A little wife well willed,
> A little house well filled,
> A little land well tilled,
> Is heaven enough for me."

If Christ had only promised an hundred wives instead of one as he did an hundredfold of other things that had to be forsaken, the exchange would have gone on successfully, and there would not have been the first difficulty in the way. So it is plain that it is the desire for a husband or wife, and partial goods that unmans the man — makes him a sinner instead of a saint — takes him to hell instead of heaven. But when in the end he finds that all his wife-seeking, and woman-loving, and lust-indulging not only lose their relish, and fail to give him happiness, but leave him vacant, lonely, desolate, weary, Christless, Godless, and midnight darkness, he will close in with the song of the poet.

> "Though wisdom often sought me,
> I scorn'd the lore she brought me;
> My only books
> Were woman's looks,
> And folly's all they've taught me."

SCRIPTURE ANALYSIS — PRE-EXISTENCE OF CHRIST.

There are two apothegms, the truth of which, I doubt not, will be conceded by all thinking men

First. All mankind are blinded by passion in proportion to its indulgence.

Secondly. All are enabled to perceive more clearly the truths, or principles, that antagonize with the passions, in the proportion that they may subdue or deny the passional efflux. Let me explain.

Love and hatred, truth and falsehood, flesh and spirit, antagonize. So far as we yield to the spirit of hatred, we lose the possession and sight of love. When we allow ourselves to run into falsity, we lose sight of truth. To the extent we indulge the flesh and allow its dominion over us, just that far we lose sight of the spirit, and are shorn of its benign influences.

It so happens that mankind have allowed the lower passions to have the ascendancy over them, some ignorantly, others willfully, insomuch that they have become almost wholly blinded to spiritual truth, and go groping about like blind men under a noonday sun ; and the sole reason is, that they have allowed their lower passions, instead of the spirit of God in their consciences, to govern them. Whilst under the influence of hatred toward any person or thing, it is impossible that we should love that person or thing, Lord Bacon's paradox to the contrary notwithstanding. He says (paradox No. 10) : "The Christian loves *all men* as himself, and yet hates some men with a perfect hatred." Now, I differ with the learned man. It is impossible for a man to love *all*, and at the same time to hate any part of all ; for the moment he acknowledges that he hates a *part*, he not only contravenes the assertion that he loves *all*, and renders it nugatory, but makes it palpably false, and, false as it is, it is nevertheless in perfect keeping with all his paradoxes, numbering 34 ; and not only so, but it is very similar to much that is said to be believed

9

by the professing world. This is equal to saying he can cause "the same thing to be and not to be at the same time," which Locke says is impossible with God.

One of two things must be true in this case of the Baconian Christian : Either the men he hates with a perfect hatred are not a part of the *all men* whom he loves, or else he must *hate himself* with a perfect hatred in order to enable him to love all men as himself. If he hates himself with a perfect hatred, and then loves all men as himself, he then not only hates *some* men with a perfect hatred, but he hates *all men* with a perfect hatred, which makes him a *devil* instead of a Christian. So the Reverend Lord only mistook the title; but a rather serious blunder taking a devil for a saint ! But in this he has proven that hate can have no part in the Christian. Likewise, the "flesh and the spirit being contrary the one to the other," we cannot be in possession of both at the same time, nor can we alternate with them and be Christians ; yet this is the case with the professing world living in the flesh, claiming to be in the spirit, and wishing to be called Christians or followers of Christ, who, though tempted, did not live in the flesh. And as they have no works by which to show forth their right to the title, they come with the Bible as their voucher, and attempt to prove by it that they are what they are not, and expound the Bible to make it coincide with their ideas of what constitutes a true Christian.

If men would honestly take the Bible and search for truth, instead of searching to find support for some creed, or fanciful notion of their own creation, there would not be such a diversity of opinion as at present exists. But, "the natural man (the man who lives in the earthly order, professor or profane) receiveth not the things of the spirit of God ; for they are foolishness to him ; neither can he know them, because they are spiritually discerned."— 1 Cor. ii, 14. Hence, the Jewish Sanhedrim and all the Councils from that day to this, with all the Kings, Popes, Bishops, Cardinals, and laymen, and all commentators on the Bible text, being earthly and carnal men, have failed to unite on the plainest truths which are recorded in the good book. They have been for more than a thousand years, with all their extensive learning and research, "darkening counsel without (spiritual) knowledge," and instead of upholding truth, have been blinding each other, and those of the multitude, sometimes ignorantly, but often for sinister purposes, seeking to maintain and support their own peculiar creeds and dogmas, at the expense of truth, until they have made infidels almost without number.

It was well said: "Canst thou by searching find out God?" It may be asked: If not by searching, how shall we find God? I answer by obedience to the light within — to the dictates of "God within the mind." By so doing, step by step, we will increase in the knowledge of God, and "find him out to perfection;" and finally "have our lives hid with Christ in God" Col iii, 3. Jesus said: "I thank thee, Father, Lord of heaven and earth, because Thou hast hid these things from the wise and prudent, and hast revealed them unto babes. Even so, Father, for so it seemed good in thy sight." Matt. xi, 25, 26.

The wiseacres of this so-called Christian world have not only failed to find God for themselves and their flocks, but have placed themselves in the condition of the Pharisees who were always scraping the *outside* of the platter; of whom Christ said "Woe unto you scribes and Pharisees — hypocrites! for ye compass sea and land to make one proselyte, and when he is made ye make him twofold more the child of hell than yourselves" Matt. xxiii, 15 This will seem a heavy charge against those who are honestly (?) trying to benefit the race, and it may be asked. How is it they make him the child of hell? I will answer. because they lead off from the only true source, thus directing souls in the wrong road, in which the further they travel the more they are separated from God; and they acknowledge themselves sinners, which is true, and that *they* cannot live free from sin in this life, which is false. Thus they not only lead them into untruth, but make them feel justification in sin, as it were giving them license to sin; and every one they commit only adds to the Alps which are already between them and God They make them believe, that notwithstanding their "sins are as scarlet, Christ's righteousness will be imputed to them " Thus, with their sanction and support, the flocks go on sinning, "believing a lie that they may be damned " This is reason enough.

Before I proceed to the analysis of the scriptures, which are believed to declare the pre-existence and supreme Godship of Christ, I will, for the benefit of the young student, make a brief statement of the different kinds of reading he must encounter and consider, and of which the Bible is chiefly composed; and if he comes to the task unbiased by creed, his studies will be rendered comparatively easy. It may be summed up under the following heads:

I. HISTORY. — Relation of past events or facts.

II. METAPHOR. — Words used with other meanings besides the ones originally affixed to them, such as *head* of a person or church; *body* of a person, or *body* of the church; god, angel, serpent, vulture, eagle, sun, moon, stars, lion, lamb, bear, fox, dog, and other things; beasts and fowls, applied to man, which are not uncommon throughout the Bible. These should rarely be taken literally — only where the sense is unequivocal and plain; otherwise reference is had metaphorically to man, which I shall hereafter more clearly exhibit.

III. ALLEGORY. — Continued metaphor.

IV. EMBLEM. — Corporeal objects standing for moral properties; as the *Dove* is an emblem of meekness.

V. TYPE. — One object made to represent another mystically.

VI. INSPIRATIONAL. — Things supernaturally induced.

VII. DEVOTIONAL. — Duties to God. Acts of worship.

VIII. PROPHETICAL. — Foretelling future events.

IX. DOCTRINAL. — Positive teaching — true or false.

X. THEOLOGICAL. — The science of Divine things.

These, with the addition of *figure*, which is applicable to all the rest, comprehend the principal points of study. The whole book, the historical as well as other parts, abounds in metaphor and allegory, but from the days of the Florentine down to the honest Bishop Colenso, the metaphor of its history has been ignored to the great disparagement of the whole Book — some of which I will notice in a subsequent discourse. But when it is known that the whole relates to *man* and the works of God *in* him, and *with* him, for his progress, elevation, and happiness, and not to blind him by a mysterious reference to foreign angels, foreign bodies, foreign beings, a foreign God, and natural beasts, birds, reptiles, etc., the difficulties of understanding it, fixing and analyzing the parts, will be greatly lessened, and, by keeping this in mind, the student will generally be led to the true exegesis. But in no case should one explanation neutralize another. Our reason must decide when it is metaphor, and when it is not.

When reason revolts at the literalization, we may generally know that it, figuratively, relates to man. Locke says: "He that believes without having any reason for believing, may be in love with his own fancies, but neither seeks truth as he ought, nor pays the obedience due to his Maker, who would have him use those discerning faculties He has given him to keep him out of mistake and error. * * *

True light in the mind can be nothing else but the evidence of the truth of any proposition; and if it is not a self-evident proposition, all the light it can have is from the validity of the proofs upon which it is received. * * * If reason must not examine the truth of revelation or persuasion by something extrinsical to the persuasions themselves, inspirations and delusions, truth and falsehood, will have the same measure, and will not be possible to be distinguished." But to the texts. As an evidence that there were "sons and daughters of God" existing somewhere in space before Universe was made, we are referred to the 38th and 39th Chapters of Job. These chapters are among the most beautiful and well-written allegories in the book, and have no reference to a period previous to the creation of the visible universe. The visible and material earth, sea, etc., are used while the entire reference is to man and the old earth and heavens, that are to pass away. (What I mean by the old earth and heavens, is the work of God in and with man anterior to the first Christian dispensation, also the condition of all those who live in the heavens and earth that man lived in then.) Especial reference is had to the texts which read: "where wast thou when I laid the foundation of the earth? declare if thou hast understanding. Who hath laid the measure thereof, if thou knowest? Or who hath stretched the line upon it? Whereupon are the foundations thereof fastened? Or who laid the corner stones thereof, when the morning stars sang together, and all the sons of God shouted for joy?" Now consider: "Who is this that darkeneth counsel by words without knowledge?" Who can conceive of pillars, and corner stones, and foundations laid for earth or moon? Where is the way where the light dwelleth? What earth were the wicked shaken out of? What stars sang together, and what sons shouted for joy? What light from the wicked withholden? What wicked? What high arm broken? What gates of death opened? What doors the shadow of death? What paths to the house of darkness? Who were the bottles of this " old heaven " that contained drops of dew, or water to moisten the clods, and what clods, of the old earth ? Or to melt the stony heart ? Were all these questions now asked with regard to the present existing churches, there are few so dull as not to be able to answer them correctly. Then, why not apply them in the same manner to the order of God in the old heavens and earth ? It is easily done. These are allegories, and refer to man in the old heavens, at which time there were veritable sons and daughters " to sing and shout for joy " for the order of God then established with its pillars and corner stones, as the new earth and heavens are now likewise established, which are the antitype of the old. We need not go to the moon, nor the stellar heavens, nor refer to our globe, for an explanation of any part of it. The metaphor is very common in the language of our own time. To speak of persons being pillars of the church, stars of the first magnitude, lion of the day, etc., is common. If it is necessary to use such metaphors now, with the profusion and richness of the English tongue, how much more must it have been necessary in the infancy and great poverty of language that existed then, in the very days of sign and symbol, when the first characters of inspiration were written on scraps of parchment on leaves, and the inner bark of trees ? All commentators on the Bible text have not heretofore given half enough attention to its historical metaphor ; and any, who persistently cling to the literalization of the chapters noticed, are as simple as the woman, who insisted that the earth was flat and stood on a pillar of rock, and upon being asked what the pillar rested on, replied : " O, it's rock all the way down. "

Secondly. " Moreover, brethren, our fathers were all baptized unto Moses in the cloud and in the sea, and did all eat of the same spiritual meat, and did drink of the same spiritual drink ; for they drank of that spiritual Rock that followed them, and that Rock was Christ."—I Cor. x, 14.

These texts are easily understood without any reference to the Godship, or pre-existence of Christ. To be baptized unto Moses, was to be baptized into the spirit of the Law administered by him, just as Christ's disciples had to be " baptized into His death, etc." The spiritual meat and drink were the spirit and the life of the work He daily administered. The same as to eat the flesh and drink the blood of Christ is to receive His word and doctrine in order to have His life in us. As Moses was the God-anointed and appointed agent in the old heavens, this food came from him , *he* was that Rock, and therefore the *Christ* of the law dispensation. In fact this positively denies the pre-existence of the Christ of the new heavens, because Moses was the type of the latter, and the type must precede the anti-type ; whereas, if the Christ of the regenerative order had existed previous to Moses, that would destroy his typeship

Thirdly " Christ was the power of God and the wisdom of God." It is asked if these were Christ Jesus ? I answer affirmatively. Power and wisdom are attributes of Deity. Jesus did or did not possess them. If he did not, he was not the Christ ; if he did, he was the Christ. He showed forth God's power in the works he wrought, and his wisdom in all he did and said. He was, therefore, *the Christ*—a partaker of the divine nature, of which, also, each and all of his followers must be partakers — II Pet. i, 4.

Fourthly. " But thou Bethlehem Ephratah, though thou be little among the thousands of Judah, yet out of thee shall he come forth to me, who is to be ruler in Israel, whose goings forth have been from old, from everlasting."— Micah v, 2. I see nothing in this text declarative of the Supreme Godship of Christ or of his pre-existence In the first place it says that he who is to be ruler in Israel shall come out of Bethlehem (I say this with the knowledge that the best critics say he was born in Nazareth) ; secondly, the coming forth into existence is future ; thirdly, when that future time arrived a child was born named Jesus, who claimed to be the very ruler spoken of by the prophet. This text is quoted in Matthew ii, 3, where the word everlasting is omitted. But if it is insisted on, I will remark that the term " everlasting " signifies eternity, past and future So that if his goings forth were from the infinite past, the Supreme must have been meant, who could not have come forth from Bethlehem only in the subordinate sense, for he (the Supreme) existed there before Bethlehem did. But it is insisted that the Infinite Being, in his humanity, came forth from Bethlehem. This may be admitted with the following explanation : God, who was from everlasting, was in Christ Jesus, who, it is said, came out of Bethlehem. But this does not make Christ Jesus the Supreme, nor affirm his pre-existence. Again : If we notice the context we will find that the prophecy had reference to a man. " And this man shall be the peace when the Assyrian shall come."

Verse three, speaks of his having brethren: "Then the remnant of his brethren shall return, etc." It would not be sensible to say that God the Supreme was a man, and had brethren to return. For further proof I would cite the student to John vii, 42: "Hath not the scripture said that CHRIST *should come out of the seed of David*, and out of the town of Bethlehem, where David was ?" It is conclusive that if Christ was to come of the seed of David, he could not have come from everlasting, for David nor of "his seed were from everlasting. Again, if he came from David's seed, he could not have existed prior to David. So pre-existence is flatly denied.

Fifthly. "After me cometh a man which is preferred before me, for he was before me."—John i, 30. It is only necessary to notice here that it was a *man* spoken of as coming *after* him. *Jesus* was that man coming after John, who was *preferred* before him ; for he was (chosen to be) before him, and *is* before him (in "the gift of God."

Sixthly. "A body hast thou prepared me," does not mean either Mary's body, nor Jesus' personal body. The prepared body was the body composed of those who received him — "For his body's sake, which is the Church," — Col. 1, 26. The Gentiles should be fellow-heirs of the same *body,* for the perfecting of the saints, for the work of the ministry, for the edifying of the *body* of Christ ; the whole *body* fitly joined together. Saviour of the body—Eph. iii, 6 ; iv, 12, 16 ; v, 23. But now hath God set the members, every one of them, in the body as it hath pleased him. There is no schism in the body, but the members should have the same care one for another. *Now ye are the body of Christ* (which God has prepared for him, for the indwelling of his holy spirit) and the members in particular.—1 Cor. xii, 25, 27.

Seventhly. The first *man* is of the earth, earthy ; the second *man* is the Lord from heaven. — I. Cor. xv, 47. It will be perceived that it is *man* spoken of as being the Lord from Heaven — not the supreme, nor some foreign spirit, but the second *man* — the *spiritual man Christ Jesus,* in contradistinction to the first earthly man Adam. This spiritual man was Lord in the finite, dependent, and subordinate sense. To come from, or go to heaven or hell, has no respect to altitude, nor latitude. To ascend into heaven is to rise, as Christ did, above earthly things and conditions. To descend to hell is to sink into evil habits and practices, the bottomless pit of self-sought pleasures, that render us miserable. Thus our hell or heaven is made within us. To be sent from God or heaven, is to be commissioned or appointed by Him to communicate His will or heavenly tidings to man. "As is the heavenly, such also are they that are heavenly."

Eighthly. "If David then called him Lord, how is he his son?" — Matt. xxii, 45. The reason the Pharisees could not answer, was because they were carnal men, and knew nothing about the things of the spirit. The learned of this day seem to be equally in the dark with the Pharisee — "carnal and sold under sin" of their own confessing. No man in "that crowd" was able to answer him; but had one said: "Thou art David's *son* by *generation*, but the son of God and David's *Lord* by *regeneration*," Jesus would certainly have responded — thou hast answered truly

Ninthly "I am the root and offspring of David" — Rev. xxii, 16. This, as with all the rest we have quoted, fails to convey to my mind an idea of the Godship of Christ or his pre-existence. It is thought that Christ could not have been the root of David without *preceding* him He could not have been the offspring of David without *succeeding* him This proves at once that Christ was not the Supreme It is impossible that the Supreme could have been the offspring of David, in any sense. He, who is infinite in every thing and finite in nothing, and to whom nothing can be added, and *from* whom nothing can be subtracted. But the text is easily reconciled in both its parts. Christ *preceded* David in the *spiritual* order; He *succeeded* in the *natural* order He was therefore the root of David by regeneration, and the offspring of David by generation. In accordance with this the Prophet says. "And there shall come forth a rod out of the stem of Jesse, and a branch shall grow out of his roots, and the Spirit of the Lord shall rest upon him, the spirit of wisdom and understanding, the spirit of counsel and might, the spirit of knowledge and the fear of the Lord, and shall make him quick of understanding" — Isa. xi, 1 to 6. Thus we must perceive it could not have been the Supreme who had the fear of himself resting upon himself in order to make himself quick of understanding Also, the coming of Christ, this Branch, from the root of Jesse, makes his pre-existence impossible "Why speakest thou, O Israel? Hast thou not known

10

that the everlasting God, the Lord, the Creator of the ends of the earth, fainteth not, neither is weary? He giveth power to the faint, and to them that have no might He increaseth strength. Even the youths shall faint and be weary, but they that wait upon the Lord shall renew their strength; they shall mount up with wings as eagles; they shall run and not be weary, and they shall walk and not faint."

PRE-EXISTENCE AND GODSHIP OF CHRIST.

To the unprejudiced and unbiased mind, the further prosecution of the subject of the Godship and pre-existence of Christ must seem supererogatory — a waste of time and unnecessary trial of their patience. To all such, nothing further can be necessary. But to those who have had these false ideas ground down deeply into their very souls by a hireling priesthood, from early infancy to old age, it seems something more should be said; for it appears, that so long as one single text of scripture remains unexplained, they will still fall behind that, as an impregnable rampart, which truth dare not assail, forgetting that they have already yielded their strongest fortifications, and that it is folly to still try to save themselves behind their weaker ones. So firmly fixed has been the idea that Christ Jesus was super-human, and hence not a practical example for mere mortal man, that, after yielding points and principles which destroy their stereotyped but false notions of Him, they still remain obstinate, and will not yield until they are left without argument, or, so long as they can find in Holy Writ one single prop to sustain their confessedly false position.

I introduce to your notice all those texts of scripture which are claimed to support the false dogma of the Godship and pre-existence of Christ.

I. It is said, in order to prove the eternity and Godship of Christ, that He was a " Lamb slain from the foundation of the world." Rev xiii, 8. If this has reference to a pre-existent spirit or angel, we have no knowledge of such spirit or angel having been slain, and if such spirit had been anointed the Lord's Christ, and was slain, this slaying must have been the work of God, which is neither sensible nor probable, and if it be further contended that such Christ was God Himself, and was slain, God then must have committed suicide! To such absurd conclusions do wrong positions lead us. If it has reference to Christ — " the man, Christ Jesus " — it will not be contended that he was slain before Christ Jesus came into existence; hence it must either have been prospective, or reference had to the New World, not the old; in which case the sentence must contain an ellipsis, to be supplied thus: A lamb slain from the foundation of the (new) — or, as elsewhere expressed, *before* the foundation of the world (was completed), which foundation was not completed previous to His second appearing.

II. "Jesus Christ, the same yesterday, to-day, and forever." Heb. xiii, 8. It is supposed that the apostle here affirms the *immutability*, and consequently the Godship of Christ. By reading the context, it will be readily discovered that it was only His constancy, or fixedness of purpose, and unwavering devotion to the will of His Father. He sets before them this virtue for their imitation: "Be not carried about by divers strange doctrines; for it is a good thing that the heart be established with grace."— Heb. xiii, 9. As to fixedness of purpose, constancy and unflinching integrity and adherence to truth, His immutability is not denied; nor can the same be denied of other good men and women who reside in His new Heavens; for, "Herein is our love made perfect, that we may have boldness in the day of judgment; *because as He is, so are we in this world.*"—1 John iv, 17.

III. "Where two or three are gathered together in my name, there am I in the midst of them."—Matt. xviii, 20. It is supposed by this that Christ attached to Himself the attribute of *omnipresence.* This can the most readily be explained by reference to other texts. Paul says: "For I, verily, absent in body, am present in spirit, having judged already as though I were present" (in body).—I Cor. v, 3. "For though I am absent in the flesh, yet I am with you in the spirit, joying and beholding your order, and the steadfastness of your faith in Christ."—Col. ii, 5. So, then, if the former proves the ubiquity of Christ, the latter proves the same of Paul. What is true of one is true of the other.

IV. *Omniscience* is thought to be ascribed to Christ by the apostle where he says: "In whom are hid all the treasures of wisdom and knowledge."—Col. ii, 3. In turning to the text, we find it not only applicable to Christ, but God is included. Verse 2 reads: "That their hearts might be comforted, being knit together in love, and unto all riches of the full assurance of understanding, to the acknowledgment of the mystery of *God* and of the Father, and of Christ; in whom (God and Christ) are hid all the treasures of wisdom and knowledge."

But if it be contended that it only has reference to Christ, I would then cite you to what the apostle says to the Romans: "I myself am also persuaded that ye are also filled with *all knowledge*." — Rom. xv, 14. Again: "I thank my God always on your behalf, that in every thing ye are enriched by Him, in all utterance and in *all knowledge*." — I Cor. i, 4, 5. What is proved for one is proved for the other. If the former gives to Christ the attribute of *omniscience*, it gives the same to both Romans and Corinthians. Besides, Christ denies the possession of this attribute, by telling us that there were many things He did not know

V. "I am Alpha and Omega, the beginning and the ending, said the Lord, which is, and which was, and which is to come, the Almighty." — Rev. i, 8 This is either willfully or ignorantly referred to Jesus Christ, who, it is said, declares He is the Almighty. But, as the text itself says, it is the Lord that speaks, we need not refer it to another. It is admitted, that verses 16. 17, and 18, refer to Christ — "A sharp, two-edged sword (of truth) goes out of His mouth," etc., and if He is first and last, it must refer to the new creation, of which He is first and last; as, also, "the author and finisher of our faith." And if "He that now liveth was dead" (verse 18), it cannot refer to the Almighty, of whom it cannot be said He was ever dead in any sense of the term

VI. I have heretofore commented on and explained the first chapter of Hebrews and Colossians, where it speaks of God making the world by Christ, etc, but I did not notice the eighth verse of Hebrews: I. "But unto the son He saith: Thy throne, O God, is forever and ever; a scepter of righteousness is the scepter of thy kingdom." The ninth verse shows that the Godship spoken of is in the subordinate sense · "Thou hast loved righteousness and hated iniquity; therefore God, even thy God, hath anointed thee with the oil of gladness above thy fellows." It is easily perceived here that there was a God above Christ that anointed Him, and if Christ was the Almighty, or some high created spirit, it would be a question of some importance to learn who His *fellows* were, above whom He was anointed.

VII. "Unto us a child is born, unto us a son is given, and his name shall be called Wonderful, Counsellor, the Mighty God, the everlasting Father, the Prince of Peace." — Isa. ix, 6 It will be perceived that it was a child and son to whom these titles were to be given. A son — somebody's son — was to be called the Mighty God, etc. This prophecy has been fulfilled to the letter; for the "Son of Man," Christ Jesus, has not only been called the Mighty God, but many have gone so far as to call Him the Almighty God! I need only further remark, that anybody's son having been called, or being called the Mighty or Almighty, does not make him such, in our sense of these terms. There is but one Almighty Moses and others were called God — even magistrates were called Gods. Again: The prophet Jeremiah, speaking of the Son, says: "In his days, Judah shall be saved, and Israel shall dwell safely, and this is the name whereby He shall be called: the Lord our righteousness" — Jer. xxiii, 6. Also, the same prophet, doubtless referring to the second appearing of Christ in the female, says: "This is the name wherewith she shall be called: the Lord our righteousness."—Jer. xxxiii, 16 If the first proves the Son to be the Almighty God, the latter proves as much for the Daughter, but it does not prove this of either. "Hear, O Israel, the Lord our God is one Lord."—Mark, xii, 29

VIII. "Let this mind be in you, also which was in Christ Jesus; who, being in the form of God, thought it not robbery to be equal with God."—Phil. ii, 5, 6   The question which arises here, is. What mind was it that was in Christ which Paul wished also to be in the Philippians? According to the text it was evidently this: "To think it not robbery to be equal with God." He says Christ thought so and wishes and advises them to be of the same mind. If to be of this mind made Christ God, the same mind made God of the Philippians. This is only a different form of expressing the same idea which Christ Himself expressed—that *He* "was one with the Father, and the disciples one with Him," so that those who are one, in and for any purpose, are in that purpose in a certain sense equal. Christ more clearly expressed it than Paul, though both evidently meant the same thing, as Paul was citing Christ as their example in all things. Hence it was no robbery for the faithful to consider themselves equal with Christ, nor Christ with God, in the sense in which they were *one* — "God being in them all to will and to do," further, who being in the form of (or conformed to) God, the faithful being also in the form of (or conformed to) Christ, to God Nothing mysterious about it. Again: "Being found in fashion as a man (whilst He was in the form of God), He humbled Himself, and became obedient unto death; wherefore (in consequence of this obedience), God hath highly exalted Him, etc., that every tongue shall confess that Jesus Christ is the Lord, to the glory of God the Father; wherefore, my beloved, as ye have always obeyed (as Christ did), work out your salvation with fear and trembling, for it is *God that worketh in you both* (Christ and you), to will and to do for His good pleasure."—Phil ii, 8–14. By what has been said, it is easily seen in what the equality consisted. Whom God commissions, what *he* does, *God* does, in which they are equal without robbery. "The Father in me and I in you"—all one Adam Clarke, Tillotson, Whiston, and others deny the present rendering, making it appear that Christ did not arrogate to Himself to be equal with God; but I feel no necessity of availing myself of the advantage of their rendering.

IX. "He that hath seen me hath seen the Father."—John xiv, 9 Jesus did not expect Philip to understand that He was both the Son and the Father, personally, nor that He was the Father of the Son; but that He manifested the attributes and fatherly character of God, which they could see. Whosoever sees the attributes of God, sees God. Jesus manifested these attributes; whosoever therefore saw Him, saw God. Hence Jesus told the truth in saying "He that seeth me seeth the Father"

X. "In him (Christ) dwelleth the fullness of the Godhead bodily."—Col. ii, 9. The essential signification of the term *Godhead* is "*Divine nature or essence.*" That this dwelt in Jesus none will be inclined to deny; but it does not make Him the Supreme. This same essence is in all true Christians 2 Pet. i, 4

XI. "God manifest in the flesh, justified in the spirit, seen of angels, preached unto the Gentiles, believed on in the world, received up into glory"—1st Tim iii, 16. This text is also doubted, and has other renderings; but I will only say it cannot be denied that God was manifested in the flesh (of the man Christ Jesus who was), justified in the spirit, preached to the Gentiles, believed on in the world, and received up into glory.

XII. "Yet Michael, the Arch-angel, when contending with the devil he disputed about the body of Moses, he durst not bring a railing accusation," etc. Jude, 9.

If there are any who think that this Michael, to whom Jude referred his brethren, was a pre-existent, spiritual Christ, who was going about in the wilderness *incognito* and there met with the devil, the great enemy of God, when a contention arose between them about the corpse of Moses, I would suggest that they had not found the true exegesis. When we turn to Deuteronomy, we find an account of the death of Moses, and his burial, in the land of Moab, over against Beth-peor, and the people mourning about it; but we find no account of the contention spoken of by Jude. The place of his sepulchre was kept secret, but those who buried him must have known where the remains were interred, and if they were secreted from the multitude, it was, of course, by order of his successor, Joshua, who was the one that ruled in the matter.

The idea is extremely ludicrous to imagine that a foreign angel, Michael, wrested the corpse from the people, and another foreign, invisible angel, seeing it, comes in on the side of the people to restore it to them, when a contention ensued between these foreign invisibles in "the woods," somewhere in the land of Moab. I cannot close in with such literalization of the words of Jude. He was evidently speaking to them, as he says, of things they had known, and cited Michael's conduct, under the most trying circumstances, as an example for their imitation.

But the corpse of Moses was not the body referred to by Jude. That corpse could not be called the body of Moses after he had put it off, any more than any other lump of clay. The body of Moses spoken of, was that which was instituted and made under the Mosaic law. Here, then, is where the contention existed. Christ himself arose out of the body of Moses, and Christ's body, or Church, was formed out of it, which was an all-sufficient cause to create a contention between him and the devil in the Pharisees, or devilish Pharisees; and that such disputation as spoken of did exist, both Jude and those whom he addressed very well knew, and if Christ is to be understood as meant by the term Michael, it must have been the anointed Jesus to whom Jude pointed them for an example. No mystery about it; no pre-existent Christ; no unoriginated devil, *sub rosa.*

XIII. "Thou lovedst me before the foundation of the world." It must not be forgotten, that these expressions have reference to the *new* world that was made by Christ. Notice Timothy: "According as He hath chosen *us* before the foundation of the world."—2 Tim. ii, 9. What the text proves for the *me* that was *loved*, it also proves for *us* that were *chosen*. Further: "God hath in these last days spoken to us by His Son, whom He hath appointed heir of all things; by whom also He made the (new) worlds."—Hebrews, i, 2. It may be thought this cannot refer to the new world without conflicting with verses 10 and 11: "And thou Lord, in the beginning hast laid the foundations of the earth, and the heavens are the work of thy hands; they shall perish but thou remainest; and they shall wax old as doth a garment, and as a vesture shalt thou fold them up, and they shall be changed," etc. Whether we consider that the new heavens in the *last* days, in verse 2, and that which the Lord made in the *beginning*, verse 10, were the same or not, I see no conflict, for the new heavens of the first appearing of Christ *did perish and pass away* as predicted. The same may be said of the *old heavens;* they also waxed old as a garment, and passed away from all who entered the new heavens.

XIV. Paul says: "Jesus was made a little lower than the angels" (as the first man Adam was) I am asked: "If Jesus was made *lower* than the angels, can *He* be the person of whom it was said: 'When He bringeth His first begotten into the world, let all the angels of God worship Him?' this must, after all, be God Himself, as He only is to be worshiped." If this is the pivot on which the question turns, the claim to a "pre-existent spirit Christ" is destroyed; but reference is had to neither. The term worship is used in a modified sense. According to Webster, "to respect; to honor; to treat with civil reverence," is to worship. Hence the anointed Jesus was the man to be thus respected by angels; for He being made, as we were, a little lower than the angels, "yet for the suffering of death (of the carnal nature), He was crowned with glory and honor;" (v 2, 9), and thus, being made so much better than the angels, Hi by inheritance obtained a more excellent name than *they* —(Heb. i, 4.)

"Therefore when He, the first begotten, was brought forth (born out of a sinful nature) into the (new) world" or order, "then let the angels of God respect Him." Thus it was, the anointed man Jesus became an object of veneration to the angels, by virtue of His own good works. No being who is higher than another by virtue of his or her creation can be, for that reason, an object of veneration; because they merit neither honor nor dishonor for that which they could not avoid. The old saw, "pretty is, as pretty does," will hold good in things spiritual as well as natural.

XV. It is truly affirmed, that Christ, the *second Adam*, was a "quickening Spirit." I am asked: Was *this* Jesus? I answer: Most certainly, the *anointed Jesus;* but flesh, blood and bones

11

were not Jesus, any more than such are the real person of any one of us. Jesus was *inside* of all that The hands, the eyes, the brain, and organs of speech were the *manifesters* of the anointed Jesus, or Christ. The commissioned, the anointed, the quickened Jesus was the *manifested* and the "*quickening Spirit.*" It would be just as pertinent to ask in relation to the *first man* who "became a living soul:" was that Adam? We can, with the same facility of reasoning, call Jesus a "quickening spirit," as we can call Adam a "living soul." Again: If the *second* Adam, whom we say was the *quickening spirit*, was created before the old world or visible universe, when was the *first* Adam created? Or was the *first* Adam created *after* the second? If so, he whom we call the first Adam and *type* of the second Adam must have been created after the *antitype*, the *print* made before the *type!* the *second* created *before* the first!! Lord Bacon himself, with all his metaphysical subtlety, could not reconcile this as a paradox. But after all, this quickening spirit was a *man* — "the man Christ Jesus" and not the Supreme, nor a foreign pre-existent spirit. Thus, it seems to me, we cannot so sufficiently blind our eyes to truth as not to see the absolute impossibility of reconciling the Godship and pre-existent theory of Christ either with the Scriptures or with reason.

But further. If Christ was God supreme, or pre-existed with God, and was created before the first earthly Adam, it is impossible that He should be the *second* Adam, or second to Adam in any sense He, being a pure spirit, cannot be second on this point; and, being *first* in point of time, it is therefore impossible that He should be *second* in any sense This being admitted, He cannot be the antitype of any person or thing Thus not only would the typeship of Adam be destroyed, but the typeship of the thousand other things that the professing world claim as types of Christ would be annihilated, seeing He existed with God anterior to them all. Thus do the priesthood by adhering to this absurd position, like children, make utter shipwreck of their castle of cobs, leaving it strewn around in hopeless confusion.

XVI. I am asked: If Jesus, the "carpenter's son," was the Christ of the first gospel dispensation, by what species of metamorphosis or metempsychosis do we make Ann Lee *His* second appearing; seeing He was man and she was a woman? how could *He* thus reappear, without undergoing a generic transformation? I answer: He reappeared in her Godly life and searching power;

in her self-denial; in her humiliation; in her willingly suffering afflictions and persecutions; in her patience; in her wisdom; in her long sufferings; in her deep, intense, and agonizing labors of soul, night and day, for mankind; in her renunciation of, and overcoming the world, as He (Jesus) did; finally, in *all* the fruits shown forth by Jesus in His anointed capacity, did He reappear in the *anointed* ANN. You talk of miracles. We need not speak of small things; but herein, indeed, has the "woman compassed the man," leaving behind her a standing miracle in the eyes of the world, of far greater magnitude than any thing wrought by the Saviour during His sojourn on earth, or by His immediate followers; and that is the existence of a number of organized and established societies or churches of her faithful followers, dwelling together in harmony, and living the spiritual life of Christ, around which all may cluster, and into which all who are willing to forsake the world for eternal life may come, of every nation, kindred, and tongue.

It would be just as proper to say that Elias did not come the second time; therefore John the Baptist was not that prophet — was not Elias — as to say Jesus did not reappear. Jesus Himself settled this matter. He said: "This is Elias that was to come." Thus we see it was not necessary for the same flesh and bones, nor the same person to come, in order for Elias to reappear; but another person to come in his spirit, power, and gift; and this truly was the case (though the whole world may sneer) with our loved MOTHER ANN LEE.

If Jesus the Christ, or Ann Lee had been created on a higher plane, or scale of existence, than the rest of the human family, it would have been decidedly disadvantageous to them. If Jesus Christ had overcome, by virtue of a higher creation, every one of His followers who arose from a lower estate, male or female, deserves greater adoration than He, and He would himself bend the knee in worshipful homage and respect to them, because they overcame with less advantages than He enjoyed. But this is not the case. Jesus Christ, that blessed man and Son of God, was the pioneer in this glorious work; who, by constantly and unflinchingly obeying the light of God, unfolded within His consciousness, arose from our lost estate, thereby setting a practical example for all men; and Ann Lee, the blessed and honored daughter of God, was the pioneer in His second appearing — the first *woman* — the first *person* — that overcame, in the second manifestation, and arose, as did Jesus, out of the lost condition of man; thus setting a practical example for all *women*. Thus are the two foundation pillars established, to which the types refer, as I shall, in subsequent discourses, clearly set forth to you. These, the parents, the Father and Mother, in God's new creation, are now with their children "co-workers together with God" for the salvation and redemption of the world.

One thing is certain: this is either true or it is false; if it is true there is nothing in the world so important and so necessary that you should know; if it is false, then a falsehood has accomplished more than all the truths and philosophy of the world have been able to do from Adam to the present day. I do most conscientiously beg you to look this thing in the face; for if it is a delusion, think what amount of delusion it would take to get any to forsake the pleasures of sense and lead a Godly life, and how much it would take to get them to obey even what light they already have given them! Do you not continually "resist the holy spirit? As your fathers did so do ye."—Acts vii, 51.

I speak unto all as unto wise men; as men of deep research, of knowledge, of understanding. I make the appeal to all as philosophers, as biblicists, and as reasonable men — as men and women of broad, comprehensive powers of mind—as candid, and as *honest* men and women. I earnestly repeat it and entreat of all not to cast it behind as unworthy of serious thought, saying it is only a figment of the fancy of some dreaming idiot or fanatic set of monks or nuns or superstitious bigots.

Christ has either made "His second appearing without sin unto salvation"—Heb. ix, 28—or He has not. If He has, those to whom, and in whom, He has appeared, are saved, as He was, from the sins and lost estate of the world. If He has not, then none are so saved. Do you call this a superstitious illusion? If so, I would ask: What amount of superstition can make any of us forsake a life of animal pleasure and lead the life of Christ? What amount of bigotry would make us adhere to it? To men and women of candor I solemnly appeal, and ask: If in the person of any one, the fruits and essential characteristics that accompanied Jesus Christ, have appeared, is this not as much and as really the *second* appearance of Christ, as was John the Baptist the reappearance of Elias? No man of sense and candor will say not. The mission of Elias was to turn the hearts of the children to the fathers, and to the observance of the broken law of Moses.

John the Baptist was the same, hence Jesus said *he was that Elias.* Jesus Christ's mission, as I have heretofore shown, and will yet more fully show, was to call mankind from the rudimental to a higher life — from the natural, carnal, selfish, partial, to the spiritual, unselfish, universal, and Godlike—leading the way Himself, in His practical life, from all self indulgence and pleasure, to abnegations, saying to the world, "follow me." This work and life fell away as predicted, and the world remained without Christ for more than twelve hundred years, when, lo! it was revived and exhibited a second time by a *woman* — and that woman's name was ANN LEE

If the properties and qualities and life of Christ were manifested by her out from the triple darkness that enveloped the world, who, I ask, with any pretension to fairness and reason, can hold up their heads and assert that this was not as much and as really the reappearance of Christ as was John the Baptist the reappearance of Elias? I feel sure no reasonable person can or will deny it. Then those who go with me thus far are bound to do one of two things — either to prove that these fruits did not appear and were not manifested by ANN LEE, or else confess that Christ has appeared the second time, as promised, "without sin unto salvation"

We testify to the world boldly that these fruits did appear in her, and that the fruition of all her hopes and expectations is being realized in her true and faithful followers. I wish it to be especially noticed that I am not asking any to believe a mystery. I am not running into other spheres beyond the clouds and wandering among the stars to fix the sense on some chimera or plausible hypothesis I ask no one to believe a mystery. I wish not to fix attention on the regal splendor of some topless throne in Jupiter; but rather to draw the mind back to the heart, to God in the soul, and the demands of Christ upon our daily life, and realize that the "kingdom of heaven [or of hell] is within." as we make it by our own action in this sublunary sphere.

"And they shall be mine, saith the Lord of hosts, in that day when I make up my jewels; and I will spare them, as a man spareth his own son that serveth him Then shall ye return and discern between the righteous and the wicked, between him that serveth God, and him that serveth Him not "—Mal iii, 17, 18

"Hear, O Israel; the Lord hath a controversy with the inhabitants of the land, because there is no truth nor mercy therein

By swearing, and lying, and killing, and stealing, and committing adultery, they break out, and blood toucheth blood. Therefore shall the land mourn, and every one that dwelleth therein languish, with the beasts of the field, and the fowls of heaven."—Hos. vi, 1, 2, 3.

Hear then, O earth! (Ye lions of the forest in the wilderness of sin), and ye eagles that cleave the clouds (ye great ones of the earth), sheath your bloody talons and draw near to Zion and receive ye the spirit of the *Lamb* and the *Dove*, or the *Lamb* and the *Bride*, and permit a "little child" to lead you into the kingdom of your HEAVENLY FATHER AND MOTHER.

CHRIST THE SON OF GOD.

If my manner of speech is offensive to the refined tastes of the more cultivated part of society, I must beg charity, as I am but a "plain, blunt man," and am not able to convey my ideas with that mellifluous euphony and oily sweetness to which some may have been accustomed to listen. To present understandable truth, unvarnished, being my main object, I cannot take time to polish phrases, were I able to do so, although I should be happy to please all Innumerable falsehoods are covered by much learning and a finely wrought phraseology, of which Locke thus discourses: "All artificial and figurative applications of words that eloquence hath invented are for nothing else but to insinuate wrong ideas, move the passions, and thereby mislead the judgment. It is evident how much men love to deceive and be deceived, since rhetoric, that powerful instrument of error and deceit, has its established professors. * ᵔ It is to fence against the entanglements of equivocal words and the great art of sophistry that lie in them, that distinctions have been multiplied, and their use thought so necessary. * * But it is not the right way to knowledge to hunt after and fill the head with abundance of artificial and scholastic distinction. * * For in things crumbled into dust, it is in vain to affect or pretend order, or expect clearness. ᵔ * ᵔ Words being intended for signs of my ideas to make them known to others, it is plain cheat and abuse when I make them stand sometimes for one thing, and sometimes for another; the willful doing whereof can be imputed to nothing but great folly or greater dishonesty. * * * They who would advance in knowledge, and not deceive themselves with a little articulated air, should lay down this as a fundamental rule: not to take *words* for *things*, nor suppose them to stand for real entities. * * When men have clear conceptions, they can, if they are ever so obtuse and abstracted, explain them and the terms they use for them. If they *cannot* give us the ideas their *words* stand for, it is clear they have none."

It seems to me that nothing can be more true than these words of the pious philosopher. Who has not noticed in forensic debates, where the opposing parties were of equal intellectual endowment, that by their eloquence or rhetorical flourish of words they would, in turn, carry the minds of the audience from side to side like a leaf tossed in the wind, and not unfrequently so conceal the truth as to entirely exculpate the wicked and punish the innocent? "Crucify him, crucify him." It is equally disastrous in theological or religious controversy, even when both parties conscientiously believe they are defending the true faith; but some have even gone so far in their blind zeal as to think it justifiable even to tell willful falsehoods in defense of the faith; forgetting that "God does not require men to misuse their faculties for Him, nor to lie to others nor themselves for His sake." To see the truth of this, it is only necessary to listen to the debates and discourses of the advocates of the thousand different creeds; and when you take up their books and analyze the sentences and give to their words fixed and determined significations, you will find them to cross their tracks as often as Reynard does when pursued by the hunter. Hence, as he says, it is a cheat and abuse, when, in the same discourse, we make a word have two different meanings in order to carry a point. Wherefore all men should adopt this fundamental rule: not to take *words* for entities until we have clear ideas of the entities themselves. This rule being adopted, any one can give the ideas their words stand for. But this is not adhered to by the professing world; they have their *creed* — the *creed must be supported* at every hazard — and teachers of each sect commence torturing what they claim to be God's word into their support, until there is no end to the zigzagging and abuse of our mother tongue. They write books, and when they find their own doctrines do not harmonize, they straightway tell you not to scrutinize its *parts*, but to look at the *spirit* of it, get the general drift, and take it as whole — that is, swallow truth and falsehood all together. A late Rev. author, of New York city, has written a large book to prove that God was *in* Christ and *out* of himself, and that God was outside of the visible universe, "operating on the chain of cause and effect," as it were, rolling up planets and tossing them around like the school-boy does his ball! And still this same author adheres to the idea of the infinity and omnipresence of Deity (!) and wishes us to look at his book as a *whole*, just as though the *whole* were not made of *parts.* If the *parts* will not connect and hang together, the whole will not. If we cannot depend upon the parts that *make* the whole, how can we depend upon the *whole?* It is the very pith and essence of weakness and dishonesty to try to cover up falsehood in this way. What, then, is to be done, we ask, seeing there are no perfect books? I answer: take only the good parts, such as will connect, and make a craft of that, as best we can The inadhesive parts and unsound planks and timbers are of no advantage to the bark. Let me illustrate:

I engage a man to build for me a ship in which I expect to cross the ocean. He builds it, and finishes it with a handsome exterior I send a scientific man to examine it, to ascertain if it is sea-worthy. When he arrives and wishes to look at its parts, the mechanic, knowing there are faulty pieces or joints, says, you must not examine its parts, but take it as a whole This man would be just as consistent as the one who would ask you to take his book as a whole without examining its parts. It would be the duty of the man sent to examine to know that all the timbers were sound and well put together even though he had to cut through the paint and varnish for that purpose; else I could not trust myself aboard for the voyage. If rotten timbers were found, they would have to be taken out, and sound ones replaced, and all unnecessary pieces removed; then I could trust the whole ship, because the parts were good. I should consider myself as dishonest as the ship-builder, were I to advise any one to take these discourses as a whole without scrutinizing their parts, and if one part conflicts with another part set it aside as worthless

I was early taught to cultivate a veneration and love for truth more than love for my mother; so that now I feel in a measure indifferent to any position, however pleasing and plausible it may appear, which admits of a doubt. Perhaps I am ultra; if so, it is consoling to know that such ultraism cannot have a very dangerous tendency In my humble opinion it would be well if this were the condition of every one — all the while feeling within ourselves ———

> "If I am right thy grace impart
> Still in the right to stay,
> If I am wrong, O teach my heart
> To find that better way "

I have thus far endeavored to keep my promise, to use the same word steadily to represent the same idea or object, so that

12

none may be misled in regard to my position. But, alas! for poor humanity. It is painfully evident that some do not wish to hear the plain truth uttered, because it comes as a two-edged sword, not only into their false systems, but also against their carnal and ungodly lives. Such ones prefer the pleasures of sense to their union with God, or the spirits of "just men made perfect," to whom the words of the Apostle Paul will apply: "They are more the lovers of pleasure than the lovers of God, having the form of Godliness but denying the power."—2 Tim. iii, 4. They even fearfully fill the poet's picture:

> 'Now conscience chills them, and now passion burns,
>   And atheism and religion take their turns;
> Are very heathens in the *carnal* part,
>   Yet still are good, sound Christians at the *heart*."

But knowing as I do, that such so-called Christians will not yield their false positions as long as they can find in Holy Writ one prop to sustain them, I must return to the further elucidation of the Scriptures, and show up some of the inconsistencies and incongruities of their teachers.

It is said that Christ is declared to be "the resurrection and the life," and if Ann Lee has manifested His second coming is she also the resurrection and the life? Most certainly; and so are all who are resurrected by coming into and living the life of Christ. To come into the resurrection, is to come into the life of Christ. To be resurrected is to be raised from spiritual death into spiritual life. To come then into Christ in His *second* appearing is a resurrection as effectual as it was in His *first* appearing. Next, I am asked if Christ did not have an advent in the Adamic dispensation through Seth, Enoch, and Noah, and in the Law dispensation through Abraham, Moses, and Joshua, and afterward through Jesus? I reply: If Christ was a pre-existent spirit, and did make those advents, what consistency is there in calling the one through Jesus His *first* appearing?!

The simple truth is this: Christ is not a foreign spirit, but the "Lord's Anointed." Jesus was pre-eminently the Christ, because He was anointed and appointed to lead in the work of the regeneration and salvation of the human race. Other anointed persons, appointees and successors in Christ's church, imbued or clothed with the same powers, are His Vicegerents.

When Christ was about to leave the earth, He said to His disciples: "Yet a little while and the world seeth me no more, but ye see me."—John xiv, 19. I am asked, if the man Jesus was the Christ, how is it that He could be seen by His disciples and not by the world? I answer: The disciples themselves saw the *person* of Jesus for some time before they saw the Christ; that is, before they saw that He was the Lord's anointed. Seeing the exterior, and comprehending the character, mission, or office, are very distinct; so there were a great many worldlings in that day, who were even conversant with Jesus, who saw not that He was the Christ; they saw only the carpenter's son, while the enlightened saw more—they also could perceive that He was the Lord's Anointed or Christ. So it ever will be.

I am asked if there might not have been an *element* or *essence* from God contained in the person of Jesus, otherwise called the blood of Christ, which we must drink in order to have His life in us? or may not *this* have been the Christ which the disciples saw, that the world could not see?

I answer, not at all: (1) This element would have to be an entity — an intelligent something, commissioned of God for a special purpose before it could be called Christ. (2) If it were such entity, He must be subdivided for all to drink or swallow Him (!) and this would destroy the entity. An element is a constituent principle, not an intelligence. There is no mystery about drinking the blood of Christ; He tells us it is His word and doctrine you must imbibe — "the flesh profiteth nothing, etc." The element which the disciples saw was this. It was His element to do His Father's will and not His own—and we must drink in this same element or else not have His life in us—*live His life*—"the blood is the life thereof."

I have now analyzed and explained all the texts of scripture that have been presented to my notice which are claimed and supposed to be declarative of the Deity and pre-existence of Christ; and it must be seen, that, by a fair and rational construction, they not only fail to yield it any support, but absolutely deny such hypothesis. I must now expose some of the absurdities that professors have been led into by striving to support this false dogma; after which I will quote a few texts from a multitude which declare the true idea that the anointed man, Jesus, was the Christ, and that He was not the Supreme, but simply the Son of God by regeneration.

The absurdities are many, and yet I dislike to enumerate even a very small portion of them, lest I might be censured for insincerity, even to mention them; for they are glaringly inconsistent. They are driven to such extremely absurd conclusions as these: That Jesus was the *Son* of God and also the *Father* of God! that He was not only the Son and Father, but "He was very God of very God!" that He was Father and Son at the same time, and whilst He was both the Father and Son, He was His own Father, making God His grandfather! that infinite as He was, He humbled and contracted His being to the germ of an embryo infant, and was afterward born of a virgin; and yet, the mother of Jehovah had to make the usual offerings for uncleanness and remain without the appointed time for purification for bringing her own Maker into the world! and also that she remained a virgin thereafter! that God grew up from an infant of a span's length, to five feet ten, and then permitted some wicked men to kill Him, and then make this murder a necessary link in the redemption of man! Thus the pious Watts has it —

"God the mighty Maker died."

The universe of course was left without a God while He was dead; but how He was resuscitated, we are not explicitly informed. Of course, the least creature of life was of more force and value than a dead God. All this (and even this is not a tithe of what might be said) is not only childish, heathenish, and ludicrous, but it is extremely ridiculous.

In relation to Christ as the Son, they are equally unfortunate. They assert that Jesus Christ was of the lineage of David, and that He existed before David himself! that Christ was the "*second* Adam," but existed before the *first* Adam; consequently the second was the first! I will only add, in this connection, that the pre-existent theory destroys all the types of Christ, claimed to be such by professing Christians, from the fact that He existed prior to them. It will not help the matter to say He has existed before them as God, and subsequently as the Son of God; for it is asserted He was all the time God. Besides, if He was ever the supreme infinite God, he could not at any time be any thing less. Such subterfuge would only, if possible, still the more confuse and complicate the doctrine. It would be adding mystery to mystery, and making confusion more confounded to the end of the chapter.

All this kind of sense, or I should say, nonsense, is of heathen origin, and has been introduced since the falling away of the first Christian church, and from this source mystery on mystery has been introduced and adopted by the priesthood, until neither the learned nor the unlearned can understand or expound the faith of their own churches

I will now introduce some of the texts declarative of the simple and easily-understood truth that the anointed man Jesus was the Christ, and to whom no idea of pre-existence can be consistently applied:

"Jesus saith to His disciples, whom do men say that I, the *son of man, am?* They answered, some say John the Baptist, some say Elias, etc." "He saith unto them whom say ye that I am'" — (*I, the son of man, am?*) "Simon Peter answered and said, Thou art the Christ, the Son of the living God." Jesus replied: "Blessed art thou, Simon Barjona; for flesh and blood hath not revealed it unto thee (that I, Jesus, am the Christ), but my Father which is in heaven" (hath done it) —Matt xvi. 13, 17

It will be observed that Jesus was careful to call himself *the son of man,* it would seem, in order to prevent a misunderstanding. Again: The high priest asked, "Art thou the Christ, the Son of the Blessed? Jesus answered and said, *I am*" Did Jesus speak the truth or not?

Again: "O fools, and slow of heart to believe all that the prophets have spoken! Ought not Christ to have suffered these things and enter into His glory?"—Luke xxiv, 26, 66. It is only necessary to observe it was *Christ* that suffered —the *anointed man Jesus.*

To continue: "The woman saith unto Him, I know that Messias cometh, which is called Christ. Jesus saith unto her, I that speaketh unto thee am He" (am the Christ). Could there be any words in the English language more to the point? less ambiguous? Jesus, the man, was speaking, and says to her. "I am He, the Christ or the Messias you are expecting to come" He did not say, a pre-existent foreign spirit in Him was the Christ; but I, the speaker, am He. John iv, 26, and v, 42. The Samaritans said: "We have heard Him ourselves, and know that this is indeed the Christ, the Saviour of the world." Also. "Hath not the scripture said that Christ cometh of the seed of David and out of the town of Bethlehem where David was?"—John vii, 45 "We believe and are sure thou (Jesus) art the Christ, the Son of the living God"—John vi, 69 "But these things are written that ye might believe that Jesus is the Christ, the Son of God."—John xx, 31. "Who is a liar but he that denieth that Jesus is the

Christ?"—John ii, 22. Now any man, professor or profane, who pretends to believe the scriptures, with these plain declarations before him, that the man Jesus is the Christ, must be convinced of the falsity of the pre-existent theory. Every one knows that the *man* Jesus did not pre-exist. The son of Mary had no existence previous to His birth; and this man Jesus is declared emphatically to be the *very Christ* that was promised. So void of mystery is this subject that "he that runs may read, and though a fool, he need not err therein." But more: God hath sworn with an oath (to David) that of the fruit of his loins, *according to the flesh,* He would *raise up Christ.* Acts ii, 30. The question is, did God swear the truth or a lie? Do we not all know what is meant by coming from the loins of a progenitor according to the flesh? God, not only said, but *swore with an oath,* that *Christ* should so come. What greater pains could the Almighty Himself have taken than did the spirit through the inspired one, to prevent our being ensnared with the lying schemes of anti-Christ, and made to disbelieve these plain and positive declarations of Holy Writ?

"Therefore let all the house of Israel know assuredly, that God hath made (as He had sworn to do) this same Jesus whom ye have crucified, both Lord and Christ." The Apostle Paul alleges "that this Jesus whom I preach unto you is Christ."—Acts xvii, 3. And he further "mightily convinced the Jews, and that publicly, showing by the scriptures (*i. e.*, the old Testament) that Jesus was the Christ."—Acts xviii, 28.

Thus, I see not how we can avoid agreeing that I have demonstrated from every reliable source of history, reason, and revelation, the truth of the proposition that Christ signifies the anointed: and that the man Jesus was that anointed, and therefore the Christ, which man could not be the Supreme, nor one-third of the Supreme; nor could He have pre-existed before the man came into being; nor was He the Christ, only prospectively, until He was commissioned, anointed, and appointed for the special purpose of opening the way of salvation and redemption to a lost world, which appointment did not take place previous to the baptism of John.

But this man Jesus was the Christ of whom the prophets prophesied and "angels sang," that was to come; but He was no high-created being from the "pleroma" or "Christ-sphere" of high-created intelligences which some have imagined, and palmed on the world. But, thus swallowing *one* mystery as a truth opened the way for another, and another, and in this way were all the host of mysteries saddled upon the church and sectarian world — as history, both sacred and profane, plainly indicates — a small portion of which I may hereafter notice.

Not being able to detect a shadow of the false theory in the scriptures, its origin must be looked for elsewhere; and if there are any who yet remain unconvinced of its falsity, I trust I shall be able to satisfy their most minute inquiries, as I expect to present nothing but what is true and that which the common capacity can understand and fathom.

There never was any thing done. either miraculously or otherwise, but that there was a *way* in which it was done; and when the *way* is ascertained, the miracle ceases. The process of salvation is no longer a miracle, because the *way* to obtain it has been ascertained. The first mortal man like ourselves who ascertained it, and was successful in its accomplishment, solved the problem and showed that it was possible for *all men;* and the first mortal woman who was successful solved the problem, and showed that it was possible for all *women.* The Apostle Paul said : " It behooved Christ to be made in all things like unto His brethren."-- Heb 11, 17. Who believes this ? I ask not the simple nor foolish , but men of deepest thoughts and most critical acumen. Particularly mark the language: "*made in* ALL *things like His brethren* " Acknowledge this to be true, we only need to know how the *brethren* are made in order to know how Christ was made What we know of the former we know of the latter. We cannot say two watches are made alike in all respects if one is made of gold and the other of brass. Again : He was "tempted in all points" — not some points only, but in all points "as we are " Now, then, if we know how we are tempted, we also know how He was tempted He resisted and overcame the tempter, and we. in order to continue like Him, must also resist and overcome the tempter, or else be excluded from His presence. This is the legitimate conclusion If no mere mortal like ourselves had accomplished the work of his salvation to a successful issue, the way would still be the great unraveled problem of the world, and the fact of its being done, would still be among the enigmas, mysteries, and improbabilities, if not the impossibilities to the human race. We might then in sad reality,

"Make dust our paper, and with rainy eyes
Write sorrow on the bosom of the earth "

But, thanks to God, this is not the case; the way has been learned and the thing has been accomplished. Jesus was the first man and Ann Lee the first woman who were successful; thus we have an example and are left without excuse. They *solved* this problem for the human race. God will not save the soul of any one in a mysterious way. He has no "under-ground railroad." The way — the plan — the process that has saved one soul, will save any soul, and is the plan that will save all souls. The way — the plan — the process that will damn one soul will damn any soul; consequently there is only one way to be saved, and only one way to be damned, and both are comprised in two words, viz.: *obedience, disobedience* Jesus Christ was Himself saved by obedience to God; while disobedience would have damned Him, just the same as it will any soul of man. Do any say God does not speak to him? Simple creatures! He might just as well say he has no conscience! To obey God in the conscience, where we are, is the first step in the right direction; and if persisted in faithfully, it will lead us to Christ's church or body, where alone full redemption is attainable, for "thither will the eagles be gathered together," — Luke xvii, 37 — where all will be thankful to yield their spirits to the guidance of the more advanced in spiritual truth, just as they would the intellect to the guidance of a superior intellect when in pursuit of scientific truth. God speaks frequently by agency — but at all times does he speak internally through the conscience But alas! it is too seldom regarded. "How long, saith God, will the scorner delight in his scorning, and fools hate knowledge?"

"Turn ye at my reproof; behold I will pour out my spirit upon you, and make known my words unto you: I have called and ye have refused I have stretched out my hand and no man regarded; but ye have set at nought all my counsel, and would none of my reproof." — Pr 1, 22, 26. "But ye are they that forsake the Lord. * * Therefore will I number you to the sword, and ye shall all bow down to the slaughter; because when I called ye did not answer; when I spake ye did not hear, but did evil before mine eyes, and did choose that wherein I delighted not." — Isa lxv, 12. Thus God pleads, promises, threatens every day, but many disobey. Therefore, let none say that God does not plead with them in every act of their lives, when to hearken and obey would be the very salvation that Christ gained. But to disobey is to bring upon ourselves the very damnation which He escaped. O! then, as you desire your union with God, or hope for heaven, or to escape the penalty of the wicked, hearken to His kind, affectionate, and parental voice:

"Come unto me all ye that labor and are heavy laden, and I will give you rest. Take my yoke upon you and learn of me; for I am meek and lowly of heart, and ye shall find rest to your souls."

13

TYPES OF CHRIST.

" But God hath chosen the foolish things of the world to con-found the wise ; and God hath chosen the weak things of the world to confound the things which are mighty."—I Cor. i, 27.

Notwithstanding the great veneration that people seem to have for truth, it is still a difficult pill to swallow when it interferes with any idol of the human heart, or crosses any cherished or loved opinion. Still the cry is: *Let us have* TRUTH. Our object is, to endeavor to show that all the types and symbols of the *Old Testament scriptures have their fulfillment in the Bridegroom and Bride — in Christ's first and second appearing* — not such a Bride as some have made from Rev. xxi, 2, who give this name to the Church; but a real counterpart for the Bridegroom.

The apostle does not say that he saw the Bride coming down from heaven, in the form of a Church, but the "New Jerusalem coming down adorned as a Bride." But the Bridegroom was a man : the Bride must be a woman — even a woman clothed with the sun, and the moon under her feet.— Rev. xii, 1.

Having mentioned the second appearing, we will quote the promise (Heb. ix, 28) : "So Christ was once offered to bear the sins of many ; and unto them that look for Him shall He appear the second time without sin unto salvation," we will further add that, in order to have a second appearance, it is not necessary that the same identical flesh and bones should return, neither that it should be the same gender. In fact it were more apropos that the gender should be different in order to have co-ordinate counterparts. The first, the bridegroom ; the second, the bride. This is well exemplified by Christ himself, who said of John the Baptist : " This is Elias that was to come."

The second appearing consists in the reappearance of the same gift, spirit, power and substance, for the same purposes — to execute and carry out the same work. John was the second coming of Elijah, because he came in the same gift and power of that prophet. And the reappearance in and manifestation by Ann Lee of the same spirit, testimony, life, power and wisdom which

was exhibited by Christ, as much constituted His second appearing as that which constituted John the second appearance of
Elias. This is plain.

And now we here boldly testify that all the fruits shown forth
by Jesus in His anointed capacity did reappear, in the anointed
Ann, and show that she was baptized with the same spirit Such,
then, manifestly, was Christ's second coming Thus are the two
foundation pillars established, to whom the Scripture types refer,
which we will now proceed to set before you, and compare with
the substance they were designed to represent.

It is said in Rev. x, 7, "That in the days of the voice of the
seventh angel, when he should begin to sound, the mystery of
God should be finished." To finish a mystery is to explain it,
which is a part of the work now before us. We need not seek,
nor have we any need to know, the precise time of the formation
of our planet, nor the origin of primal man : these are hidden
from the world, and we have no revelation disclosing the secret.
God hath revealed by Moses, recorded in Gen. i, that in the
beginning he did thus and so, but when that beginning was, no
man knoweth. But it is proper that man should know when the
"old heavens and earth were created that were to pass away,"
and when "all things were to become new and all things of God "
This can be ascertained by noticing the *generations* of the heavens
and earth, treated of in the second chapter, which has special
reference to man, and is given for our instruction Here we may
easily arrive at the precise time of the first called or created man
from the primal structure, or "dust of the ground" of animal
promiscuity.

It is generally admitted that the first chapter treats mostly of
the creation of the universe in six periods of time called days, and
if it is observed that the second chapter treats of the generations
of the earth with respect to man, we then hold the key to unlock
the mystery, and have no difficulty with the commands given to
man in the first chapter, and those given to the first called man
in the second chapter, of Edenic order, with whom we very
readily perceive was God's first covenant, called the "old
covenant," which was the type of the new, in that, man was
raised from a lower to a higher condition

This was the beginning of God's special dealings with his
creature man. "He breathed into him the breath of (spiritual)
life (the inspiration of lives), and he became a living soul " Here,

it is evident, is the commencement of *the types of Christ.* The first called man was the first type, and corresponds completely with the second called man, Christ, who is his antitype. The first " a living soul ;" the second " a quickening spirit." The first " to multiply and replenish the earth ;" the second to multiply and replenish the heavens. The first called man was the head of the orderly, natural, Adamic church ; the second called man was the head of the Spiritual church.

Cain was the first apostate from the Adamic church, and was the type of Judas, the first apostate from the Spiritual Christian Church. The first church arose from the lower order of the world to that of orderly generation. The second, or spiritual, arose from the plane of orderly generation to that of regeneration. The first forsook the old, disorderly, animal world. The second forsook the orderly, natural world for the spiritual. The twain were to become one flesh in the natural order — the twain to become one spirit in the spiritual order — having risen above, and forsaken the natural, " father, mother, brother, sister, houses, lands, and all that pertains to that partial relation."

Thus the types agree with their antitypes, and show clearly the distinction between the two orders. From our basis, it will be perceived that the first man Adam, who was taken from the pre-Adamic body to institute a new order of things, was the beginning of the " old heavens and earth that were to pass away ;" — having no reference whatever to this planet, being

> " into heaps of ashes turned
> When Heaven itself the wandering chariot burned,"

but to the earthly order then created, at which time all those who come into this order, and embraced this gospel, were " Sons and daughters of God."

As Adam was raised up from among the brethren of the pre-Adamic body to establish the old heavens and earth, so Jesus was raised up from among the brethren" of the Mosaic body to establish " the new heavens and earth." And all who embrace this order are the sons and daughters of God, and sing and shout for joy at the establishment of this new order.

Thus far we see the types and antitypes are perfect, and as the first called man was a perfect type of the second called man, so Eve, the first called woman, was a perfect type of the second called woman. As the first Eve was taken out of the sleeping body of Adam — from among the disorderly flesh there — to be with the man Adam one flesh, so the second Eve was taken out of the sleeping body of the world — from among the disorderly flesh there — to be with Christ one spirit. Thus do the types and antitypes agree.

A letter from our pen is not the antitype of the pen, but a printed letter is the antitype of the metal face — their faces must correspond. So it is with all types and their antitypes, their faces must agree. Then, if one is understood, the other will be also. While the first Adam and Eve of the natural order were types of the second Adam and Eve of the spiritual order, they could not have been types of a pre-existent Christ nor Christ spirit, as this would make the type come after the antitype, which is impossible.

Let us repeat, that the first man, Adam, was made of the ground on which pre-Adam or Adamkind stood, and was thence called a " living soul." The second was made of the ground on which the Mosaic body stood, and was called a "quickening spirit." And the first Eve was taken from the flesh of the sleeping Adamic body for a help-meet for the first Adam, and was called the " Mother of all (the) living ; " that is, all living the higher, natural life. The second Eve — *Ann Lee* — was taken from the flesh of the sleeping anti-christian body, for a helper for the second Adam, Christ Jesus ; and she is called the Mother of all living the higher, spiritual life. Thus we see what becomes of the "wisdom of this world," who have three male deities, with neither type nor anti-type.

Such metaphorical expressions as we have noticed are very common. How often do spiritual leaders inquire what ground we stand upon ? How often cite to the " hole of the pit whence we were digged, and the rock whence we were hewn." The simple truth is, God made man out of the ground *then*, as He "digs them out of the pit and hews them out of the rock, *now*. Whoso is wise shall understand these things, and whoso is prudent shall know them," although they may confound the wisdom of the wise !

But it is said : " The Bridegroom hath the Bride," long before Ann Lee had existence ; and we are asked : How could she, who yet had no existence, fulfill the conditions ? In answer we would say, he had her prospectively. Such expressions are frequent in holy writ: " This day I have begotten thee ; " " Before Abraham was I am;" but which simply means I am before what Abraham was.

Joshua said the Lord had delivered the enemy into his hands, before he commenced the battle. Just so the Bridegroom, Jesus, had the Bride Ann, prospectively, but was as sure of her as Joshua was that he would conquer the enemy. This is true, although it be to the "Jews a stumbling block," and to the Greeks "foolishness." It may be observed that Ann Lee, of Manchester, England, was the first person that was baptized and quickened into the spiritual life of Christ, to rise out of nature's loss and order, to live above these, and to proclaim the higher life to the world. Hence she has the honor of being the Bride, the "Lamb's wife." Being ignorant of this fact, some have supposed that the Bride, which the Bridegroom had, was a spirit from some foreign world which he had in Him; but it is time that the mystery of such a chimera was disposed of; to admit which, would spoil the agreement of all types and their antitypes.

When the indisputable truth becomes known, that Christ, in any age of the world, was no mysterious being, but simply a God-anointed, or which is the same thing, a *God appointed* or *commissioned agent* for a special purpose, all this chimerical, mysterious chaff will be blown away, no more to disturb a dreaming world.

Abraham and Sarah were types of Jesus and Ann; not only in their obedience to the Adamic Gospel, but they were of one stock or race — begotten and born alike, equal as to mode of existence, as man and woman may be heads of a family "Abraham hearkened to the voice of Sarah." But what did this hearkening typify? It was, that, in the new covenant, the man should hearken to the woman; even so it is. In the second appearing, where a "woman compassed the man," all hearkened to the Bride, Ann; while, under the *old* covenant, the law is, "Thy desire shall be to thy husband, and he shall rule over thee."

Millions find this true to their sorrow, and see no way of relief; but there is a way. To all who wish deliverance from such bondage we would say: Leave the rudimental — come up-stairs into the new covenant.

Some orthodoxans tell us, in justification of the saved-by-faith doctrine, that Abraham's faith was "counted to him for righteousness." So it was, because *it was accompanied by good works.*

" Faith without works is dead ; " and who can be saved by a dead faith ? They tell us also, that the offering up of the ram was symbolical of the sacrifice of the " Lamb slain from the foundation of the world." Now the theological student is considerably advanced when he can tell the difference between a typical ram and a typical lamb. Then there is some hope of him.

If they had told us that the ram offered up was a symbol, that the ram that had ruled the world from Adam to Christ had to be slain and burned up; they would nearer have approached the truth. But Sarah called Abraham her Lord, or head. *So Ann called Jesus.* Not only so, they were types in sacrificing that which was most dear to them, typifying, that, in the gospel of Christ, that which was most dear to the natural man and woman must be sacrificed.

But you will say, Isaac was not sacrificed; but the ram was taken in his stead. This is true, and agrees perfectly with the antitype. Isaac was saved, and Abraham was promised an hundred fold in the seed of Isaac. So it is now. All the Abrahams and Sarahs that come into the gospel of Christ must offer up their little Isaacs, who will thus be saved; and they shall receive an " hundred fold of Isaacs and other gospel relations, and in the world to come eternal life " Such is the promise of Christ — the type and antitype complete. But the ram was put on the sacrificial altar, and was consumed with fire. This typified that the animal passions must be sacrificed and utterly consumed by the fire of Christ's gospel. Could types and antitypes be more complete ?

The rite of *circumcision* typified that in Christ the works of the flesh must be cut off. The mystery makers contend that they were types of Christ, because " Isaac was begotten by promise." Isaac was not begotten by promise. He was begotten by Abraham — " Abraham begat Isaac." There is no mystery about it. He and Sarah propagated children according to the law of generation. Jesus and Ann propagated children according to the law of *re*-generation. The first natural ; the second spiritual. Thus were Abraham and Sarah the types of Christ Jesus and Ann Lee, in being, in call and work, whose offspring are the seed of the " Free Woman," who are " the weak things of the world, whom God hath chosen to confound the things which are mighty."

Moses and Zipporah were plain and perfect types of Christ in His first and second appearing. We will repeat what Moses said to the fathers: " A prophet shall the Lord raise up unto you *of your brethren like unto me.* Him shall ye hear in all things whatsoever He saith."—Acts iii, 22. Some, in order to keep this mystery from being explained, have left or omitted the words "of your brethren" in their writings, and, also, where it is said the " sanctifier and sanctified are all *of* one" the preposition *of* has been omitted, lest we should get a peep into the fact that they were of one stock or race, and so save one prop to the miraculous story — well knowing that, if they were of one stock, this would be wiped out. We have no apology to offer for such omissions.

The preposition clearly shows they were of one race — the human. But Moses not only truthfully declared from whence Christ should arise, but he was an eminent type of Christ, in that he was called to deliver his people from Egyptian bondage. Some say Moses was not a perfect type of Christ — an imperfect type is no type at all. But Moses was a perfect type of Christ. He was begotten by a man, and born of a woman; *so was Jesus.* He was raised up from among the brethren; so was Jesus. He was called to deliver his people from Egyptian bondage; Jesus was called to deliver them from the bondage of sin. Also Zipporah was a type of Ann. She was raised up from among the Sisters; so was Ann. She forsook her people and followed Moses, suffering the toils of the wilderness, while journeying to the promised land, and became a Mother in Israel. So Ann Lee forsook her own people and followed Christ through the sufferings and toils of the wilderness of this world for the Kingdom of Heaven's sake, and, thus conjoined to Him, became the Mother of spiritual Israel.

Of animals and things, we may go through the good book and find agreement in types and symbols throughout. The "two cherubim covering the mercy seat with their wings, and their faces one toward another," were excellent types of Christ Jesus and Ann. They were wrought gold of beaten work; not only so, but were out of *one piece.* So plainly does every type represent the pure, simple truth, that the two foundation pillars, male and female, in whom they have their fulfillment, were alike and equal in all respects — no more mystery about the one than the other.

The two silver trumpets, the two tables of the Covenant, the two olive trees, the two olive branches, the King and Queen, the son and daughter, etc, all have their accomplishment in Jesus

Christ and Ann Lee, the Bridegroom and Bride of the new creation of God.

We look in vain among the lower-floor churches and our theological seminaries to find agreement of the types with their antitypes. With all their learning and worldly wisdom, they only pile mystery on mystery, and the further we follow them the more dense the fog grows, until we reach a cloud of impenetrable darkness.

" But God hath chosen the foolish things of the world to confound the wise, and the weak things to confound the mighty " Thus, under the seventh-sounding angel, this mystery of God is finished. It would seem that enough had now been said to satisfy the most carping critic of the falsity of the miraculous statement, and of the far-fetched, foreign Christ theory. It is a rule in mathematics that, when there are unknown quantities to be found, they must be ascertained from quantities which are known. The same is true in logic — truths may be ascertained by reasoning *a posteriori* as well as the contrary Types and antitypes come directly under this rule; so if we know what the antitype is we may learn what the type is, and *vice versa*. Thus when we see a printed letter we know what the face of the type was; or when we see a type's face we know what the letter will be. The question recurs . Have you known data? Ans. — We have. Of types we have shown, in person and work.

Of the antitypes we have Ann Lee, to whom the female types pointed, and in whom they have their fulfillment She is the known quantity, whom anti-Christ cannot mystify. We know she came into being by the same law of all her typical females The two must agree. So, in like manner, of types we know the law by which they came into being, and, from this, the law which brought the antitype Christ into being There is no possibility of evading this conclusion. And as Elijah was a type of Christ, and left his mantle behind for Elisha, so it was with his antitype Christ, and so it continues to this day. " All power to save was committed to the Son, who committed the same to His successors "

Jesus testified : " All that the Father gave me have I given them." And the call is now, to the whole world, of every nation, tongue and kindred, to come; accept Christ's terms and be saved. To be saved does not mean to be saved *in* sin, but *from* sin ; and all its deathly and damning effects, which can only be done by forsaking the world, finding God's order of finite agencies, and there

14

confessing, forsaking, and repenting of all sin, and becoming "crucified to the world and the world crucified to us," and, henceforward, living the life of the Redeemer.

We purpose further to institute a comparison between the modes of the first and the second appearing of Christ, showing their similarity as well as their equality in person and commission. But, by way of leader, will remark that, from what has been previously said, it must be perceived that in every succeeding order among men, from the first record to the present time, the instruments must have arisen out of a previous body by a higher unfolding and increased inspiration of the spirit of God; and hence every order has superseded the previous one.

CHRIST'S SECOND APPEARING.

Witness, as shown, the creation or call of Adam and Eve from primal, animal Adamic body — the rite of marriage first instituted — and orderly generation enjoined on pain of the displeasure of the Creator. See this order building and establishing the first old heavens and earth that were to pass away, and shadowing forth the new. See what gospel was preached and lived, by those who constituted the Adamic church — Seth, Noah, and others, until Abraham, with whom God renewed His covenant, shadowing forth the increasing steps in the new and everlasting covenant

Circumcision was instituted under the old covenant, which is a type of what should take place in the new that of cutting off all the fleshly works of generation and becoming " eunuchs for the kingdom of heaven's sake." Advances were made in the old heaven gospel which shadowed forth the gospel travel in the new, and it was practiced and lived until Moses, when God's covenant was again renewed with additional sacrifices and self-denial, and which, being kept, brought renewed blessings. These were enjoined and kept by some, with little modification, until Christ, with whom the new covenant was made. The substance now appeared, and the work of forming the new heavens and earth was begun — the creation of the new world, which the apostle says truly, was made by Him, which we now enjoy with increasing light and power in His second appearing in Ann Lee. Thus we see what God's uniform law and order are: First the Adamic arose out of the dust of the pre-Adamic body ; the Abrahamic out of the Adamic ; the Mosaic out of the Abrahamic ; and the Christian out of the Mosaic, and the second appearing in Ann, out of the so-called Christian, which was fast asleep when she was taken out of that body, and it is snoring yet

We will now call attention to the history and biography of Jesus, and examine the manner of His call, to which we beg especial attention It so happens that we have no reliable history of Him until he was about thirty years old ; precisely what kind of life He lived previously to that time is unknown to history and mankind ; nor is it necessary that we should know it ; but John the Baptist doubtless knew all about it, by His confession, as well as Jane Wardley knew all about Ann's. In turning to the New Testament we find the gospels beginning with the call of God to one John, the son of Zacharias, who was to be the forerunner, to prepare the way for the man Jesus, the son of Joseph. John did not come with a new gospel, but in the power and spirit of Elias. and " was that Elias," to turn the hearts of the children to the fathers, to revive the spirit of Moses' gospel or law, from which many had backslidden — to administer the gift of repentance and forgiveness of sins to all such as would honestly confess and forsake them, and return to the law. The account reads thus :

" The word of God came to John, the son of Zacharias, in the wilderness ; " hence it is truly said " a man sent of God," just as Christ was. God sent John for one purpose, and Christ for another, both being God-commissioned agents — one to revive an old institution, the other to create a new one; one to baptize with water, the other with fire. It is further recorded : " Multitudes came confessing their sins (violations of the law), and were baptized into the spirit of repentance " And here is where we get the first reliable account of Jesus, who was among the brethren there, and who came for the same purpose that the rest did— to acknowledge the gift of God in John, confess and repent, as it was impossible that He should supersede John without acknowledging and accepting the gift of God in him, who was as yet before Him

From St John's account, it would seem that the Baptist did not know Jesus to be the chosen one that was to supersede him, even from His confession, as he said, " I knew Him not."—John 1. 32 But He was pointed out by the descent of the Holy Spirit. Then says John . " I saw and bear record that this is the Son of God " It would be warping the record, as the Gnostics have done, to say the descending Spirit was the Christ, for John testified he knew the coming Christ stood among them, before He was pointed out to him by the descent of the Holy Spirit

Jesus could no more have superseded John, without submission to the order of God in him, than Ann Lee could have superseded that of James and Jane Wardley, without confessing, acknowledging, and complying with the order of which they were the heads Thus we may see the first steps that Jesus took toward the priesthood or Christship was His childlike humility in bending before the gift of God in John, setting us an example in the very beginning of His work. We have no more right to dispute Jesus' confession to John than we have to dispute His being baptized by him unto repentance, of which His soul-melting prayer on the banks of the Jordan gives ample proof. It is all plain.

Do any of us think that we can get to heaven with less humility than Jesus did? If we do we are wofully mistaken. He is our exemplar, and as He worked out His salvation so must we; and we shall be called to take no mortifying step, that our Father and Mother, Jesus and Ann, have not taken before us, but these we must take or never be saved. God will not provide one way for their salvation and another way for ours; hence they say, follow us. To follow one is to follow the other, for they are one — their example and teaching the same; both, after their anointing, lived free from sin

The reason "Jesus was anointed above His fellows" (mind He had fellows), was because He was the best of His class — "loved righteousness and hated iniquity" more than any of them. It was written of Him thus· After His temptation, He returned in the power of the Spirit to Galilee, and thence to Nazareth, where He was brought up; and, as His custom was, He went into the synagogue and stood up to read. And there was delivered to Him the book of Esaias, and when He had opened it He found the place where it was written:

"The spirit of the Lord is upon me to preach the gospel to the poor, to heal the broken-hearted, to preach deliverance to the captives, to set at liberty them that are bound, to preach the acceptable year of the Lord"

He then closed the Book, gave it to the minister and sat down. All eyes were fastened on Him. An electric flash from a cloudless sky at noonday would not have shocked them more than the next words He uttered from his seat: "*This day is this Scripture fulfilled in your ears.*"

Thus was announced to an astonished world for the first time that the Christ they had so long expected was then sitting in their midst! At first they were pleased with the gracious words that proceeded out of His mouth; but after a few home thrusts, and the affirmation that *He* was the man to whom the prophetic word applied, they became enraged, and wanted to kill Him. A young man whom they had known, to presume so much! He was now *Jesus, the Christ*, the commissioned of God, according to His own declaration. There was no *miraculous dove* talking or speaking through Him, as the Gnostics have reported. He was now at home among His brothers and sisters and young acquaintances, and well He knew they would suppose He had faults as well as they; so He took the start of them by saying: "You will say unto me this proverb, 'Physician, heal thyself.'" But there was one thing that, perhaps, His relatives did not know, and that was, the physician had healed himself in the order of God under John. Thus, in short, we see the mode of His first appearing; the second must be like unto it.

Thus it was with Ann Lee, who went through the same ordeal, setting the example for womankind, that Jesus did for men, since which time the church has rested on these two pillars, no more to be overthrown. Thus, the "mystery of God, in the blazing sunlight of this day, is finished." Amen; it is finished. These truths may set hardly with some who have considered Jesus to be superhuman; but such must remember that He was one of the brethren, after His baptism, and not at all ashamed to call them so.

But we are told that, although tempted in all points as we are, "He was without sin; and that He always did the things that pleased the Father." The same may be said of Ann, who manifested the Mother in Deity. She was without sin, and always did the things that pleased her Mother and Lord after she was commissioned. So it was with Christ; for Jesus became the Christ by virtue of His appointment. He was not Christ before that time, but simply, as the Apostle John said, "Jesus of Nazareth, son of Joseph."

But the anointed man was tempted in all points as we are, for, saith the apostle, "we have not an high priest who is not touched with our infirmities." Now, it is a fact worthy of note, that all temptations must come through some department of our nature. It is impossible for any one to be tempted by an external presentment unless he has something within him which desires it. The serpent that tempted Eve only showed something she desired; and Adam could not have been overcome but for the fact that he had as strong a desire for the fruit as Eve had; and his throwing the blame on her was simply cowardly and contemptible.

Now, if we know how we are tempted and what tempts us most, we know how Jesus was tempted and what tempted Him most; but that He successfully resisted ALL temptations after He became the Christ none will dispute. This, and this alone, is the apostle's declaration, and is true. This adds an hundred fold more lustre to His brow than to admit the Gnostic doctrine, that a Christ came from some unknown world, entered into Him and rendered Him impeccable.

Little is known of Jesus' history previous to His baptism by John; but if we examine the word of the apostle closely we shall find that they thought Him not impeccable previous thereto: "In that He died, He died unto sin once," as we also must die. We cannot die to a thing to which we have never been alive "*He was as we are* in this world.*" Do we not know how we are? "He learned obedience by things He suffered," as we must Also Peter iv, 1, 2: "For as much as Christ suffered for us in the flesh (not in our stead), arm yourselves likewise with the same mind, for he that hath suffered in the flesh hath ceased from sin [as Jesus did], that he no longer should live the rest of his time [as he had done a part of his time] to the lust of men, but to the will of God."

What sublime pathos in the soul-melting out-pouring of the spirit through the prophet Isaiah, in which it is shown that Jesus did the work for himself. Who is this that cometh from Edom, with dyed garments from Bozrah? — this that is glorious in his apparel, traveling in the greatness of his strength? Wherefore art thou *red* in thine apparel? * * (His answer is enough to draw tears from a stone.) "I have trodden the winepress alone, and of the people there was none with me: And I looked and there was none to help, therefore mine own arm brought salvation unto me " — Isa. lxiii, 1, 2, 3, 5

It would seem that enough had been said showing the similarity between the first and second appearing; but people do not readily believe if one stone is left unturned. It could not be said to be a *second* appearance if there was any essential contrast, either in the mode, effect, operation, or ultimate. We have shown that it was unnecessary for the same flesh and bones to reappear, to constitute a second appearance — but that Christ was manifested, and reappeared, in Ann's testimony, her searching power, her self-denial, tribulation, etc ; in fact all the evidences reappeared in her that appeared in Jesus.

He did not come with the nature of angels, but the seed of Abraham. She appeared likewise, not with the nature of angels, but with our nature; hence Jesus and Ann are alike in their natures. As there was a forerunner in the first appearing to prepare the way for Jesus, so there was in the second appearing to prepare the way for Ann.

Previous to the second appearance, anti-Christ began to be weakened by that memorable division called the "Reformation," by which a way was opened for man to contend for his long lost liberty. About this time, many religious revivals broke out in various parts of Europe, particularly in France and Germany. The remarkable revival which occurred about the year 1689, in the province of Dauphiny and Vivarais, in France, excited great attention. The subjects thereof testified that the end of things drew nigh; they preached repentance, stating that the kingdom of God was at hand — that the marriage of the Lamb would soon take place.

These witnesses increased until about the year 1706, when a few of them went over to England, where many were united to them, and both their numbers and powers of ministration, like the sea, ebbed and flowed for forty years, when a small number of the most faithful were led by the spirit to unite themselves into a small society, near Manchester, under the ministry of James and Jane Wardley. These were the John Baptists of the second appearing of Christ, to whom the people came and were baptized into the spirit of repentance, confessing their sins; and Ann Lee was among the rest, and she came for the same purpose the rest did; and as Jesus confessed to the forerunner in His day, so likewise Ann Lee confessed to the forerunner of the Second Advent, and came up through that order, as Jesus did through that of John. So that the forerunners declared her to be, first a woman "coming *after* them, but was preferred *before* them, for she was before them."

Thus it is seen that the second was the reappearing of the first; hence, as promised, Christ has appeared "the second time without sin unto salvation" to all who will accept, believe and obey. The little handful continued to increase in light and power until the year 1770, when by a special manifestation of divine light the present testimony of salvation and eternal life was fully revealed to Ann Lee, and by her made known to the society; and thus she rose above them and became the anointed and acknowledged leader of this faithful band. From this time forth Ann knew herself to be the Bride, the Lamb's wife, being baptized with the same spirit, and, by implicit obedience to the light received from God, she became conjoined to the Bridegroom, and was a co-worker with Him in the regeneration and redemption of the race — He the Father and She the Mother in spiritual Israel.

And now let us ask: Are these too humble, lowly and mean to be honored with the leadership of God's people? or shall we, Gnostic-like, look high up among the stars for a greater? It were folly to do so We trust it is now seen that all the types and symbols under the shadowy dispensations of the law and the prophets are completely fulfilled in the "two anointed Ones" who stand as the first foundation pillars in the new creation — Jesus Christ and Ann Lee, whose ultimates are the same — the first appearing ultimated in a living body or Church, which had all things in common; the second appearing ultimated in the same. Hence we see in *every particular*, from the first shadowing forth — from the first promise of God that a Redeemer should appear, through all prophecy up to the substance, the first and second — that the male and female are perfectly equal in type and symbol, in prophecy and person, in call, in character, in operation, in substance, in effect, in culmination and in ultimate. Equality! is ineffaceably stamped upon them, never more to be blotted out.

The same spirit now calls that called then; the same doctrine is taught now that was taught then; the same exhortation is made; the invitation is given now to all kindreds, nations and tongues that was given then: "Look unto me and be saved, all ye ends of the earth."

The last silver trumpet is now sounding to the inhabitants of the earth, and may its shrill and piercing notes reach every mountain-top, penetrate every forest, echo in every land and extend over every wide sea, till the whole earth shall know that now is come salvation and strength and the kingdom of our God and the power of His Christ.

15

THE DEVIL NOT SELF-EXISTENT.

TEXT—Have I not chosen you twelve, and one of you is a Devil?—[John vi, 70.

I propose to-day to fulfill the promise which I made in a previous discourse, by calling your attention to the consideration of the great being named in the text. He has been made an important factor in the world's history from creation to the present day. So much importance has been and is (shall I say ignorantly?) attached to him by pulpit orators and others, that he is now considered by many to be co-equal in existence with God, and sufficient in power to frustrate the designs and thwart the plans of the Almighty. That while God's kingdom is a kingdom of light, his is a kingdom of darkness, from which he emerged in our world's infancy, and, in the absence of Deity, made shipwreck of his noblest work, causing the fall of man and taking him captive; and the destruction was so great that God has not been able in 6,000 years to fully repair the breach then made; and His own unappeasable wrath became so enkindled against man that He has given nine-tenths of his posterity to his Satanic Majesty, to be by him roasted in Plutonian fires through all eternity! That, finally, He saw no plan to defeat the Devil and keep him from taking the whole, but to humble Himself and come down to earth through a woman, who in turn had to appear before a sinning priest, make confession and offer a sin offering for the uncleanness of that which God Himself had imposed on her; and for which sinful act she has not only been canonized, but made the fourth person in the Godhead by the greatest of all the lower-floor churches. These glaring inconsistencies alone ought to be sufficient to satisfy every thoughtful and rational Bible student that the whole miraculous statement was a forged interpolation. But this humiliation on the part of Deity was to show the devil that, in the form of man, He could withstand his wiles and not be overcome by him, and for this cause the spirit led him into the wilderness to receive his temptations. Here He was made not only to fast forty days and forty nights, but was

SORELY TEMPTED BY THE DEVIL,

who took Him from the wilderness upon a high mountain, where He could view the surroundings, and in a twinkling showed and offered Him "all the kingdoms of the world and the glory of them," if He would forsake the Lord and worship him. Not satisfied with this refusal of the God-man, the devil took Him back to Jerusalem and set Him on a pinnacle of the temple, and, though sorely tempted, He stood His ground. Still, one would think He should not have been very greatly tempted by such offers when He had the whole universe in the hollow of His hand. Now, temptation is an impossibility to any one who has nothing in him which covets or desires the thing offered. And as the God-man was tempted, it follows that He had within Him a desire for the things offered Him by the devil, and which desires had to be resisted and overcome; thus it is evident that His *desire* for these things was the devil which had been worrying Him, and not some great external bugaboo. The error of the pulpit is in looking at this scene as a literal and external transaction, as impossible as it would have been. They contend that the fasting in the wilderness, His being taken by the devil on to an exceeding high mountain, and afterward being taken back by him to Jerusalem and set on a pinnacle of the temple, are *prima facie* evidence of the self-existence of the devil. But with little careful thought the student will discover its literal impossibility. First — It was a spiritual fast. While under the influence of these internal temptations in the wilderness of doubts in regard to the efficacy and success of the work He was called to, He could receive no spiritual food; but after He had resisted all those temptations and banished all vain desires, angels then could find access, and "came and ministered to Him" the bread and waters of life. We know that He was not bodily set upon a church steeple, nor bodily carried on to that high mountain. These were only the self-exalted notions presented in His mind, which He found it His duty to banish before He could receive the blessing of angels. Thus it will be seen we have not found the external monster yet, either in or out of the Bible, but in man only. Hath not God chosen hundreds, and are not some of them devils? Every hypocrite, every thief, every liar, every backbiter, every fomenter of discord, every debaucher, and *all* who obey the lower instead of the higher impulses, may be classed with Judas as devils. So, then, if any have a curiosity to see the devil, I would advise them to look within, and if he is not there, they need not fear him.

But I must come more directly to the subject and consider the possibility of two independent, self-existent beings, and notice some of the arguments in its favor. It is asserted that all existences have their opposites, as light and darkness, heat and cold, life and death, good and evil, God and devil, and that we have the same evidence for the existence of one that we have for the other. The error here consists in taking conditions and qualities for entities. Darkness is not an entity, and heat and cold, life and death, are conditions of matter; good and evil are qualities only.

God is infinite spirit; but infinite devil is a chimera, as I will hereafter show. Besides, we have not, as asserted, the same evidence for the existence of a devil, external to man, that we have for the existence of God. For the latter we have the harmonious universe. For the former, or devil, we have no evidence of his existence only in the actions and deeds of man, which go far to prove that he has no existence exterior to finite creatures. "Have I not chosen you twelve, and one of you is a devil?" But it is affirmed that the "free agency of man pre-supposes the existence of two opposite powers, controlled and directed by two primary antagonistic intelligences or beings." But this conclusion does not follow, but the reverse. This is a sophism that logicians call *non causa pro causa* — the assignation of a false cause. Two equal antagonistic powers cannot cause free agency or any other active condition to exist. There is no living thing whose existence can possibly pre-suppose two antagonisms. On the contrary, such existences pre-suppose something harmonious. A thing made and destroyed does not pre-suppose two antagonisms, but simply the power to make and destroy. But 'tis argued that God made his free agent, man, "very good," which supposes a good maker; but now man is made very bad, and this supposes a bad maker or devil, since God could not be the maker nor author of any thing bad. Hence, if the good man is proof of a good maker — God — the bad man is proof of a bad maker — devil — thus the existence of the great antagonist of God is logically proved. Not so fast. Logic wrongly applied is worse than no logic at all.

In this there is no agreement between premise and conclusion. That God's free agent had the power to misuse the good faculties given by his Maker, and thus become a bad man, affords no evidence that another being external to himself had any hand in it. So we still have no necessity for God's great adversary.

But it is further asked: "If God gave man the inclination, or that which caused the inclination, to do wrong, knowing he would do so, does this not make God Himself responsible?" By no means. God could not do an impossible thing. It was necessary to progression that man should be free, which could not be without investing him with power either to do or not to do at pleasure. If he had not this power he would be relieved of the responsibility; but, having it, makes him a creature of rewards and punishments. He is thus accountable for all the words and deeds of life, and may either become a devil or saint, as he may elect "For the Son of Man shall come * * Then He shall reward every man according to his works."— Matt. xvi, 27 But the querist continues. What caused the man to choose to follow the bad inclinations, if the devil did not come to tempt him? In reply I would ask: What caused him to listen to the devil? When this is answered, the other will be also. It is evident that, if man had not the inclination to deviate from a straight line, or as he was acted on by his Creator, he would simply be a machine without accountability If it still be supposed that the good man would not have erred but for the interposition of a foreign being called devil, this would still deny his free agency. No reason nor logic can show that either the machine or the man could become a free agent by being placed between two opposite forces, whether these forces were equal or unequal. It they were equal, the man or machine would be made to stand still and be held in equilibrio If the forces were unequal, he would be moved and guided by the strongest power, and, as the majority of mankind are in "evil continually," it would follow that there is a power greater than God Then why strive to obey the weaker power? To this would the acceptance of a self-existent devil lead But it is added: What meant Christ in saying to the Jews, " Ye are of your father the Devil" (John viii, 44), if he did not mean, My Father is God; your father is the devil? Are not Christ's plain declarations to be relied on? Most certainly. But Christ added: "Your father's lusts ye will do " His meaning would have been more clear if He had said: " My Father is the Spirit, your father is the flesh, and his lusts ye will do " "Ladies and gentlemen." as you are pleased to style yourselves You are free agents Flesh or spirit? Both cannot occupy the same chamber. Lower floor or upper floor? Carnal life or spirit life? God-spirit father, or flesh-devil father? We will all show our choice by the lives we lead. That devils do exist none will dispute. "Have I not chosen twelve, and one of you is a devil?" But his unoriginality and self-existence are denied. The moment investigation begins, we see it involves the following

PARADOXICAL SOLECISMS :

Two equal infinities, creator and destroyer. Two supremes, two first causes, two necessary self-sufficient existences, two originals, two almighties, all of which are absurd and impossible. But were these true, the universe could not have been created at all, for two equal forces, whether of mind or matter, would have brought every thing to a stand-still. While it would have been the mind of one to create, it would of necessity have been the mind of the opposite to destroy, and, being equals, no world could have been made; but the universe denies the proposition. It is sufficient to say here, that which has no beginning can have no ending, and if the devil is a self-existent being he must continue forever. An unoriginated being is a necessary existence, and must be just what it is — must exist because of the necessity of such existence; consequently must be *good*. His goodness is as necessary as his existence. He could not be evil because evil is unnecessary, not needed; consequently not unoriginated. Pursuing the thought, we discover that a necessary being is necessarily from everlasting, without beginning, without ending, self-existent, self-sufficient, almighty. Such being must of necessity be wise, his wisdom be infinite, as there is the same reason for the infinity of his wisdom as that of his being, and, being infinitely wise, he must perceive that goodness is infinitely better than evil, love than malice. In a word, being independent in his existence, and consequently in his action, he must of *infinite necessity choose* to be *good*. Hence we assert, with mathematical and logical certainty, that a necessary being is necessarily *good*, *wise and perfect*. All of which is proved from the mode of his existence. How then is it possible for a sane mind, after tracing matters thus far, to admit that another being, whose mode of existence is precisely the same, can, notwithstanding, possess a nature diametrically opposite? Whoever asserts that an eternal, self-existent being can be absolutely malicious has no argument to prove that another being of precisely the same mode of existence is absolutely good. So thus logically stands the case: If a self-existent being be necessarily good, as proved, there can be no self-existent evil being. Thus his majesty

VANISHES INTO THIN AIR ;

for, unless the axiom that the same cause must always produce the same effect be given up as false and absurd, we are compelled to admit that those primary beings whose mode of existence is the same must be similar in their character and nature. Thus we see that, by the admission of so great an absurdity as the existence of two or more primary beings, we gain nothing by it. We have not found an eternal source of evil at last. For two eternal independent beings cannot be admitted. When the mind has rationally traced out as shown, the existence and attributes of one necessary being, it cannot logically suppose another; because one being of infinite power and wisdom is fully sufficient to account for creation. So in strictness of language and logic, there can be but one eternal, self-existent, infinite and necessary being. There can be but one infinite space. If we supposed two, we set bounds to each, and thus destroy the infinity of both. Just so is it with infinite beings. By admitting two we destroy the infinity and un-deify both. But it may still be affirmed that after having found an efficient cause for the existence of all created good, we still want an efficient cause for evil, and argue that, since one necessary being is necessarily good and perfect, to suppose that evil originated from Him would be to deny his necessary goodness. However distressing the necessity may be to discover the origin of evil, we cannot remove the difficulty by supposing an eternal self-existent evil being, for in so doing we create a greater absurdity than we remove. The good Apostle James points out its origin in the following emphatic language: "From whence come wars and fightings among you? Come they not hence even of your lusts that war in your members" (where the flesh-devil reigns)—James iv, 1. He further says: "Resist this devil and he will flee from you." But whenever we assert that a necessary being is not necessarily good and perfect we do away with the necessity of an evil being, because such being may be the author of both good and evil; so then the case would logically stand thus: If a self-existent being be necessarily good, there can be no self-existent evil being. But if a self-existent being be not necessarily good, it would follow that God is not necessarily and unchangeably good, and may, therefore, be the author of evil; consequently, we would have no use for a self-existent devil. According to the first proposition, the existence of such a being is impossible. According to the second he is wholly unnecessary. Thus his non-existence is proved to a demonstration.

SPINOZA.

I might stop here, but will tax your patience a little further by reading a quotation from the Hebrew philosopher Benedict de Spinoza, as follows: "If the devil be an entity contrary in all respects to God, having nothing of God in his nature, then he can have nothing in common with God. Is he assumed to be a thinking entity, as some will have it, who never wills and never does any good, and who sets himself in opposition to God on all occasions, he must assuredly be a very wretched being, and, could prayers do any thing for him, his amendment were much to be implored. But let us ask, whether so miserable an object could exist even for an instant, and, the question put, we see at once that it could not, for from the perfection of a thing proceeds its power of continuance. The more of the essential and divine a thing possesses, the more enduring it is. But how could the devil, having no trace of perfection in him, exist at all? Add to this that the stability or duration of a thinking thing depends entirely on its love of and union with God, and that the opposite of this state in every particular being presumed in the devil, it is obviously impossible that there can be any such being. And then there is, indeed, no necessity to presume the existence of a devil, for the causes of hate, envy, anger and all such passions are readily enough discovered, and there is no occasion for resort to fiction to account for the evils they engender."

This I consider true. It were indeed absurd to refer to a foreign power that which man is able to perform of himself, and which it is well known he has performed in all ages of the world. The passional nature of man is sufficient to account for all the evils of the world — past, present and to come. But men will reluctantly yield opinions imbibed, as it were, from their mother's bosom, and, with all that has been or can be said, will feel somewhat like the darky who said: "Sah, you need not tell dis niggah dar is no debbil. Kase, if dah was no debbil, how does da make de picters so zackly like him? Wid dem big claws and dat great chain around his neck and de angel a holden him in de pit till God gets ready to let him loose. When dat time comes, see if you will den say dar is no debbil." I am cited to other texts of scripture than those quoted, which, now to notice, would be too great a strain on your already overtaxed patience. I will, therefore, close with the words of our Saviour, which plainly show where we may look for the devil, and the origin of evil. He says (Matt xv, 19): " For out of the *heart* of man proceed evil thoughts, murders, adulteries, fornications, thefts," etc Not from some foreign source, but from the heart of man. Then let us all " turn the battle to the gate," " purify the heart," drive out our own little devils, and then we shall have no cause to fear the big one.

16

BIBLE METAPHOR.

When any person appears before an audience of intelligent people to address them, he should be induced to do so from one of two motives, viz.: either to exhort them to greater holiness of life, or to enlighten their understandings. I am vain enough to be moved by the latter on this occasion. That which men have most overlooked in regard to the Bible is its metaphor — its beautiful tropes, figures of speech and symbol. Its richness in these excels any other book. A want of comprehending them has made many things appear to be miracles when they were not, and has caused many to throw the book aside as useless rubbish. The orthodox are at one extreme, that of worshipful veneration, and the generative spiritualists and infidels at the other, that of insolent contempt. Both conditions are caused by either the want of comprehension, or of close, candid and unbiased inspection. I am not vain enough to suppose that I or any other person can reconcile all that is contained in the good book, either metaphorically or otherwise, with the scientific knowledge of to-day. But, in my judgment, it has fewer faults than the infidel supposes, and more than the orthodox are willing to admit. Much that is deemed faulty by the former is true when properly understood, but with a very different meaning than that applied by the latter. A few of them, and very few out of the many that can be made plain to the common mind, I now propose to notice. I will begin with the statement of the creation of man, 6,000 years ago, which is so lustily berated and disputed by scientific evolutionists and generative spiritualists, and see if the Bible be not sustained. That the species *homo*, or man, has existed on this planet at least 100,000 years prior to the event here recorded the honest explorers of this field have fully proved. But this does not invalidate the Bible story in the least degree, because it speaks of a different creation. The term " create " has two significations — one to make anew, the other to change. To change is to create a new condition; hence, the new condition is a creation. The

story reads thus: "Let us make man in our image." — Gen. i, 26.
So it seems that, previous to this, man had not been in God's
image, and, in order to make him so, it was necessary to make
him differently from what he had been previously. Some writers
say that, because they were created male and female, this feature
was God's image; but this would have wrought no change, for
primal man was thus from the beginning Besides, this whole
planet, mineral, vegetable, and animal, was created male and
female, previous to the existence of man. Were this God's image, then the beasts of the field were in God's image before man
was created (!) Verse 7, of the 2d chapter, says · "And the Lord
formed man of the dust of the ground, and breathed into his
nostrils the breath of life, and man became a living soul " This
shows that previous to this he was a *dead* soul But God made
him of the dust of the ground. What dust? Answer. The dust
of promiscuity and animalism. There was no other dust to make
him of. God being spirit, He made the internal, the real man
spirit also — " breathed into him the breath of life " — quickened,
changed him from death unto life; hence in His own image.
Any other construction would conflict with known truths The
common orthodox rendering seems to me to be as ridiculous as
that of the negro who said . " De fuss man God made was black
He took some good, rich, black dirt an' mold him up, den set him
up 'gin de fence to dry, and blowed bref into him;" whereupon
one of his hearers ejaculated: "Who made de fence?" But
creation did not stop here. It was found that the newly-made
man, who was chosen and appointed to lead in the advanced
order, had no counterpart There was no woman made anew
with a living soul, and God saw that it was not good for the
quickened man to be alone. So the account goes: He brought a
deep sleep on Adam, when a rib was taken from his side, of which
a woman was made. I would remind my readers of the fact that
the Hebrew word Adam is a noun of multitude, as well as a
noun proper. It is like our word man, which may mean either a
single man or mankind; so Adam may mean either the man
Adam or Adamkind. Hence it is reasonable to conclude that it
was Adamkind that slept from whom the rib or binder was taken
for the man Adam's counterpart. She was then the newly made
woman, quickened as the newly made man, who were intended
for the higher order of marriage, which was now for the first
time instituted.

Thus it was that man and woman were created more than 6,000 years ago, according to Bible history, which is shown to be consistent, and not in conflict, with any known truth. The whole story of man's creation, of his rectitude, of the Garden, the serpent, etc., is a beautiful allegory, and no less beautiful than true, and all the derision and cant which has been cast upon it is only so much wasted breath. I will pass the plagues of Egypt, the serpent-rods, the Red sea, to Joshua. One of the greatest stumbling-blocks to Bible-readers is that of Joshua commanding the Sun to stand still on Gibeon, to lengthen the daylight from twelve to twenty-four hours, in order that he might slaughter all the women and babies as well as men that dwelt in the land. But the first question in order is: Did God have any thing to do in directing a war so merciless? This, I think, is not altogether unanswerable. God, for man's edification and instruction, is within him; His word is there, and whosoever obeys that word, impressed on his higher consciousness, obeys God. If Joshua thus obeyed the operation of God's spirit within, it would follow that God directed the warfare, as when any of us obey the highest light vouchsafed to us, we obey God, and are, for the present time, justified, though ever so imperfect. But whether Joshua did this or not, I am unable to say, and therefore drop this part of the subject. It seems that the rulers in Gibeon had, by deceit and hard lying, entered into a league with Joshua, which so incensed the five adjacent kingdoms that they combined together and brought up their armies to chastise them for it, and, although Gibeon was the greatest, the five against him would certainly have conquered him, but they sent runners to Joshua, whose army was encamped at Gilgal, to ask his aid, thinking that with the help of his army they might be saved from destruction. Joshua consulted the Lord and was ordered to go up to Gibeon. Arriving there, he would not accept Gentile assistance. The account runs thus: "Then spake Joshua to the Lord in the day when the Lord delivered up the Amorites before the children of Israel, and he said in the sight of the children of Israel: Sun, stand thou still upon Gibeon and thou Moon in the valley of Ajalon, and the Sun stood still in the midst of heaven and hasted not to go down about a whole day." Josh. x, 12, 13. There can be but little doubt but what such transaction occurred, and that the Sun and Moon, spoken to by Joshua, obeyed him, but they were not our day and night luminaries. If the Sun was up in the stellar regions the Moon was there also; but it will be observed that the Sun spoken to was on Gibeon, and the Moon addressed was in the valley. Exactly here is where the two Gentile armies were, the greatest on Gibeon, called the Sun, the secondary the Moon, which obeyed the command of Joshua and stood still in the midst of heaven, or extreme happiness, the whole day, to see Joshua slay their enemies without their aid. It is no wonder the Sun was in heaven all that day. Now, had it been our luminary that Joshua addressed, it would have required nearly fourteen years for the command to have reached his burning and anxious ear. Astronomers tell us that if one end of a chain could be attached to the sun and the other end to this planet, and they should start opposite directions, it would take about one decade to tighten the chain. But orthodoxans ask: Could not the Lord hear Joshua, and so stop the sun at once? What the Lord could have done I cannot say, but in this case the most convenient thing would have been to apply the brakes to our own little car-wheel, and stop its revolving on its axis, without calling to an object 95,000,000 of miles distant!

Thus it seems to me that we cannot fail to see that the metaphorical exegesis is the only consistent and correct one. We would be startled at such literal construction now, when we make use of the same kind of metaphor that was used then. We call a fearless, brave man a lion, without dreaming of his having four legs; a meek one, a lamb, and so on, and make nothing strange of it. Suppose our late war had been recorded in the Bible, how many miracles could have been manufactured to astonish future generations.

For instance, the walls of Sumpter were said to be sixteen feet thick, of solid masonry, three or four times the resisting power of the walls of Jericho, and see how quickly they tumbled down at the sound of the voices of three little swamp-angels! This was the printed literature of the day that went all over the world — yet the event at Jericho is said to be a great miracle, because the walls of that town fell at the sound of seven rams-horns.

Now, any wall of a given thickness has a certain power of resistance per square inch, which must be overcome ere the tumbling down will commence. Historians give ample proof of the Jews' mode of battering down walls. Jericho was not an exception. Those troopers, with the rams-horns, were doubtless the watch for those engaged in fixing their usual battering-rams to be moved by two or three thousand men, at a given signal, which was when the seventh long blast was sounded. The account is doubtless true, that the walls fell at that signal. It is no benefit to sacred writ, for designing men to try to make the scriptures more than true to stimulate our gaping marvelousness. Had there been no elementary force besides the rams-horns brought to bear on the walls, they might have galloped and tooted till the crack of doom, and not one brick would have moved from its resting place. Again, look at our metaphor, in war times, slightly clothed in Bible language. Behold, the enemies of the Lord in the Southland trained a band of Louisiana Tigers, fierce and powerful, to tear in pieces God's chosen army (?). But the "Lord fought for Israel," and defeated them with great slaughter, and the remnant fled in utter confusion to their dens, canebrakes and swamps for safety, and the Lord triumphed! But the enemy, not wholly subdued, trained a host of Copperheads and tied fire-brands between their tails, and sent them to "burn the shocks" and supplies of the armies of Israel. But, instead, lo and behold! God turned their weapons against them, and burned the whole region with fire, and smote it with the sword, from the land of cane and cotton even to the great sea! All this only goes to show with what ease metaphor may be made to resemble fact. The prophet's she bears only differed from the Louisiana Tigers in gender, and Samson's foxes had just as many legs and tails each as the Copperheads, and no more. To be tied by the tails is to be joined by the lower passions for evil. To be tied by the heads is to be joined by the higher and nobler faculties for good. It was well said that Samson's foxes were tied together by their tails with fire between them. Had it been four-legged foxes, they would have had more concern for their tails than for the shocks of the Philistines. But the orthodox would have us believe that God could so fix the fire-brands between their tails that it would neither burn them nor the string with which it was tied! It is this kind of literalizing impossibilities that makes infidels by hundreds. Wherever it is possible, we should take a common-sense view of Bible history, and not strive to convert it into impossible marvels. There are many apparently miraculous statements in the good book that admit of a rational exegesis, to some of which I may hereafter refer, but cannot do so now. The orthodox call this meddling with God's word. But it is well to remember that it is a child that has been lost and found, and

has been greatly meddled with by various Sanhedrims and councils of carnal men, for many centuries past, the most of whom
were inclined to exaggeration — to color and magnify, if not to
mystify, the word; and the great wonder is that it has come
down to us even as perfect as we now find it.   It is at the present
time undergoing another manipulation at the hands of a lot of
sinners in England, and whether it will be improved or worsted
we shall perhaps learn in the future.   They are doubtless tainted
with the Nicene fraud, and it is not difficult to rearrange nouns,
verbs, adjectives and adverbs, so as to give them a meaning at
variance with the original

The things to which Bible statements refer are either possible
or impossible.   If impossible in either the literal or metaphorical
sense, they are fraudulent interpolations by designing men.   I
do not mean to say that all we cannot comprehend is fraud   I
refer only to that which is comprehensible and yet impossible.
But the orthodox, in defense of the whole as it is, tell us that
with God all things are possible   This, I say, not irreverently, is
a mistaken declaration.   It is impossible for any power to cause
a thing to be and not to be at the same time, or to make two particles of matter occupy the same point in space at the same time.
It is no sacrilege to affirm that things which are absolutely impossible are as much so with God as with men, but this is not
affirming that there are not things possible with God that are
impossible with men.   In Bible history, as I have endeavored to
show, there are many statements, which, if taken literally, seem
absurd and impossible, but when metaphorically considered are
found to be in harmony with scientific truth.   This should cause
us all to hesitate in condemning that which we do not yet understand   Truth, as a whole or in parts, is a harmony either natural
or spiritual, or both together, and wherever there is the least
clashing there is error either on the one side or the other, or both.
Too carnal to understand spiritual things, some great writers call
us back from the inspired word to nature   John Weiss, a gospel
minister, so called, and one of the most able writers of the age,
after having given orthodox revivalism in the Radical Review a
severe scourging, has nothing for us to fall back on but nature.
He says: "The spasms of lecture rooms and tabernacles cannot
galvanize a soul back into that corpse whose crime has been that
it lived by false pretenses on the human heart.   If a great people
would tingle with revival, let it stand in the circuit of nature and

permit the element to steam through it," etc. This is just what the infidel world has been doing for centuries, and what have they to show for Nature's revival? Intellectually, something. Spiritually, nothing. Nature alone, without God's internal inspirations, would take the whole world back behind the fig-leaf dispensation. The difficulty with this class of giant intellects is, they keep looking into nature in their search for God, and find just as much as a bat does, and seem to think intellect is spirit. All such will yet have to learn that in order to be saved they must find God in His order of finite agents, and where He has "placed His name for salvation." Zion is that place. (Isa. xlvi, 13.) God is consistent with Himself; He will not establish an order for the redemption of man, and then save him standing in nature waiting for her tingling inspirations.

" But the natural man receiveth not the things of the Spirit of God; for they are foolishness unto him, neither can he know them, because they are spiritually discerned." — I Cor. ii, 14.

CONCEPTION OF CHRIST.

The text I have chosen to-day may be found in John iii, 6: "*That which is born of flesh is flesh; that which is born of the spirit is spirit.*" We extend the text, and say, that which is begotten of the flesh is flesh, and that which is begotten of the spirit is spirit.

Mankind are divided into many classes, but may be reduced to two. Materialistic evolutionists make them the same, contravening the assertion of Locke that matter cannot think, and that no new property is added to it by change of position and relation. I. In proof of their position, they assert that matter invisible is sensitive, because certain plants will shrink from human touch; hence the matter of its formation must have contained the sensitive quality before the plant was formed. II. They further assert that some plants are carniverous, and destroy animal or insect life for their growth and sustenance; and here the evidence of thought begins and extends in the higher growths, to animal and man, all of which are matter. "All flesh is grass." This year the grass grows; it is turned under, and next year it is corn, and the next it is animal, and the next it is man. Thus evolution makes man, with sensation and thought, from the "dust of the ground," and in this it triumphantly tells us that it stands on Bible ground. But how will it do to say all flesh is spirit? Here the evolutionist steps off of Bible ground into impenetrable darkness, because he ignores the great, grand over-thought, the cause of the first atom and the first thought; or, he might recognize the further Bible doctrine of the breathing in something distinct from matter, and learn that whatsoever is born of the spirit is spirit, and not matter; and thus not lose sight of the philosophy which teaches that these are contradictory substances which are neither blendable nor interchangeable. There are substances in matter that cannot be really made to touch nor intermingle without the introduction of a third

Where the touch is complete, a real union is formed. Could

17

you bring two boards into full contact, you would need no glue to hold them together. But I am wandering. Spirit and matter, being contradictory substances, tactualization becomes impossible. That which is born of the flesh is flesh. Jesus was born of a woman who was flesh; consequently, Jesus was flesh. But He was afterward born of the spirit. "Marvel not that I say ye must be born again," [as I have been]. It is not rational to suppose that Jesus could have been born like us, unless He had been begotten like us. In support of this, I will cite you to Bible testimony. It is said, Rom. viii, 29, that Christ was the first born among many brethren. This has reference to the spiritual birth — being born of the spirit out of a sinful nature; and all that receive this new birth are brethren. That which is born of the spirit is spirit. Again, I Cor. v, 20th: "Christ is the head of the body, the first born from the dead." To become His brethren, then, we must be begotten and born from the dead, spiritually as He was. Without this we cannot be called His brethren, neither could He designate us as such. No one can be numbered with, and become one of His brethren while living the worldly life, whether he be professor or profane. But now Christ is risen from the dead and become the first fruits of them that slept. For since by man came death, by man also came the resurrection from the dead.— I Cor. xv, 20, 21.

The lesson to be learned from this is, first, Jesus was a man born of the flesh, like His brethren were; and, second, that He had been dead to that spiritual life into which He rose. He could not have risen from the dead except He had been dead; but being born of the spirit, by obedience to God, His spirit arose from the dead, and this was His true resurrection, to which He always had reference, and not that of the material body; and this must be the resurrection of all who are ever saved — for whatsoever is born of the spirit is spirit. Having led you along thus far, I will now call your attention to the two first chapters of Matthew's and Luke's gospels, which treat of the miraculous conception of Christ, noting the fact that, of the four gospels, two are silent on the subject, a very great and culpable neglect surely, if the statement be true.

That it has been clearly shown to be spurious by able writers, precludes the necessity of my going outside the sacred volume for evidence pro or con. I would, however, thus far deviate as to let you know that the oldest Greek copy now extant is in the

English Museum in London, and is written in Greek capitals. In this copy the four gospels all begin alike, at the baptism of John, showing that the story has been introduced and added to Matthew's and Luke's gospels at some later period. But this I leave.

The first Scripture text which is generally admitted to refer to Christ is found in Deuteronomy—the last book of the Pentateuch, v. 18, chap. 15, and reads: "A prophet shall the Lord your God raise up unto you, of your brethren, like unto me, Him shall ye hear." This is to the point and sustains the text. "That which is born of the flesh is flesh." The prophet spoken of by Moses is acknowledged to be the Christ, who was not only to be like Moses, who was the Christ of the law dispensation and type of Jesus, but like Him "raised up of the brethren"—that is, of their stock or race; of the seed of Abraham and David. It then cannot fail to be seen that these first words spoken of Christ deny the miraculous story. But further, Isa. xii, 1· "And there shall come forth a root out of the stem of Jesse, and a branch shall grow up out of his roots, and the spirit of the Lord shall rest upon him —the spirit of wisdom and understanding." This was clearly and literally fulfilled in Jesus, both in the natural and spiritual point of view. Let it be observed, He was to come of Jesse, not from the stellar regions, but was to grow up out of his roots, thus flatly denying the miraculous statement. Again, Jeremiah, xxiii, 5: "Behold, saith the Lord, the days come that I will raise unto David a righteous branch; and He shall be called the Lord our righteousness." And Micah, v, 2. "But thou, Bethlehem Ephratah, though thou be little among the thousands of Judah, out of *thee* shall He come forth to me that is to be ruler in Israel." Thus we see the Prophets are in harmony, and a unit in denying the miraculous story, and point directly to Jesus, the *man* Jesus, as the Christ; one who was begotten and born of the flesh as other men. Much more might be cited to the same effect in the Old Testament, but I must not be too tedious.

I turn now to the New Testament, beginning with Matthew, i, 1: "The book of the generation of Jesus Christ the son of David, the son of Abraham." Now let me ask: Who does not know what *generation* means? Then the son of David, the son of Abraham, and consequently, beyond denial, the son of Joseph, to whom he is traced. Thus is the story denied before it is told; and x, 25: "It is enough that the disciple be as his Master, and the servant as his Lord." Now please notice particularly : If the disciple was as his Master — and we know how the disciple was — we then know how the Master was. But further, see John i, 45 : We have found him of whom Moses and the prophets did write, "Jesus of Nazareth the Son of Joseph." Thus in one brief sentence does the beloved apostle nail the whole story to the counter, and confirm what the prophets foretold.

But I am reminded that this same apostle has also said that He was "the root and offspring of David ; " and am asked : How could He be the root of David without having preceded him ? And I would ask : How could He be the offspring of David without succeeding him ? But I will explain : He was born of the Spirit before David, and spiritually preceded him — and was, therefore, the root of David. He succeeded him in being born of the flesh, and hence was the offspring of David. He was, therefore, the root of David by regeneration, and the offspring of David by generation. So the apostle said truly : " He is the root and offspring of David," which could not have been said of Him had He not been flesh — born of the flesh.

So readily do all the texts of the good book come to the support of the truth when properly understood. But still more, viii, 40 : " But now ye seek to kill me, a *man* that hath told you the truth which I have heard from God." It seems that none but the willful can possibly mistake the meaning of the good apostle John, who declares in plain words, that Jesus was the son of Joseph, and Luke and Matthew, put the story at variance with itself. In chapter 1, verse 32, the angel Gabriel is made to use the following emphatic language to Mary : " Thou shalt conceive and bring forth a son, and the Lord shall give unto Him the throne of His father David." He did not say of His father Holy Ghost, nor His father God, but His father David.

The angel Gabriel did not so much as hint that He should be miraculously conceived. Also chapter 2, verse 41 : " His parents, Joseph and Mary, went yearly to Jerusalem ; " and verse 48 : " Son, why hast thou dealt so with us ? Thy father and I have sought Thee sorrowing." She did not say, Thy Holy Ghost father, nor Thy father God, has been seeking Thee. Evidently it was Joseph and Mary who were the anxious and sorrowing couple. Chapter 2, verse 23 : " And Jesus being the son of Joseph, the son of Heli." I would further cite you to Acts, ii, 30 : " God hath sworn with an oath to David, that of the fruit of his loins according to the flesh, He would raise up Christ." Jesus was this fruit; and xiii, 23, is plainer still. " Of this man's seed hath God, according to His promise, raised unto Israel a Saviour, Jesus " It is perfectly clear, if the apostle knew what he was talking about, that Christ could not have been miraculously conceived. Romans, i, 3: " Concerning His Son Jesus Christ, which was made of the seed of David, according to the flesh, and declared to be the Son of God, with power according to the spirit of holiness by the resurrection from the dead " How clear these words are to the unbiased mind. First—Made of the seed of David according to the flesh; born of the flesh and was flesh Secondly—Declared to be the Son of God, by his resurrection from his former dead estate; born of the spirit and was spirit; now a spiritual, instead of a natural man.

Thus have I given you a chain of evidence showing the perfect harmony of the Old and New Testaments on this subject, and proving, beyond dispute, that Jesus was not miraculously begotten nor conceived. This miraculous story is a Catholic teat, from which the Protestant churches have been drawing nutriment from the days of Luther down to Beecher Tertullian, one of the early Catholic fathers, born about one hundred and fifty of our era, has given the most plausible and ingenious mode of Christ's introduction into this world, to sustain the story, that I have anywhere noticed It is this: " As the branch is not separate from the root, the river from its fountain, nor the ray from the sun, so the word (Christ) is not separated from God, and this ray of God, passing into a certain virgin, became flesh in her womb, and was born a man mixed with God; the flesh, animated by the spirit, was nourished, grew, spoke, taught, operated, and this (flesh) was Christ " This fictitious story is told in the most serious earnestness by the author of many volumes, he being one of the most learned divines of his day. But it will be perceived that, while he favors the miraculous story, he admits that Jesus was the Christ.

But where did the animated flesh come from? Was the ray that entered the virgin matter, or spirit? If it was not separated from God, how did it become His Son? If the ray that came from God and became flesh in the virgin was not separated from God, but a part of Him, then God is Himself matter, because spirit and matter are not interchangeable. If it was spirit, it could not become flesh. Besides, God cannot become mixed up with flesh.

And if God is omnipresent, He was in Mary before the ray. The question would then arise : Whence came the ray ? He says from God. But where was God ? On all these points, the Holy Father leaves us in Cimmerian darkness. The subject, at least, is awfully mixed, and asseverations senseless; at the same time, it is the best argument extant favoring the postulate that Christ was miraculously conceived; and the world must, indeed, be in its babyhood to accept such cob-house for a real abiding place. The logic, syllogistically, stands thus :

FIRST — Sumption .... God is immaculate.
SECOND — Subsumption .... But Jesus is God.
Ergo .... Jesus is immaculate.

But the second premise, or subsumption, is false in the sense intended. The same false logic is applied to Mary. Pope Pius IX made the discovery that Jesus, in His conception and birth, could not be free from taint, while His Mother was tainted, and he decided that Mary must also have been free from taint, and so told one lie to cover another; and, thus emblazoned, stands the false logic:

FIRST — Sumption .... The Mother of Jesus was immaculate.
SECOND — Subsumption ...... But Mary was the Mother of Jesus.
Ergo .... Mary was immaculate.

The church ratified it. The bull was published, and thereafter all who disputed it were accounted heretics. So there was another lie saddled on the church. It is true that Jesus became immaculate; but the means by which He became so are ignored by the whole learned world. He became so by accepting the order of God in John, who preceded Him, and by confessing, forsaking, living above, and free from all sin. And all who are to be redeemed, must become immaculate in the same manner. There is no climbing up some other way; we must climb up the same way that Christ did. The dogma of the foreign origin of Christ was first promulgated by Cerynthus, a learned Greek scholar of Rome. This was a short time previous to the death of the beloved Apostle John, about the year 100. They met in Ephesus, where the former was promulgating his new doctrine of the super-angelic origin of Christ — that He was a high-created spirit that came from the Pleroma and took possession of the body of Jesus at the baptism of John. It was at this time that the aged apostle, who had leaned on the bosom of Christ at the last supper, and who was the only one of His disciples that attended him and witnessed His crucifixion, and who had the best right to know of any one then living, denounced the doctrine in the most vehement language.

In the first epistle to his brethren he said · "I have not written because ye know not the truth, but because ye know it, and that no lie is the truth Who is a liar but he that denieth that Jesus is the Christ? He is anti-Christ." Thus the good apostle met it at the threshold with such testimony as should have put a quietus upon it for all time. But he passed away, and it was persisted in to escape the odium of the false accusation that the Christians worshiped a dead Jew.

Thus it became engrafted on the church, and proved to be the entering wedge that rent the church asunder. Since which time the Christ subject has been classed among the mysteries. We are asked such questions as these: Which is the world's Saviour, Jesus or Christ? Was not Jesus a medium for the Christ spirit, etc.? To which I answer: First—Jesus the Christ, or, as the apostle has it, "The man Christ Jesus," is the Saviour of the saved. He cannot be the Saviour of the lost, and none are or can be saved except they follow Him. He calls to the world and says follow me, not Moses, nor John the Baptist, but ME   Secondly—He could not be the medium for the Christ spirit, because He was Himself the Christ or Messiah We might as well ask: Was Jesus not a medium for the Messiah? The *Christ spirit* and *spirit* of *Christ* are convertible terms; what one means the other means If, by denying myself and following Christ, I have so far changed my spirit, temper, desires and habits as to be moved and actuated as Christ was, then I shall possess and have in me the spirit of Christ or Christ spirit—not a double entity, but simply have my spirit changed from the worldly to be as Christ's spirit was. This is clear.

The saying of the apostle that "Jesus Christ is in you, except ye be reprobates," does not mean that we are to literally have the man Jesus, soul and body, within us His true followers are in Him, and He in them, in all the works and walks of life—"as thou, Father, art in me and I in thee, that they may be one in us, that the world may believe that thou hast sent me."—John xvii, 21. This is the key to unlock the mystery about Christ being in us, etc. Jesus never spake of such a thing as a foreign Christ spirit inhabiting His person and controlling Him · but says thou, Father, art in me, etc

Christ Jesus obeyed God in always doing the things that pleased the Father instead of doing His own will, and we must obey Him, and walk as He walked, or fail of salvation. This a child may understand. It seems obvious that we cannot follow a spirit which was created impeccable — pure, spotless and sinless, from some foreign world, who knows not experimentally any thing about our trials, lusts and divers temptations. Such angel could not succor us: could not know how to sympathize with us. We must have just such a high priest as was Christ Jesus, of whom the Apostle Paul says: "For we have not an high priest which cannot be touched with the feeling of our infirmities, but was in all points tempted like as we are." — Heb. iv, 15.

If Christ was a foreign spirit which entered into Jesus to control His action and speak through Him, what credit can Jesus have? How did His own arm bring Him salvation? We are enjoined to follow Him, and "walk as He walked." How can we know how a Christ from a foreign world walked? Where He came from and whither He went? And, if Jesus had to be miraculously begotten and conceived in order to enable Him to obey the Father and be an example to the world, what must become of us who were "conceived in sin and brought forth in iniquity?" To put us on grounds of capability, and enable us to work out our salvation as He did, we should all have been miraculously begotten and conceived.

It were unreasonable, very, to require us who were conceived in sin to follow one who was "conceived by a ray of light from the body of God;" or begotten by some angel sent from His throne for that purpose. We may rest assured that this is the work of the deceiver, to make us believe that we may "continue in sin that grace may abound" — that we cannot follow Christ, and must be saved by His merits. We may hug this delusion to our bosom, and nestle it in our heart of hearts, but sooner or later to our sorrow we must learn how much we have been deceived, and realize the truth of the text, that whatsoever is born of the flesh is flesh, and whatsoever is born of the spirit is spirit, and that such was the case of our Exemplar, who was first born of the flesh and afterward of the spirit.

The way is now open for every sin-sick soul to enter the new birth and to be made a new creature; and now is the loud call. The trumpet's blast from Zion's God is come, and the Father and Mother say come, "The Spirit and the Bride say come; and let him or her that is athirst come; and whosoever will let him or her come and take the waters of life freely."

ORTHODOXY AND SPIRITUALISM.

All creedal, religious denominations consider their own to be orthodox and those who differ with them heterodox ; and as in what I propose to say to-day, no one particular profession of religion will be singled out, I will, for brevity's sake, use the new term orthodoxan, which, in this discourse, will include all religious professors who hold to one dogma in common, to wit : the trinity of the Absolute, or three Gods in one. No blame is attachable to any individual, nor any organized body now existing, for entertaining it ; because it is a kind of spiritual heir-loom which has been handed down from generation to generation for fifteen hundred years. After the falling away of the primitive Christian church at Jerusalem, heathen rites, ceremonies and doctrines were introduced, among which was the dogma named above — and the poor, but true followers of Christ were banished. In the year of grace 325, Constantine, the bloody Emperor of Rome, called a General Council at Nice to settle the disputes that had arisen and establish the doctrines which were to be received by the so-called church. It was at this council, with about 2,000 persons in attendance, after much heated controversy, which lasted nearly three months, that this false dogma in part was forced upon the world ; here it was "conceived in sin and brought forth in iniquity," and was full fledged in another council held at Constantinople about a half a century later.

It was here decided that Christ was not "raised up from among the brethren" to be an example for them to follow according to the scriptures, but that He was God Himself, who had descended and assumed the proportions and form of man, and was no longer "an example that we should follow His steps" 1 Pet. ii, 21 Here, by these bloodthirsty sinners, Christ was regularly installed, the second person in the God-head, or God No. 2. After the dispersion of the Council, it was discovered that the Holy Ghost, who had overshadowed the Virgin at Christ's conception, had been sadly neglected, whereupon a dis-

18

cussion arose in the churches which could not be settled without calling another council. This God was, by some, considered to be feminine, and it was a question of difficult solution whose wife she should be, whether of the Father or of the Son — of God No. 1 or No. 2!

Finally the second Council was convened at Constantinople in the year 381, when the Holy Ghost was installed as God No. 3, without regard to gender. Thus was saddled upon mankind the most inconsistent and impossible dogma that man could invent, and it has been tenderly nursed in the arms and suckled at the breast of the Catholic and Protestant churches from that day to this. These half-heathen sinners, after they got their gods arranged in working order, proceeded to give each one His high office, with distinct duties to perform. The Holy Ghost was to act as a kind of suavitor, or soothing sweetener between the other two. Christ was to be a reminder of No. 1 of His crucifixion and death — a kind of interpleader for the human race, for whom He left His throne and became man, to redeem. As false and absurd as it is, even to-day your clergy, your Moodys and Sankeys, with their psalm-singing and swelling sobs and melting tears (themselves confessedly co-sinners), implore others to come to Jesus — " O, come to Jesus!"— Only believe, and save your poor souls from hell-fire, "where the worm dieth not and the fire is not quenched."— O, sinners, "to-day, if you will hear His voice harden not your hearts;" "don't delay, come now." "Only believe, and Jesus will take you in His arms and you are safe!" and much more of the same sort, fully justifying the scathing ridicule of the poet Burns in "Holy Willie's Prayer," which is a true portraiture of the effects of the acceptance of the triune doctrine, and of being saved by proxy. The Catholics still had another step to take. About twenty years ago a Council was called by Pope Pio Nono, when the "Returning Board" finished their work by introducing the fourth person into the God-head, and Mary, the mother of Jesus, was fairly installed. Protestants need not complain of this, because the thing cannot be worsted, and seeing there were two males there already, it were well to have two females also to aid in the good work of redemption! But long since many became restless and dissatisfied with the Nicene creed, and other creeds were made with but small improvements. About the beginning of this century rents were made among the orthodox, and to-day they are trying to weld the fragments together. The noted outpouring of the Spirit in the great Kentucky revival had much to do in breaking the creedal bonds with which they were fettered ; and in consequence of the corruption and the failure of the churches to satisfy the soul-cravings of mankind, thousands have left it, while many refuse to unite with them, and are now turning their attention to Spiritualism, which I now propose to examine in as succinct a manner as possible.

In the year 1838, a great outpouring of Spirit power was bestowed on all the societies of Shakers, with the daily visitation of the spirits of departed friends, who became visible to many This was about ten years before something of the same character began in the world outside of Shakers. Hence, we are justly called Spiritualists But there are two classes of Spiritualists — the *regenerative* and the *generative* We are the former ; the Spiritualists of the outside world are the latter. These two classes stand on different planes. The generative stands on the same plane with the Orthodoxans ; and it is a question which of the two are nearer the kingdom of heaven. They both practice the same works in actual life — both, perhaps, with equally good intent. The orthodox hold to Christ in some shape. The spiritualists discard Him as a chosen, heavenly teacher, but weigh Him in the scale with moral reformers, and find Him wanting The orthodox have a head to their bodies ; the spiritualists have none For aught I see, the generative spiritualists must keep company with the generative orthodoxans in the rudimental state and on the lower plane, until they become willing to unite with the regenerative spiritualists on the higher Christ plane. Spiritualism has only existed with us of the regenerative order in its highest phase, which is that of operating upon and using the organs of human beings to communicate their mind and will to us , whereas, it began in the outside world by raps, and moving ponderable substances, which still continue with them It was but natural that they should rejoice in having their minds disabused by their spirit friends in relation to the great forged lie of the Nicene Council and the fear of being thrown into a hell of burning sulphur the moment they were released from the mortal tenement This should have made them humble and thankful, but, instead, many of them are puffed up, boastful, lustful and proud, and do not seem to be nearing the Kingdom of Christ. Failing, sometimes, in argument, they, like the orthodoxans, depend on miracles ;

those of the former being wrought by God, of the latter by spirits and hidden law, both striving to convince the world and bring it to believe in impossibilities. The orthodox far exceed the spiritualists in startling story, beginning with making a woman of a man's rib, and coming down to Noah's Ark, serpents from rods, the stationary sun and moon, the banking waters of the Red Sea, and hundreds more; none of which are miraculous when the metaphorical language of the book in which they are recorded is properly understood.

The spiritualists seem equally eager to impose on the world impossible things. Their bottom plank is spirit materialization and dematerialization, both of which are impossible. Some have gone so far as to marry a materialized female spirit to a male in the body. I presume they left off the part of the usual ceremony, " until death do us part." The officiating clergyman affirms that he had the pleasure of kissing the spirit-bride before the dematerializing process commenced. The spiritualists seem to cling as adhesively to this impossibility as do the orthodoxans to the miraculous conception of Christ, both of which are equally false. After the oft-repeated exposures that have been made, their faith seems to remain unshaken. For the present it must suffice for me to take under examination one of their most noted and reliable mediums, viz.: Cora V. Richmond, whose inspirations in the year 1875, while under the control of the spirit of Prof. Mapes, were in accordance with truth on this subject.

The Professor then said : " I now retract all my former theory on this subject. I find spirit to be in itself an essence, which by no possibility of combination in matter can either be material or created. In my reasoning I shall take the basis of the non-spirituality of atoms." And of spirit-forms he says : " Do not mistake these forms for the actual spirit forms of your friends ; they are neither composed of the same substance nor in *any way* constructed as is the spirit in the spirit-land, etc." Here, by one of the most reliable instruments now living, the possibility of materialization is flatly denied, and also the real appearance of spirit friends to the normal eye. This is most undoubtedly true. We also have corroborating testimony from Brother Peebles, who has carried the spiritual flag around the globe, and who, when he was visited by the spirit of Aaron Knight, he, (Brother P.) supposing he was materialized, remarked to the spirit : " How strange it was that he was so materialized." But the spirit answered and said :

"Not so much materialized as thou art spiritualized." What must we now think of Sister Cora, two years later, speaking for another spirit and making the following declaration : " Facts are better than hypotheses. Spirit materializations do occur; they take on every appearance of human beings; are created for a time and disposed of at the end of a given time. They come out of seemingly nothing, and disappear again into nothingness, except where by special permission, some piece of raiment or lock of hair is retained as a *souvenir* of the materialization." Now, which is to be believed — the former or the latter declaration ? Both cannot be true. That the latter cannot be true admits of easy proof. If spirit is a different substance and distinct from matter, as the former statement avers, they are contradictory. If they are contradictory they can neither tactualize nor blend ; neither can one become the other On the other hand, if spirit is not a distinct substance from matter, then God is matter, for God is spirit. This, the most thorough-going spiritualist will not deny, and, being unable to deny it, the whole spirit-materializing theory falls lifeless to the ground — dead, *dead*, DEAD, asserted facts to the contrary notwithstanding ; and thus philosophically and logically failing renders it certain that any declared materialization of spirits is a deception or fraud, or else the asserter, being conditioned, supposed the spirit was materialized when it was not This will hold good in the face of millions who may suppose they have seen spirits with the normal eye But if they really do see objects with the normal eye, supposed to be spirits, they may know it is a fraud. So I fear not to affirm that no person now on earth, or that ever was on earth, ever saw or ever will see a spirit with the normal eye The contrary assertion is as gross a blunder in the generative spiritualists as that of the orthodoxans in claiming the possibility of the infinite becoming finite ; so they should cease their boasting until they get on more solid ground. Impossibilities cannot be made possible by any metamorphosing, although millions may believe. But the spirit, through the medium, goes on to inform us that " spirit is the vitalizing substance of the universe, man included " This spirit vitalization of matter contradicts spirit materialization because it vitalizes something besides itself. The spirit continues · "Spirit is not the outgrowth of matter, but matter is deducible from spirit " To help out materialization, the editor of the *Banner of Light* steps in and says : " Atom is the *ne plus ultra* of divisibility and because we have no term for the divisibility of matter, we have a right to predicate non-materiality of matter." This is a sheer assumption ; because we have no name for its condition, we have no logical right to postulate a judgment which supposes it to have changed its properties and assumed others. This is reducing logic to a point the consistency of which can neither be discerned by the natural nor spiritual eye ; but to such extremes persons are always driven who hold a position which they are determined to prove to be true. Locke says we should not even wish a thing to be true until we have proven it to be so. We can have no conception of the *ne plus ultra* matter, any more than that of space. But the spirit further instructs us through Sister Cora : " By the spirit's presence atoms are attracted and food is assimilated. The spirit, separate from the body, is alive, has veins and arteries of etherealized substances, and it only takes one or two grades more of material to make the spirit form palpable to the senses ; hence this is the process of materialization." That is to say, the spirit, separate from the body, has material veins and arteries, and, with a trifle more of matter added, spirit materialization is accomplished ! ! Should we not be thankful for this information ?

But the spirit sayeth further : " This matter which is added to the spirit is gathered from the medium and those surrounding him or her, who give off what is known as *psychic force*, or *nerve aura*, which the spirit attracts to itself." Now *psychic force* is *mind force*, and *nerve aura* is *dead matter* discharged from the nervous system ; the two are not identical. But it goes on to say that " books, jewels, solid iron rings and human beings have passed through solid substances, into and out of rooms without any visible apertures. The inverse of the process to materialize enables the spirit to dematerialize." Of course, were one possible the other would be also. To dematerialize is to remove or take away from an object all the matter it contains. When this is done that which is left passes through the solid door. In the case of the iron ring and such like things there is nothing left — then nothing passes through the door. But it is insinuated that the matter somehow follows, and is again formed into a solid ring on the other side of the door. It is then said the solid ring went through the solid door. Such is the mode of dematerialization ! One can hardly treat such reasoning seriously. This puts to blush all the occult magic of China and the East Indies. After trying to fool mortals into the belief of such stuff, the spirit then coolly informs us "that we must remember that between our ignorance and their knowledge there is a vast step." This is cool, indeed. They must show better reasoning than that offered, or we will feel bound to transpose the sentence. But I am asked: How are we to account for these appearances if they are false and unreal? I have not so pronounced them. This has been already answered in part. I entertain no doubt but that spirits do appear and converse with mortals; but in all such cases the change is in the mortal, not in the appearing spirit. Such mortals are conditioned by interpenetrating spirit influence, so as to enable them to see, hear, and feel spirits, *spiritually*, but which, at the time, may seem to them to be natural. Perhaps some would be pleased to be informed whether I ever had any experience in that line—to which I will simply answer affirmatively, although at the time I thought I was in a normal condition; but after it passed by, my reason taught me better. To admit the possibility of the interchange of spirit and matter would be fatal to all religion, all pure spirituality, and to the idea of the existence of an infinite, all pervading, omnipresent spirit, imminent in all worlds, and places at all times. Hence it would be wisdom in all spiritualists of both orders to abandon the idea at once and forever; as every phenomenon pertaining to it can be as satisfactorily explained without its admission as with it.

TYNDALL CRITICISED.

The saying that the brave are always generous may be fittingly applied to the illustrious Tyndall—brave, fearless, candid. The excerpts given us of his eloquent inaugural, delivered before the British Association at Belfast, Ireland, are like meteor flashes from among the stars—a grand pyrotechnic of richly-worded, well-weighed, and nicely-rounded phrases. *It is the first time in the world's history that an association of that magnitude and materialistic tendency could dare to stand up in open day and boldly ask the religions of the world* to "stand from under"— get out of its way—so bold and daring, that religion's arm seems palsied, and her votaries stand aghast, terror stricken.

I do not accuse all the members of that body of being materialists; but the general tendency seems to be in that direction, as I think, can be shown from the address of their President. Enough is given to attract the attention of the thoughtful, and to show the materialistic, not to say the baneful, tendency of that learned body of aggressives.

Attached to this Association are some of the strongest, ablest, clearest-headed and far-searching minds of Europe, if not of the world; and any thing done by it cannot fail to make its impression on the world of mind, and must have its effect for weal or woe for generations to come. But no man nor party should become so popular and powerful that their acts and sayings should go unquestioned. It seems that the Professor not only strove to steer clear of every thing spiritual, lest he might fall into dream-land and find nothing real, but proceeded to span the universe with a bridge of solid matter, and then walk majestically over it; thence plunge out into a world of atoms and "polar molecules," and go back on the atoms until the atoms should give out, while he finds nothing beyond! Unlike a contemporary of his, who, at the point where the atoms were lost, discovered God, mind, and law, above nature itself; but the Professor turns upon his heel and proclaims that in matter "*the power of every form and equality of life is found.*" His first step in this direction is to exclude the " crude beliefs in the power of supernatural beings," then speak concessively of the Empedocles theory of the existence of love and hate among the atoms, and of the hypothesis that animals are automatic, thus excluding even instinct, and making them mere walking machines in the great arcana of things natural, contravening Pope and many other able writers who .

> " Place reason over instinct as best you can,
> In this 'tis God directs, in that 'tis man "

Tyndall further says . " Scientific searchers, freed and released from the caprice of super-sensual beings, sought to place absolute reliance on law and nature." How nature came by law remains a trifle beclouded ; but this, he informs us, is the " beginning of scientific investigation—the first break from the supernatural to a reliance on the facts of nature." And finally, like the honest, brave and daring man that he is, he comes squarely to the work and says : " Abandoning all disguise, the confession I feel bound to make before you is, that I prolong the vision backward across the boundary of experimental evidence, and discern in that matter (which we in our ignorance, and notwithstanding our professed reverence, for its Creator), have hitherto covered with opprobrium —the promise and potency of every form and equality of life " This seems to have been spoken with some hesitancy. A shade of gossamer covers its face ; but, when laid bare, it becomes alarming—all sweeping. The opprobrium once removed, matter becomes an object of reverence, in which is found the power of *every* form of life—psychical, spiritual, instinctive, and physical ! Ah ! what a mistake hast thou made, thou Christ ! Ah, Paul, what a blunder ! It is no more " in *God* we live and move and have our being," but in *matter* The Professor verifies my construction by adding : " The human understanding itself is the result of the play between organism and environment, through cosmical ranges of time."

Beautifully spoken , but where is the proof ? What kind of play ? What is this but saying that the faculty within us that knows, that embodies our knowledge—the thinking, reflecting ego—is originated and brought into being by the play between our physical organism, and the matter which surrounds it ? He cannot mean any thing more subtile than matter, for this might be *inside* as well as playing around ; if so, it would be God Himself.

19

I. The power of the life of the physical being he finds in matter.

II. The knowing faculty is brought into being by a *play* between the matter, created being and surrounding matter; but how the play is gotten up, we are left to conjecture. One essential is sadly wanting, and that is, *proof*. Feuerbach nor Comte can go farther than this. The former gives an apparently plausible thesis, how the soul, if there is any, dies with the body, forgetting that a machine can wear out and be unable to move, while the power that was wont to move it may still exist. The latter has based his positive philosophy on propositions which themselves demand proof, declaring nothing to be real that is not cognizable to one or more of the five senses; when, were I asked to point out definitely the meaning of the word *unreal*, I could not do it much more truly than to say *material existences*, as any of these can be made uncognizable to the five senses. It were more reasonable to conclude that the solids underlie these ever-changing, shifting, vanishing existences, that seem to exist to-day and to-morrow are not, than the contrary. Locke's reasoning here is to the point: " Matter is not one individual thing; neither is there any such thing as *one* material being; but an infinite number of eternal cogitative beings, independent of one another, of limited force and distinct thoughts, which could never produce that order, harmony and beauty which are to be found in nature. Since, therefore, whatsoever is the first eternal being must be cogitative, and whosoever is first in all things must necessarily contain in it, and actually have, at least, all the perfections that can ever after exist, nor can it give to another any perfection it hath not actually in itself, or at least in a higher degree — it necessarily follows that the first eternal being cannot be matter. Unthinking particles of matter, however put together, can have nothing thereby added to them but a new relation of position, which it is impossible should give thought and knowledge to them "

It is not at all strange that religion comes in for a castigation at the hands of physical science, because she forsook her high domain and obtruded herself on forbidden ground into the sciences of natural things. Science soon proved her to be in error, and, having done so, led her to doubt the whole. Christ, our exemplar and founder of the true religion, did not so. He left physics to fight physics, and betook himself to the realm spiritual and there remained — where all his true followers do to this day. Religion

must remain in the realm of spirit; but if she descends therefrom to the physical, as the Professor says, she must submit
Having made this blunder, and substituted in its stead, "School
Philosophy and Verbal Wastes," she is fast becoming the
laughing-stock of the world, for we now find more than a thousand creeds and forms, all at variance, while no two truths can by
any possibility disagree. It is, therefore, impossible that there be
more than one right way. When the right way is found — and
it can be found — it will not consist of ceremony and mystic belief, but one whose adherents live in their daily walk and conversation the holy life of Christ their exemplar.

"His can't be wrong whose life is in the right"

It is undoubtedly true, that "spiritual longings did put a check
on physical science for two thousand years; which longings the
Christian religion and the Scriptures in part satisfied" The
simple reason for this was, because neither matter nor physical
science contains the elements to satisfy the soul's demands, but
having committed the error before mentioned, it lost the spirit
and substituted the "school philosophy." The world became
word-weary, and thus gave physical science the opportunity to
claim the upper seat. But the liberal and truthful Spencer says,
after all, "there is a measure of truth underlying all creeds and
systems of religion." These truths it becomes science not to ignore.

The Professor next turns to Darwin, and out-Darwin's Darwin himself. But why should this *savant* speak all the while of
physical science as though there were no other? Religion has its
science as well as physics. To ask religion to step out of the way
of science is like asking science to get out of the way of science
There can be no conflict between the truths of each As far as
I am able to go back "across the boundary of the experimental
evidence," the science of religion has the honor of the first record
Witness the metaphorical language used in stating the corresponding condition of the first pair of our species — not the first of the
race, but the first pair — the first that were paired off from promiscuous Adam to lead a higher life and restrain their passions
This shows that here spiritual science had its beginning; and, most
of the time since, the spiritual longings of the race have kept religion of some sort "in the van."

Inasmuch as mind is greater than matter, and cannot be fully satisfied with material things, the whole world will reverse the command of the Professor, and say to physical science: "Keep your place. As long as souls aspire Godward, the purely material must get out of the way." The Professor has undertaken too much, and already seems to tremble under the load. History shows that all material triumphs have been of short duration; but should materialism now triumph under its brave and gallant leader, it cannot be long before it will be found inadequate to the wants and longings of the soul, when an enthusiastic rising will occur, and again scatter it in fragments to the four winds of heaven. At length he admits the grand question of the hour is to satisfy the internal, emotional, soul-feeling of mankind. This, the highest physical science can never do. The panacea for the soul's ills is only to be found in the plane above — the spiritual.

The Professor gives the impregnable position of science thus: "All religious theories which embrace notions of cosmogony, or reach into its domain, must in so far submit to science." This is true. But as far as the cosmogony of the universe is concerned —the creation of matter and generation of worlds—all science may as well keep quiet. As far as we are able to see, it is as impossible for God to create something of nothing as it is for man to do so; and as far as we can see, matter is as indestructible as mind; and as to our real knowledge of the former it is quite as limited as of the latter. The term creation is used as correctly when meaning change, mold, form, etc., as to create something out of nothing. The former is, I think, the Bible signification and use. Physical science has proven to a demonstration the existence of man on this planet thousands of years prior to the creation of the Adam and Eve of Genesis; but still, if the metaphor is understood, the Bible and science do not conflict. The term Adam, like our word man, means both a man and mankind. And "God formed Adam of the dust of the ground." What ground? The ground that the race then stood on was animal ground—animal promiscuity and generation. From the dust of this ground, Adam, or an Adamite was taken, and raised to a higher plane—made a man of instead of animal—and while Adam —Adamkind—slept, a rib, binder or woman, was taken and made a new woman for a helpmeet for Adam, to govern and restrain the animal and lead a new life. They were inspired by the Creator, or changer, and breathed in the breath of (the new) life.

Thus they were the first created, doing no violence to scientific truth. But they failed to keep their high estate, fell victims to their passions, lost their rectitude, and on that day died to the spiritual life into which they had been elevated ; and this was the fall of man

Why, the very resurrection that Christ spake of was to rise above and relieve ourselves from the preponderating influence of matter. or material things, and the lawless sensualities of the generative life ; and the soul that is bound by them has never tasted true liberty, and knows not what it is to be free

The Professor condemns Buckle, who sought to detach intellectual achievement from moral force ; and says he gravely cried. But may he not be in error here ? As I understand it, intellectual and moral force are distinct.   There can be great intellectual achievements void of morality, and *vice versa*   God, in the infinite sense, is not an intellectual being   Intellect implies the necessity to think and reason, in order to understand and reach conclusions.   God is not under this necessity

At last, and finally, the Professor (we give him thanks) condescends to meet us halfway and says: "I would set forth equally the inexorable advance of man's understanding and the unquenchable claims of his emotional (why not say spiritual?) nature.   Then, if freed from intolerance and bigotry, in opposition to all the restrictions of materialism, I would affirm this to be a field of the noblest exercise of what may be called the creative faculties of man."   Verily, John Tyndall, " thou art not far from the kingdom of heaven "

But here our honest-hearted and brave friend finds himself in water too deep for the length of his line, and excites our sympathy, for really his knowledge of matter is nearly as limited as that of mind   The former he puts into his crucible, and tries matter with matter ; he forces it to change position and relation , gives names to the parts; gases escape, cinders remain, are examined and thrown away in despair, not knowing its generation and what it really is ; and were he not a philosopher his very ignorance would run him mad   Whilst the *ego* continues to reassert itself in every thought—demands and compels recognition—complains of the material bondage to which we willfully subject it—we plod along, ignorantly mistaking the shadow for the substance, until in God's crucible the spirit is relieved, and called to "give an account of the deeds done in the body, whether they be good or whether they be evil." Then if the spirit finds itself not in harmony with the power that caused it to exist, this will be its hell. Now, whether spirit or matter should most engross our attention, every reader for himself or herself must judge.

"THE POWER BEHIND NATURE."

The great mistake in the oft-repeated assertion that "religion has been the cause of more bloodshed and misery to the human race than all other causes combined" consists in the misapplication of the term. Religion, *per se*, is non-resistant, with which false religion antagonizes, as falsehood does with truth. Here is where the misery comes in ; and no religion can be called true which forms a connecting link and affiliates with the passional nature of man, instead of governing and controlling it. Men not being equally unfolded, see not alike, and from misconceptions on the part of either come the clash of arms. The first recorded instance, baptized in blood, was between a shepherd and ground-tiller — one supposing that God preferred mutton chops to garden sauce — and ever since that eventful period, misconceptions about the mind of God, equally futile, have arisen among men, dividing them into factions, causing angry words and bitter strifes, not unfrequently ending in bloodshed, even up to the present hour. Among all controversialists, the religiously creed-bound seem the least able to lay themselves open to receive plain, unvarnished truth. I say this, although a religionist myself, and am led to make the assertion at this time by noticing the annual address of Dr. McCosh to the senior class of college students at Trenton, N. J , in which he took occasion to contravene the doctrines enunciated by Prof Tyndall, President of the British Association of Belfast, Ireland, whose discourse I have endeavored to lay on the executioner's block.

The Doctor begins by a kind of counter-trenching in a "hide and seek" manner, and manœuvers like a certain general, whose forces, inferior to those of his adversary — were kept marching and countermarching, revealing and concealing themselves, until the enemy would so over-estimate his forces as to yield without resistance. His forces must have appeared great to the class, as the feat was pronounced " masterly." It was in bad taste, if nothing more, for the Doctor to underrate his antagonist, and attach ignorance to one of the most learned and highly gifted men of the age, as Tyndall surely is. We all live in glass houses, and should be careful how we throw stones. " The man," says Locke, " who undertakes to reason must not be in love with any opinion, nor wish it to be true, until he knows it to be so. Keep a perfect indifference to all opinions and not wish any of them to be true, lest the wish make them appear so." This advice could not have been kept in view by Dr. McCosh, as it is evident he " had an ax to grind," which proved to be the defense of a personal Deity; and this it was that caused him to deviate from the line of fair, outspoken reason, which shines so conspicuously in his rival.

It is a question which of the two discourses, if received entirely for truth, would be the most baneful to society. The Doctor, while accusing Tyndall of deception and ingenious disguises, is like the man who dug a pit for his neighbor and fell into it himself. Nevertheless, his accusation seems to be, in part, justifiable, as Tyndall has named philosophers who yield him at best but a meagre support. Tyndall makes Bruno a prominent figure, who uttered the following: " The highest contemplation which transcends nature is impossible and null to him who is without belief; for we obtain this by supernatural, not natural light, and such light they have not who hold all things to be corporeal."

But I cannot see that he attempted to " make us believe that all agreed with him ; while the Doctor begins six hundred years before Christ (might have begun one thousand years) excluding only the Brahmins, accepts the Buddhists and appropriates to himself all the philosophers of the last twenty-five thousand years ; while, outside of creeddom, none yield him a cordial, and I might say even a meagre support. This was a great mistake in the Doctor, if mistake it was, for most assuredly, of this class, Tyndall's forces greatly outnumbered his, but neither of them has a right to the claim set up.

The Doctor speaks truly when he says : " All the leading philosophers persisted in claiming the existence of some intelligent, designing cause back of nature." The Brahmins did the same ; but none, except the religiously creed-bound, agree with the Doctor in calling it *personal*. The man who insists on a *personal infinite Being* should never appeal to science nor philosophy to find support. But how the Doctor should exclude the Brahmins and accept the Buddhists I am at a loss to know. It is true the Brahmins were the more sensual, but both held to the principal doctrine of the Vedas; the Buddhists differing only in two essential points—that of abolishing caste and a privileged priesthood, and that of establishing celibacy. Both had their trinity of Gods, who were active, subordinate agents, governed by an invisible cause—or as Spencer would say, "unthinkable and unknowable," from whence all things sprung The Brahmins thus express it: "There is one living and true God, everlasting, without parts or passions, of infinite power, wisdom and goodness; the Maker and preserver of all things, incomprehensible, illuminates all, overspreads all creatures—spirit without form, self-existent, pure, perfect, omniscient, and omnipresent" This is also Buddhist doctrine; and with all their follies, vagaries, and apparently senseless ceremonies, they were more consistent in their belief than the professors of the religions of to-day generally are, who claim God to be three distinct persons, with distinct offices, who, whilst acting separately, are finite, but taken collectively are infinite—thus outraging philosophy, which they claim for support, and the Pythagorean science of numbers—absolute truth and common sense—all to support a man-made creed! And they, like the Buddhists, believe in the efficacy of sprinkling babies and baptizing in water to wash away sin, whilst it only reaches the surface, and at best, was but a type of that Christ baptism of Spiritual fire that reaches the heart We are next referred to Confucius, who taught, "one invisible being, first cause, original principle," and then to Zoroaster, who believed in "one supreme essence, invisible, incomprehensible." We are then taken to Greece, where the Doctor can find no support, only a stray shot here and there Orpheus, an early teacher, held that "One invisible God, unknown, prior to all beings, contained within himself the germ of all things" Thales the same; and Pythagoras, to whom we are especially cited, taught the very reverse of a personal, infinite God He says: "There is one universal soul diffused through all things, eternal, invisible, unchangeable, etc;" and the Sicilian Empedocles was his pupil and follower. Anaxagoras was supposed to be the first Greek who separated mind from matter; those before him, that combined them in unity, support Tyndall But this separation cannot reasonably be construed into a personal deity. Socrates and Plato both taught the "unchangeability and omnipresence of Deity, without beginning or ending" Aristotle the same—"God a spiritual substance, without extension, succession

20

or division of parts." On and on we may go, turning in vain the leaves of history to find support for a personal, infinite exist-ence. The Stoics, founded by Zeno, Spencer says, "reduced philosophy to little else than the right way of living." Sensible Stoics. To the Germans we look in vain. The Celts and Teutons "believed in the existence of one Supreme Being, by whom the whole universe was animated, a portion of whom re-sided in all things."

And the Romans adopted the religious doctrines and customs of Greece with but little modification; while the same may be said of modern as of ancient philosophers, and I see no justifica-tion in the Doctor laying claim to them. It is clearly evident that he is guilty of the crime with which he accused Tyndall; that is, of appropriating to himself that to which he had no right. He in-tended his class and the world to believe that all the great philoso-phers of the last twenty-five thousand years supported his idea of a personal, infinite first cause. He introduces early into his dis-course, that what the "Buddhists, Confucius and Greek philoso-phers taught had the tendency to secure a steady progress up to that one controlling, intelligent, personal first cause." The Doctor seems to favor the doctrine of "evolution," and supposes that it can be reconciled with scripture, while Tyndall proposes to aban-don the one or the other—the creative or the evolution theory. The Doctor's implication of evolution, as something to be "evolved from," seems to be overstrained; for, wherever admitted, it spoils the creative. The flower unrolls its own leaves and unfolds its petals. The animal evolved from the egg was itself the egg. The power behind it causing the evolution is Spencer's Un-knowable, which Tyndall himself acknowledges to be God in the following significant words: "In fact, the whole process of evo-lution is the manifestation of a power absolutely inscrutable to the intellect of man; as little in our day as in the days of Job, can man by searching find this power out." And then adds: "You will observe no very rank materialism here." Better stick to the creative, Doctor, as you must see you can get no help from evolution. But the Doctor himself comes to Tyndall's assistance when referring to the heavenly bodies and crystals seen in plants, by saying: "Whatever the original forms were, they *arrange themselves* according to definite laws." This is evolution "with a vengeance." The sneer at Tyndall for thinking the first form was an atom seems misplaced, for most certainly the first phenomenal form was an atom or atoms — if not, what was it? He next speaks of intelligence, and says: "Tyndall refers to some illustrious man who said he would be miserable without a belief in a personal intelligence back of nature," and adds "that he would like to know who this illustrious man is, since such belief is spontaneous in every reflecting person since Socrates." In reply to this, I would say that reflecting persons, outside of religious circles, who do believe it are indeed very few, and there is no wonder Tyndall was surprised at finding one. Socrates himself did not believe it. Locke, Pope, Mill, Spencer and a host of others, almost without number, may be included in the unbelieving category. All, I might say, of the deepest thinkers the world has produced believe that infinite intelligence, omniscient and omnipresent spirit, force or energy, pervades all matter in all worlds — " inhabiting eternity " — "filling immensity " — " unthinkable and unknowable" in his entirety and wholeness. It is far more impossible for finite man to comprehend the infinite than it is for a dove to swallow this planet. If, with our present personal proportion, and all the knowledge we now possess, we could increase to the size of this earth, and our knowledge increase in the same ratio, and on until we reached the proportion of the sun, and still on to that of Sirius, which is two thousand times larger than the sun (by which time we should be in possession of considerable knowledge, as well as bulk, perhaps nearly as large as the Doctor's personal, infinite God,) still we would then seem to be as far from comprehending the Infinite as we now are, and would doubtless feel less conceit of ever becoming able to do so. Yet, notwithstanding our ignorance, we feel a certitude that " He is as perfect in a hair as heart," and, as Spencer says, " cannot help knowing He exists " and unfolds in every thing, however minute. He sounds in the thunder, burns in the fire, shines in the sun's rays, " glistens in the stars as well as in the baby's eyes," and blushes in the maiden's cheek ; jabbers in the monkey, sings in the mocking-bird, squalls in the peacock, and flowers in his tail. This being conceded, it logically follows that he speaks and acts in every mortal when the passions are governed and His attributes alone prevail. But, having delegated to man freedom of thought and action, it follows that God does not prompt his evil thoughts, words and deeds. So that, between the Doctor and Tyndall, *their* relations with Deity (all mere professions aside) depend entirely on which of the two best control their passions, and are most moved in what they say or do by God's attributes. This cannot be gainsayed by religion nor philosophy. The Doctor goes on to say : " It is far easier to prove that there is a personal God, infinitely wise and good, than to prove that insensate atoms are the source of the systematic order of the world, as well as life, reason and conscience." This is exactly what we wish the Doctor to prove : First, how a person with limited mind can have unlimited attributes ; and, secondly, how a personal God can be infinite ; or, in other words, how finity can be infinity ? This would be equal to proving the same thing to be and not to be at the same time, which Locke says is " impossible with God." And thirdly, prove that atoms are insensate. For the absolute proof of these I would very willingly traverse this planet from center to circumference to find the book containing the arguments, and feel that I had obtained the knowledge cheaply enough. I freely admit the Doctor has reasonable grounds for saying that atoms are insensate ; but who can tell me why the particles of matter adhere to and form my finger in its present shape ? Not a man on earth can tell me, so very ignorant we all are ; still we strut, put on airs, and talk about our knowledge. In its present connection, the Doctor will admit there is life and sensation in the finger ; but amputate it — then, as far as we know, it becomes insensate ; but how can we prove that the particles are not sensate in a different relation ? Whether they are, or are not, is beyond our powers of demonstration. But, just here, it were sheerest folly in religion not to submit to physical science.

Materialists proceed in the same line of reasoning (though not with the same ground) to prove their position that we do to prove the infinity of space. A certain portion of space being cognizable to us, we have nothing to hinder the belief that it extends endlessly beyond our powers of cognition. Just so it is with animal or atomic life ; we see so far with the naked eye, and might suppose it ended there, but, by artificial means, are made to know that we eat, drink and breathe living creatures, unrecognizable to the senses, every day of our lives. It is not then so very strange that materialists have come to the conclusion that life in matter extends also to infinity, and hold that they have proved infinite life in matter by the same line of reasoning that we prove infinite space. But the two are hardly comparable, as one is phenomenal and the other is not. That there is attraction and repulsion in atoms cannot well be disputed ; and beginning with man, but not ending with him, and going down to animal, insect and molecule, we find the greatest attraction to be that of *sex*, governed by the law of affinity for the propagation of its kind But the Doctor—we pity him—" hath not where to lay his head" in the domain of logic, philosophy nor sound reason. Starting with a contradiction, there is no possibility of finding a spot for reconciliation.   The great thinkers disagree with both the Doctor and materialists ; for behind all matter, whether insensate or living, they find infinite intelligent power, all-controlling, inscrutable God, but not a personal God When the Doctor speaks of the God of the Bible, he should use the plural form and say, Gods of the Bible, as every careful reader cannot fail to recognize the fact that the Bible speaks of God in two senses —the infinite and finite, or subordinate sense.   Whenever God is spoken of as leaving one place and going to another, changing his mind and purpose, or of becoming angry, wrathful or passionate, it must be understood in the subordinate sense, as that of a godly man or angel ; but spoken of as " All and in all," it is then to be understood in the infinite sense.

Now, to sum up the whole matter, let us draw a short contrast between the three classes that represent the world's ideal with three representative living men — Henry Longueville Mansel, on the side of a personal infinite God ; John Ernest Renan, of the impersonal, agreeing with J. Stuart Mill, Spencer, and others ; and Prof. John Tyndall ; also Feuerbach, Comte, and others of the materialistic faith—and point out in brief what we suppose to be the mistakes of each.   The first—Mansel—a pupil of Sir Wm. Hamilton, has, in my view, given the most ingenious and the strongest argument that has come to my knowledge, in favor of a personal first cause. His strongest position is a negative argument, and so strong is it that it will doubtless lead many astray.   He draws a distinction between the Absolute and Relative, and argues that God must be either one or the other, overlooking the fact that in a certain sense He may be both, but the argument is, that God must be in relation with the universe and man, or be out of it If in relation, He cannot be out of it ; therefore, not absolute ; hence, personal If out of relation and absolute, He would then have no connection with the phenomena of the universe ; hence, could not exist as first cause, and therefore would be a useless Deity.   Taking his sense of the use of terms, his arguments would seem conclusive ; but passing under Mill's

critical eye, they vanish, as this critic pronounces it, one long
"*ignoratio Elenchi.*" But Mill's mistake is in calling Mansel
ignorant, when, with the same creed and cause to defend, Mill
could not have done better himself. Mansel is a terse and cogent
reasoner; but his cause was bad, and he found it so on taking the
affirmative, when he despondingly relinquished the contest, saying · "We are bound to believe God to be infinite (that is, impersonal), but we must think of Him as personal," (that is finite),
and, as the "*think*" and the "*belief*" are contraries, his affirmation is, that we are bound to believe a contradiction, as it is impossible for us to believe a proposition to be true and then think
the contrary is true. So we see to what absurd conclusions intelligent minds are driven, while striving to support a false
theory He had better have heeded the words of Renan, who
said : "The most eloquent language that can be used on this
subject is silence." But, secondly, Renan, having been accused
of atheism, was forced to declare *his* belief as follows : "For
myself, I believe that true providence is not distinct from the
order so constant, divine, perfectly wise, just and good which
reigns in the universe Against atheism I strongly protest; such
(my) doctrine is only the exclusion of a capricious God, acting by
fits and starts, allowing the clouds generally to follow their course,
but making them deviate when prayed to do so; leaving a lung
to decompose to a certain point, but staying decomposition when
a vow is made—changing his mind—in a word, according to his
views of interest , and, should the saddest consequences result
therefrom, the absolute sincerity, of which we make profession,
obliges us to say so" Again he says : "Men who really have
a fruitful sentiment of God have never put the questions in a
contradictory way; they have been neither Deists after the
manner of the French school, nor Pantheists. They have not lost
themselves in those subtle questions They have *powerfully felt
God* They have lived in Him They have not defined Him
Jesus occupies an exceptional rank in this divine phalanx." These
are clearly the sentiments of an honest heart, that fears not truth.
But his and Tyndall's mistake is in ignoring the efficacy of
prayer in the phenomenal as well as spiritual. They see clearly
that there can be no retro-action in an infinite existence ; hence,
they take it for granted that prayers touching phenomena are
useless and unavailing Hear a simple anecdote : A father says
to his little four-year-old, " Charlie, my son, it is bed-time ; go to

your room, but, before retiring, don't forget to kneel down and
ask God, your heavenly Father, to bless you and to give you
whatever you need " Charlie kissed his pa, and did as he was
told ; got on his knees, folded his hands, and, in much sincerity
and faith, with upturned face, said aloud . " O God, my heavenly
Father, will you please bless me, and give me a drum ? " The
father heard the prayer, and next morning the drum was forth-
coming. Now the question is: Did God answer the prayer ?
I answer affirmatively If God's attributes of goodness, love,
and mercy overcame the man's cupidity, avarice, and selfishness,
and caused him to get the drum, then what the father did, God
did ; therefore God answered the child's prayer. What this class
of thinkers have overlooked is this : That whenever a prayer
reaches the attributes of Deity, whether in man or angel, it
reaches the ear of God in a retro-active agent, who, inspired by
God in *them*, is thus sent to your relief Therefore, God comes
to your relief in answer to prayer, though He was present in you
and knew your needs before your petition was offered. But it is
ridiculously childish, unscientific and unphilosophical to suppose
that the first angel that heard you conveyed it to a second, and
he to a third, and so on until some shining throne was reached
whereon sat a personal God, who there told the messengers what
to do ; yet this is a fair deduction from the personal God theory.

In the second place, they have overlooked another important
fact : Whilst men on earth chain the lightning and change the
course of nature in many ways, it is not reasonable to suppose
that spirit existences, moved by God's attributes, are able to do
much more ! even to changing electric currents and the courses
of clouds, as are stated in Bible history ! What such agents do
being impelled by God's attributes, God does ; and to Him be all
the glory And as " every knee shall bow and every tongue shall
confess," materialists will not be an exception ; and all such, will
on their bended knees, yet acknowledge the efficacy of prayer.
It will thus be seen that the answer to special prayer does not
conflict with the unchangeability of Deity ; and it hence clearly
follows that every sound borne upon the waves of the atmosphere
to the drum of mortal ear has and must come from finite
agencies, which alone are retro-active, and no words of such
agents, only such as his attributes impel, can be the word and gift
of God. Thirdly, and lastly, the honest materialists, Feuerbach,
Comte and others, are not without a plausible argument in their

favor. Finding life in matter as far as is possible to reach, they proceed upon the hypothesis that all is phenomenal with life in itself, and, with Darwin, conclude that the greater than the atomic is caused by affinitive attraction, selection, aggregation, and cohesion—first, mineral ; secondly, vegetable ; thirdly, animal ; fourthly, man   Now, that the power of God's unfolding in nature has done all this in the manner by them set forth, I confess myself unable with any certainty to deny ; but be it as it may, it is still the work of God, by the creative, or, if any prefer, the changing power of His attributes in nature, manifesting an intelligence far superior to that of all finite creatures combined. But the *very* great mistake in these deep and honest thinkers consists in their not lifting the screen to see if something besides matter does not exist.   They stopped too soon, were too easily satisfied—only one step more and they would have learned that there exist attributes and qualities which are not phenomenal, and that the first atom, whether insensate or living, was itself an effect which had its cause ; and for which cause, we in humility bow, and say we can find no better name than GOD.

BEECHER DISSECTED.

TEXT.—*Let nothing be done through strife or vain glory ; but in lowliness of mind, let each esteem others better than themselves.*—(Phil. ii, 3.)

When a great light flashes upon the world like a blazing comet passing through the ecliptic, all eyes are turned toward it and all minds strive to comprehend its errand   Such was the case a few evenings since, when it was announced that the illustrious pastor of Plymouth Church, New York, was to appear at Liederkranz Hall, in Louisville, to enlighten the benighted understandings of the inhabitants of the Falls City, and with its great capacity it was not able to contain the eager and pressing multitude that sought entrance to the prepared feast   If the dishes set before the guests are correctly reported, some of them must have been as indigestible as the Revelator's little book—somewhat bitter, though " in the mouth sweet as honey "

Our text at the head of this discourse he declared to be the essence of his discourse, at the same time denying its possible, permanent existence with men !   Above all things, it is most important that such lights at such times should enunciate truth in clear, unmistakable language, which always can be done if clear ideas are entertained.   Many sound truths were uttered, enough to sugar-coat the oiled sophistries and cause them to be relished and swallowed with pleasure ; but no pains seem to have been taken to give them logical accuracy.   My purpose now is not so much to notice the truths, but if possible to remove the finely woven covering which beautifully arranged language and similitude have spread over error in order to make it pass for truth.

He sets out with a negative denial of the *Trinity* in its commonly accepted sense, in which the text he chose seems to justify him, and he asserts truly that " Christ manifested the Father's interior nature "   But in the next breath, either unwittingly or otherwise, he seems to lock arms with Auguste Comte, who in his Positive Philosophy makes the objective all that's real, and

21

every thing unreal which is unrecognizable by the five senses.
The pastor says: "We can imagine no other truths than those
which belong to our (five) senses," which, to settle his meaning,
he calls "objective truths." Comte goes no farther than this—
he owns no God not manifest to the senses; and the pastor
clinches the doctrine, and, in a negative manner, seems to deny
any other senses. "Can anybody," he says, "tell me there is
such a thing as taste that is not taste? hearing that is not hearing? seeing and feeling that are not seeing and feeling?" Now,
nobody can believe a thing can be and not be at the same time,
then for what purpose these questions only to deny the possibility
of two kinds of senses of seeing, feeling, etc.? If not, why all
this dust and smoke? Why question us in this adroit manner if
he really believed in any other than the five natural senses?

Now, I would have you all understand, "without vain glory
and in lowliness of mind," that there are other senses besides
those enumerated, and vastly more important, that we should
recognize. These are the spiritual, the real and subjective,
while the outer or objective may be called the unreal. Take a
block of marble: You see and feel it; it is white and hard, and
you pronounce it real. But bring it into the crucible; it is soon
red, then incandescent, next a fluid, and finally disappears from
your vision or touch. What is it now? Is it real? If so, what
and where is it? No mortal can answer the question. It was
and is not marble. Just so vanishes in the crucible of truth the
affirmation that God is only known objectively, and all truths the
same. God was in the marble as well as our minds, but where is
the marble? Our minds, being indestructible, are real, though
subjective, and God is still there. Now, to my understanding,
which God in His mercy has enlightened, subjective truths are
by far the most real and imperishable, while nothing can be more
true than that the objective or external senses, like the marble, all
vanish in time's grand retort, the spiritual and subjective senses
which are eternal, alone remaining.

When we make use of the concept *man*, we usually include the
ego and *non ego*—the subjective and objective—and what better
definition can be given to the terms than *internal* and *external?*
The former "refers to the thinking subject, the latter to the object thought of." But it may, with some plausibility, be affirmed
that when the mind contemplates itself it is then both subject
and object. This being admitted, it does not follow that it can

be made the *non ego*. It is simply the *ego* contemplating the *ego*
Neither can God in the mind be made the *non ego*. I admit the
God, whom the pastor describes as of our own making, to be
objective, and whom the simplest heathen, as well as he, " can
see in clouds and hear Him in the wind." He may, if he choose.
term all external nature the objectivity of the divine. It is what
Moses saw in nature on the " clefts of the rocks," and for want of
a better phrase, termed the " hinder parts of God?" This is
what Comte, Beecher and others call the true God, as all such
do, who affirm that He can only be known objectively, when the
best that could be said is, that it is simply the shadow of God
Spencer, Tyndall, Baring, Gould, Huxley and others know better.
They go behind nature and find an " incomprehensible potency,"
which is termed " persistent force," " Divine energy," " Divine
essence," " inscrutable Providence," an " evoluting power, etc."
Though claiming little spirituality, this stands true, and in contradistinction to the objective doctrine, and is simply what we
call *Infinite Spirit*—GOD—in a sense which cannot be applied to
any finite being or tutelary deity. This infinite, omnipresent
Spirit, enthroned in the mind—whose " kingdom is within you "
—there makes Himself known in spite of every effort at unbelief,
and this subjective knowledge is far in advance of all that externals can possibly impart. Here is where the true knowledge
of God is obtained ; and the possession of this knowledge has no
tendency to raise one above another and cause them to do any
thing through " vain glory," but on the contrary it shows us our
defects and assists us to " lowliness of mind, and to esteem others
better than ourselves " Obedience to the operation of this spirit
in the higher consciousness of our unfolding is the resurrection—
the daily rising into newness of life and a more sensible relation,
connection and union with God—more and more elevating the
soul above and weaning it from earthly things, until the Christ
plane is reached, Him received and obeyed, and full and complete
redemption obtained.

With these plain truths before us, which must come within the
range and experience of every thoughtful mind, I leave all to
imagine my astonishment at finding the Plymouth pastor, one of
the greatest lights of the world, to be so far in the dark as to
place all true knowledge of God objectively, instead of by this
internal revealment of Himself to the mortals. He must have
been led astray " through strife and vain glory, instead of lowli-

ness of mind." Why, the wild negroes wandering on the east coast of Africa, between the Juba and Cape Delgado, know as much about God objectively as does the Plymouth pastor. So all the talk about how we and they make God must pass as so much idle wind But he goes on in the same strain and says. "All conceptions of God are but extensions of human character and experience." Is this the way Christ obtained His knowledge of the Father? Did the Divinity "that stirs within" reveal nothing more than He could glean from human character? Is Christianity lowered to this platform? Truly, the wholly "natural man discerneth not the things of the spirit of God, for they are spiritually, not objectively, discerned." O, nay, Christ's advancement came from His reception of subjective truths made known by the Father As the Father taught Him, so He taught the world, "in all lowliness of mind." But, leaving speculative authority, the pastor finally gets down to his work, and quotes: "Let nothing be done through strife and vain glory, but in lowliness of mind let each esteem others better than themselves" Here he strikes bottom and stands on solid ground, and adds: "This is harder to accept and practice than any theology ever put on paper" Most true, "noble Festus," still, it is the Christian ground, and such as cannot stand on it should not call themselves Christians, in the full import of that term. It is the very thing which is put into the practice of the daily life of the consecrated Shaker.

But hear his further testimony · "This is very well in meeting-time, but when you go home there is not a man who believes anything in it." Then, I would add, there is not a Christian among them. But what seems impossible with him is altogether possible with the true followers of Christ; but, with him, I would confess its impossibility in Nature's self and selfishness. He very pertinently and correctly ridicules the idea, by some entertained, that the Infinite is some "magnificent being enthroned in the center of the universe, sitting there in crystalline splendor, with universes swinging around Him and His majesty demanding their homage and worship" He that "fills immensity" cannot have center nor circumference. If such throne exists, it must pertain to subordinate, finite creatures, with Christ for Supreme Judge. That the omnipresent Spirit is ever in the minds of all free agents is a truism to which the whole world can bear witness But after the foregoing truths, what must we think of the succeeding declaration? "God is not centripetal, but centrifugal, sending all things out from Himself." This seems to neutralize what he has just told us — it implies limit and admits the throne denied Him. To send things out from one's self implies that they go where He is not, and thus Omnipresence is denied (') The simple truth is, we are made to feel our nearness to or distance from God just in proportion to our obedience or disobedience, with no reference whatever to latitude nor altitude. Hence, the apostle says: "Submit yourself to God, draw nigh unto Him, and He will draw nigh unto you;" "humble yourself and He will lift you up." James iv, 8, 10.

Next, the pastor comes to the motherhood in God and asks. "How Christ came to tell us of the motherhood in God?" He did not do it. The time had not come for the motherhood to be declared; this was not for the bridegroom, but for the bride to declare In the first appearing it was the Lamb, the bridegroom, masculine, who manifested the Fatherhood in God The pæans were then the Father! the Father! The love of the Father! "What kind of love the Father hath?" In the second appearing it was the bride, feminine, the Lamb's wife, who manifested the tearful, tuneful, motherly love, affectionate and pitying tenderness, and the unbounded sweetness and gentleness of the motherhood in God. Now the pæans from their virgin children are· The Mother! The Mother! The blessed Mother! the love of the Mother! And what kind of love the Mother had? We should not allow a feeling of scorn nor derision to arise at the idea of a woman claiming to be the Lamb's wife: but we should, instead, hide our heads in very shame to affirm the possibility that a church, full of concupiscence and lust, could be such

Further on, the pastor draws a sad picture of this "sample nation," and says: "It is all avarice and selfishness — every man for himself in the great centers of the government." Ah! it is but too true, and instead of one-third of the human race being Christianized, there are not ten thousand Christians on the face of the globe Does not his own $25,000 a year given him for such talk as I have noticed in this discourse, exclude him from being among the number of the true followers of Christ? Reflect, and then reply. He very justly affirms the want of justice in the administration of the government, and asks: "Can any one say that our courts administer justice according to the benign spirit of Christianity?" To which none, in truth, can give an affirmative answer.

The Goddess of Liberty, holding the scales of justice over our Court-houses, is but a mockery and a sham. Pour enough gold into her lap and the scales will topple any way, and she will excuse any crime under the shining sun. The pastor has had ample evidence of the truth of his affirmation in his own case.

It must be acknowledged he began the *amende honorable* and rectification of his own wrong in the proper Christian spirit, with true heartfelt repentance and confession not only to the injured party, but to others. If it had been accepted and reciprocated in the same spirit, as it should have been, all would have ended well. When the pastor humbled himself before Tilton, he, being likewise charged, should have humbled himself and made confession to his pastor. And could he have been satisfied of the ruling of the spirit of Christ throughout, he would doubtless have taken Mrs. Moulton's advice, who was then to him really " a section of the day of judgment " But the Christians were not to be found; and he soon realized the fact that his only chance was to " fight the devil with fire " — to use the same unchristian weapons for defense as those with which he was assaulted. He staked his all in the warfare and won. Being forced to use worldly weapons, he proved himself to be master of the situation, and, in a worldly point of view, came off with flying colors.

I cannot well help, in this connection, however, calling to mind the words of an intelligent negro, who said : " Da better quit agitatin' dat subjec' 'tween Mr. Beecher an' de ladies." " Why so, uncle ? " " Case why, sah, it mout git down into de church, an' if it does it will play de debbil with de whole ob 'em." This brings to mind the saying of Jesus : " Let him that is without sin cast the first stone ; " and had the same been applied in this case not very many, in the old negro's view of it, would have been thrown.

Seeing, then, the equalizing process, it were well that we " should do nothing through strife nor vain glory, but in lowliness of mind let each esteem others better than themselves."

THE SHAKER PROBLEM.

A LETTER TO S R. WELLS OF THE PHRENOLOGICAL JOURNAL.

[NOTE BY THE EDITOR — Several of these discourses and letters would be more replete to the reader, should we present the letters and discourses to which these are intended as replies But to save voluminous ambiguities, we trust to the critical, good sense of the reader, to easily perceive from these replies what points of interest they are intended to embrace and to give a proper construction thereto   G A L]

Dear Editor: — My reasons for not sooner noticing the brackets so profusely interspersed among my answers to your twenty-five questions in the *Journal* are the sickness and decease of a brother, which claimed my attention.   If agreeable to you, I now propose to notice those of most importance.   They are like little shrubs that one grasps while falling down a declivity, which, when taken hold of, immediately give way, when one after another is clutched with the same sad result; but they serve the good purpose of easing the fall.

Now, the Shakers are spiritually right or wrong.   If wrong, it becomes the duty of those who perceive it to point out wherein; if right, it is obligatory on them to make it manifest to the world by letting "their light so shine that others, seeing their good *works*, may also glorify their Father in heaven " — Matt v, 16 It is an old saying but true: If you wish to learn your faults, listen to what your enemies say; but I prefer a candid friend, whom I take you to be, and hope that you, or some writer for your *Journal*, will continue to point them out without reserve.

We want with us in God's Kingdom only such as are striving to be good.   You say God wants (in His kingdom) all mankind — good, bad and indifferent.   What a kingdom ; what! are not the sheep to be separated from the goats ?   Are the good not to be distinguished from the willfully bad ?   You ask: Was it the righteous or sinners Christ came to save ?   He came to save sinners FROM their sins, not IN them.   The saved are those who find a visible order of God, and these confess their sins, forsake them, and live free from sin. Those who will not do this have not power to cease from sinning, are not saved, and must be classed among the goats, and cannot enter God's kingdom.

" Physical reform is best continued through right generation " While I yield to you the palm in physical knowledge, I must not be censured too severely for entertaining some scruples in regard to the position here assumed. Christ and His followers advocated and practiced the reverse ; *regeneration*, not *generation* — right or wrong. If they were mistaken, then we are. Jesus Christ, our exemplar, gave few lessons on mere physics, though He was " made in all respects like His brethren ," but of soul reform He was the teacher of all teachers. The one hundred and forty-four thousand that followed Him were *Virgins*

Of the wedding garments, you ask if we are sure that we are right ? To us the evidence is clear. Some of the invited guests could not control their selfishness. The less guilty begged to be excused , but the reply of the married was to the point : " I have married a wife and therefore *cannot come*." From these examples it seems obvious that the rejected were not self-controllers, but were " sensual, having not the spirit ; walking after their own lusts." — Jude.

You ask how we know what Zion expects ? — " Have you (we) been there ? " Most assuredly ; we are there now. You say : " Let Shakers beget Shakers, etc " This they are doing ; but not in a natural, generative nor worldly manner. That would be impossible. They must cease to be followers of Christ, and become worldlings before they can do so They would thereby become " children of this world, who marry and are given in marriage," and would cease to be among those who are counted worthy to obtain the resurrection from the dead, where they neither marry nor are given in marriage, but are as the angels (not yet angels themselves, but like the angels) Matt. xxii, 30. They would be like the young widows whom Paul advised the church not to receive ' For," says he, " when they have begun to wax wanton against Christ, they *will marry*, having damnation, because they have cast off their first faith" (which was not to marry, but to live a purely virgin life, after the example of Christ.) — Tim v, 11–14.

You say " Shakers are something beside spirits " I will notice this further on. You ask : Why we sit in judgment ? " Do ye not know," says Paul, " the saints shall judge the world ? " If the followers of Christ—"though in the world, yet not out of the world," are the saints, and those who do not follow Him are the world, why should the latter complain of being judged by the former? Or shall the world judge the saints?

You say of my fifth answer: "It is both unscientific and unscriptural, to say that there is no danger of the world being burned in the way the Shakers seem to fear."

Assertions unproved always bring more or less suspicion on one's solid arguments. It is far easier to say a thing is unscientific than to prove it to be so. The earth contains the area named, more or less, and that population increases on its surface in a given ratio is indisputable; and, though it contained double the area named, the reasoning would hold good; and although *you* may have other means to stay the tide of population, it is still evident that the proposition is mathematically scientific. It is not the Shakers who fear a literal conflagration of the external world. Now, let those who are really concerned for the continuance of the world, advocate the Shaker or Christ plan, which is to burn up the world in the human breast; and in proportion as this is done, which must be gradual, propagation will be checked, and the world continued. Either this, or wars and pestilence, greater than the world has ever known, are all that can continue the human race on the earth five centuries more! else there is no truth in mathematics, nor in effect following its cause.

"Oh, the egotism!" you exclaim, etc. "We *know* that we are of God, and the whole world lieth in wickedness."—1 John v. 19. Was the beloved apostle an egotist? If he was, so are we, because we know the same that the apostle John did.

"So few!" you exclaim; and then add· "Were *you* appointed to sort the acceptable ones?" Certainly. If the saints, the true followers of Christ, who constitute God's Kingdom on earth, are not to judge who are acceptable, who shall? Must it be worldlings? Perhaps you will say, *God.* Very well; but how? It must be God in the seeker, or God in the world, or God in the saints—which? But you say. "Go slow, Mr. Shaker, and quote the Saviour, 'Judge not, that ye be not judged'"—Matt. vii, 1. This caution Christ gave to brethren who were equals, whose first work was to remove the beams from their own eyes. Christ, while on earth, was the seat of judgment for the world. This judgment He gave to His successors when He left, and it still remains with His true followers.

22

Now, what say ye?

Christ was a Communist. Ananias and Sapphira got into their difficulty by their dishonesty. There are many Ananiases and Sapphiras in this day, who are struck dead to the spirit, carried out and buried in the world.

You ask: "Do not the Shakers own and let out land as other professed Christians do?" Not at all. We have said Shakers own no land by absolute right and title. They once had this right, but it passed away from man in the general consecration to God and His service, reserving to themselves, and to you, and to your children, and to all nations, peoples, kindreds, tongues, or color, the right of USE AND OCCUPANCY who will confess and forsake their sins, and follow Christ in the regeneration, by leading, like Him, a pure and holy life. *Any one, every one*, the whole world over, can come and occupy this consecration just as freely as those who now occupy it by living the pure life above stated. Is this the way other professed Christians do? If so then they are Shakers.

"But do they not sell land?" you pertinently inquire. If they do, the consecration only changes its form. Suppose 100 acres of land builds a house, no one nor ones have a personal right to the house any more than they had to the land. They have the right of the *usufruct*—to use and occupy it so long as they remain true to the covenantal compact and no longer. But any human being now existing between the poles has the same right, on the same conditions. Thus, you see, the principle of selfishness is destroyed to an extent nowhere else accomplished under the shining sun. Are we now understood? Is this the way other professed Christians do?

Emasculation is like Paul's circumcision, of the heart, in the spirit, and not in the letter. (See Rom. ii, 29.) Outward emasculation would avail nothing, but in the heart every thing. The eunuchs for the kingdom of heaven's sake are such as in *heart* deny themselves, not such as externally incapacitate themselves and retain an adulterous heart. Now take a vote upon this if you please.

"Those who will not follow Christ He cannot save," you repeat interrogatively.—Cannot?—If omnipotent, why not? He is not omnipotent. He is not the Father, but the Son of the Father. He is what Paul tells Timothy: "For there is one God, and one Mediator between God and man—the *man* Christ

Jesus."—1 Tim. ii, 5. He cannot be mediator between two and be either of the two Himself. Though a chosen man, He was between God and mankind. Since it has pleased the Father to bestow on man freedom of thought and action, and since salvation depends on man's obedience to the Son, it follows that the Son cannot save the willfully disobedient This is the "why not"

"Pauper children." The Shakers do not depend on pauper children to keep up the institution, but on finding a few " self-controllers " among the mass of mankind.

I will now notice your seventh proposition —"Shakers are something besides Spirits " It would have been more true and to the point if you had said Shakers are something besides *bodies*. Bodies are only fictitious, fleeting, fading tenements or present coverings for the real Shaker ; they exist for a moment and disappear. If there is any truth in philosophy, or if the deepest thinkers of this or any other age have found a truth on which all agree, it is the fact that the body forms no part of the man If this be true, then, our friend is mistaken in saying Shakers are something besides spirits. All writers, whose works I have read, have enunciated the fact that the *ego* and *non ego*, the spirit and the body, are contradictions, and distinct ; that the phenomena of each are governed and controlled by different laws.

Socrates, in his dialogue with Alcibiades, maintains it. Bacon and Descartes, fathers of modern philosophy, affirm the same Locke and his personal friend, Le Clerc, adopt the same Reid says : " They (the mind and body) are separated by the whole diameter of being."

Laromaguere : " Between an extended and unextended substance there can be no connecting medium." He, with Socrates, denies that the body is any part of the man ; and Plato says : " The soul is in the body like a sailor in a ship—that the soul employs the body as an instrument, but that the energy, life or sense is the manifestation of a different substance, etc." All agree with Laromaguere that " the unextended (the mind) can have no connection by touch with the body." He thus disposes of the plastic medium between soul and body that some contend for . " This hypothesis is too absurd for refutation. It annihilates itself, for between an extended and unextended substance there can be no middle existence, these being contradictory If the medium be neither soul nor body, it is a chimera ; if it is at once body and soul, it is contradictory ; or if, to avoid contradiction, it is said to be like us, a union of soul and body, it is itself in want of a medium."

So, my dear friends, you must perceive that we are something besides bodies But as it is to us as the ship to the sailor, it needs some attention, and, as this seems to be your greatest concern, go on and mend up the leaky vessels and build new ones; we can sail more safely in a good ship than a poor one. But let us agree as to our prerogatives ; while yours is with the ship, ours is with the sailor—then let us fraternize. While you are mending up the old hulks and making new ones, you must permit us to trim the sails and show the sailors which way to steer to the haven of rest and harbor of peace—peace, sweet haven of peace ' which none but the truly honest cross-bearer and follower of Christ can ever find.

Kind friend, I have written the foregoing with a subdued heart ; as it were by the side of a dying brother, with a deep sense of the little span of time allowed me here, sincerely and earnestly, and in the kindest spirit of true friendship for yourself and the many readers of your excellent *Journal,* hoping that some may be induced to investigate and prove if these things are so.

ANALYSIS OF SHAKERISM.

Friend V : — Your favor is received, and having leisure I will now notice its contents. Your first wish is to be rightly informed if you have misapprehended the sentiments of one whom I will term F., and, as I think you have in some cases, I shall now endeavor to comply with your wishes. This request shows to my mind honesty of purpose on your part. I will proceed to notice them in the order in which you have stated your objections in the paper you had the kindness to send me.

I. "Creative Wisdom," I presume, is only another name for God, and certainly, as F. has stated, those who most perfectly obey God, must realize the greatest amount of happiness, and inasmuch as God is *disobeyed*, " unhappiness must be the inevitable result " If the Shakers, as a *class*, obey God more perfectly than any *other class*, they, of course, must enjoy the greatest amount of happiness. You say : " In some respects the Shakers do." I ask : Is there any other class, or body of people, that do in more respects ? If so, who ? where ? when ? how ? If you will be good enough to point them out to me, I will certainly bow before them and do them reverence.

II. Instead of using the term "another," F. should have said a " higher" state of existence, in order to convey the true idea. The life of Christ being a higher life than that of the world, we have chosen *that* life ; as the apostle saith, we are they " on whom the ends of the world are come," living *now* as Christ did *then* on earth, and as we conceive the angels do in heaven. What objection can be brought against any one who *chooses freely* to lead the life of Christ, and live above the selfish and sensual elements of the world ? I can see none. This the Shakers do — I speak of them as a class ; that there are exceptions I do not deny Bro. F. is right in denying that the separation of the sexes *as sexes*, causes dissatisfaction to such as freely choose the life of Christ ; but that there is disquiet and unrest attending those who are only *experimenting* in it, I will freely admit; and that the countenances of such are indexes, to some extent, and also of the amount of happiness enjoyed by them. To pretend to lead the life of Christ, with the heart's affections placed upon the pleasures and things of this world, is by no means calculated to make a heaven for any soul, and I am not sorry that such ones exhibit their true condition to discerning visitors who come among us. But to the charge of scolding and ridiculing such ones, I must demur. Than this, there can be no greater mistake. The office of an *Elder* is not to *govern*, in the ordinary sense of that term, but to *lead*. Elders are not to be *feared*, but *loved* They are to set others an example by *governing themselves*. *Shall and shall not* are not of their vernacular — do not properly belong in the Shaker vocabulary; but, as said, the Elder's duty simply is, by *counsel, precept* and *example, to aid others to govern themselves;* and " he that would be greatest must be servant of all," must be the most yielding to the wants of others, the most forbearing, the most forgiving, the most condescending, the most upright, that others, "seeing their *good works*, may glorify their Father in heaven," and though being equals will love and obey them of choice. One substituting any other government must have studied himself and human nature to small profit The government of *force* is gone when the forces become equal. The government of *fear* is lost whenever the *fear* is gone; but the government of love is eternal This reveals the secret of what stability belongs to the government of the Shaker institution

III The affinity question is well put by F , and I am compelled to say, as I think, rather poorly answered by you. Jesus was not the advocate of marriage other than in the same sense in which the Shakers themselves advocate it The whole tenor of His life and teaching is as much against it as is ours. To all those who chose or desired to be made perfect, to become one with Him in the higher life, it was uniformly . " Forsake all — father, mother, house, land, wife and children. Take up the *cross daily*, and follow me." But to those undeveloped Pharisees, and all who chose the lower life, He cited *them* to how it was in the *beginning*, and exhorted them to be guided by *that*. We say the same, and wish all who do not choose the higher life, may live an *orderly life* with the wife of their youth.

IV. Truths never conflict; and wherever there *is* " manifest conflict," the one or the other is an error. But there may be apparent conflict, and both be right. This may be in consequence of the incompetency of those who suppose they have made the discovery. For example: The word of God to Moses and Joshua was: "*Slay your enemies;*" but to Jesus "*Love* your enemies" Is there conflict here? By no means God's word to each man and woman can be indicative of nothing more than his or her highest internal perceptions of truth and right — *i e.*, the highest they are capacitated to receive Moses and Joshua were incapable of perceiving higher truths than an "eye for an eye." God could not give them the Christ light nor life Their development or unfoldment would not admit of it It would not have been seen nor appreciated by them, had it been presented to them. According to this, you will say that Moses, who slew *his* enemies, and Christ who *loved His*, were equally justified before God Precisely so — if they were equally obedient to their highest light No man can justly be condemned for obeying his highest light. All condemnation arises from *disobeying*, not from *obeying*. "*This is the condemnation — that light has come into the world*" Again God's word to Adam was: Marry a wife, generate offspring orderly This was higher light, and a higher state than that of animal promiscuity. But to Christ it was: "*Excelsior*" — come up still higher; lead the angel life in this world He obeyed God; and, as Paul says, set us an example that we should follow His steps — every one whose unfoldment will admit of it — who perceives the higher light. Is there conflict here? Not at all. But here verily is *progress in reality* — a progress which you seem to ignore Can we live the Mosaic and the Christ life at the same time? Can we live the generating life of the *first Adam*, and the self-denying life of the *second Adam*, at the same time' "Do men gather figs from thistles?"

V If the "goodly Ann Lee" discovered that self-denial, celibacy, and chastity formed the substratum of the Christ-life, and this was *true then*—all the sophistry in the world cannot make it *false now* After having chosen and adopted this higher Christ-life, would not the choosing and adopting the most orderly Adamic-life be retrograde? What use for the Christ-life if the Adamic will answer? Or was Christ's life a failure? It to lead a life of *virtue, purity* and *chastity*, in the *present tense*, is incorporating, as you seem to indicate, an error fatal to the *future* virtue, purity and chastity of the human race, then your charge is true and logically sound, and a *sweet* fountain can send forth a *bitter* stream. But I must say it requires greater powers of discernment than are vouchsafed to me, to be able to discover how the exercise of any good quality in the *present tense* could operate against that quality and make it evil in the *future tense!* But let me beg you to note this: It is not *total abstinence* that encourages drunkenness, but it is the honorable (?) moderate drinker.

VI. If we have the threefold existence, of which you speak— *spirit, intellect* and *body*—is it unreasonable that the spirit should reign over the intellect and animal? I know you will say you go in for a harmonious combination of the three, each performing its legitimate functions and duties. This is just what we are at; but the higher must dictate the lower, and the lower be subject in its action—whether it be much, little, or none at all—or else harmony is unattainable. Should not the lower impulses be subordinate to the higher? But how is the fact with the world? Do not the animal appetites run riot in the face of protesting spirit? You must answer affirmatively. Now *true Shakerism* is honesty of purpose, the subordinating and subjecting the lower to the higher impulses; and if the spirit *should*, in the more highly developed and brightly unfolded souls, require the entire abnegation of some of the more gross and merely animal appetites, what just censure can rest on such pure-minded ones for obeying the high mandate? Really none, I think. If your unfoldment has reached this—the Christ-standard—the word of God to your soul will be: "Come ye out from among them; touch not, taste not, handle not the unclean thing," and Christ will receive you, and you will be with Him "one spirit;" but if your condition is below this, and yet on the highest plane of the natural man, the word of God will be to you: Marry *one wife,* and live in orderly generation, and be with her "one flesh;" and this is all you can make of it—simply "*one flesh;*" *nothing more, nothing less.* Next below this is animal promiscuity, with its times and seasons; lower still is unbridled license under the ordinary marital state; lower still is the same license with concubinage and the plurality wife-system; and still a deeper depth is that of ill-famed institutions of debauchery. Thus are the gradations manifest from below up to the animal, to man, to Christ, to God. He that hath eyes to see, let him see. Truly Bro. F. was right in leaving marriage to the "children of this world," *where Christ left it,* and not to suffer pressure from below to force it upon " those who are not of this world, even as he was not of this world, but are as the angels in heaven." Is this unfair?

VII. Your remarks in reference to the declaration that Shakerism brought forth Spiritualism, I think, are to the point It would read better to me reversed, and say Spiritualism brought forth Shakerism quite one hundred years ago, and has abided with it ever since—*Spiritualism* the *cause, Shakerism* is the *effect*.

VIII. I freely admit that rules which require men to bow before creeds must pass away, but not that of a *" visible lead."* One good *visible lead* is worth more to society than a dozen *in*-visible leads; and a lead of some kind is indispensable. For every man to lead himself as best suits his inclinations, is just what the world generally have been doing from Adam to the present day, with few exceptions. Nor is it dispensing with reason to yield to a visible lead, but rather the highest exercise of it. Even though the lead be imperfect, harmony cannot exist without such acquiescence I love to reason with my fellow men, and yield to the best reasons offered me on any subject. Truly, as my Bro. F. says, *" Shaking does not injure the Shakers."*

IX. You say the Shakers profess to have faith in the laws of Nature. So they do Gravity is a law of Nature So is pro-creation, you may say. But how is this to be proved? Because issue follows the act. This does not make the act itself a law of nature. We might as well affirm that the desires and will of man are laws of Nature. I frankly admit that in procreation the laws of Nature should be observed; but regret to say it is seldom the case with man. But such as choose not to propagate, do not thereby violate any law of Nature. Perhaps you will say they violate the laws of their being; if you should, the proof will rest with you, which you may find it difficult to make clear. But the most flagrant violation of Nature's laws can truthfully be charged home on those who choose to propagate, with scarcely a complaint from the reformer and advocate of progress! Can this be successfully controverted? But all this introducing and inter-larding with the God of *Nature* and *laws of Nature* seems to me is not for the purpose of liberating the *soul*, but to liberate the animal, and set it free to indulge itself in spite of the soul's pro-testations; or else it is a subtle intellectual argument in behalf of the animal, to convince the soul that it is imposing unnecessary restrictions. And hence the animal, in unison with the intellect,

23

complains, cries, speaks of prison walls, bonds intolerable, and appeals to the laws of Nature and Nature's God for relief. But all its special pleading is easily comprehended by the well-balanced and well-developed mind. Would it be amiss for me to ask what is meant by Nature's God, and what are His attributes? When this is answered, we may come to a better understanding, and learn whether we violate them or not; until then we must claim to be in harmony and unison with them.

Now, Bro. Valentine, you will perceive that I have followed your example in speaking plainly, with no design of giving offense—have simply spoken for myself, as I understand the truth, to help as I am willing to be helped by every friend of human progress.

In the cause of Christ and Humanity, thine,

H. L EADS.

"HAS JESUS ANY FOLLOWERS?"

Is asked with a flourish of trumpets, by one Jamieson, in his closing critique of the character and sayings of Jesus Christ. The announcement that the end has come will doubtless give relief to some. I have concluded, however, not to let the matter die without answering his important question that heads this article I now respond in the affirmative, with as much emphasis as he has in the negative

Every man or woman who takes Jesus Christ for an exemplar — lives His life — brings him or herself into the conditions He prescribes, as far as he or she is able — is emphatically an adherent and follower of Christ. It is, however, thought by our critic to be impossible to follow Him and obey His teachings in consequence of their absurd and contradictory character, and wrong to do so in consequence of their immoral tendency Besides, he says, "no man can represent all truth," and he wants the universe for his fountain from which to draw his portion. Now, he who best represents the attributes of Deity best represents *truth ;* for *God is truth* This, Christ did better than all the universe beside, so far as we have knowledge, which His own biography, if true, fully substantiates. The *spiritual* truth of the universe may be said to have been focalized in Him; while truths pertaining to mere matter were more or less ignored. In asserting that His teachings were absurd and immoral, it would, at least, have been commendable in the asserter to have added this clause · " If I am able to comprehend and understand them." This much modesty would have revealed a deeper vein of thought than is otherwise exhibited in his productions, and would have shown a due respect to minds equal to his own, that might chance to differ from him To my mind, his articles all show a great want of ability to comprehend the true meaning of the texts and sayings quoted by him. What seems to him a "perfect muddle," is to others of equal learning and culture, a harmonious and consistent whole.

If I am able to understand our critic, I find many of his assertions without foundation, and some, I think, untrue. The assertion that "but few of Christ's teachings were of importance, and these few came from the heathen," he must have known to be groundless, unless he has had access to heathen productions not accessible to the common public. Besides, of the few that are found in heathen works can he be quite sure that they were not interpolations by interested parties from Christ? *Assertion* is one thing, *proof* is another. It seems presumptuous to assert that Christ has no followers, because the critic thinks it impossible. I profess to be one of the followers of Christ, as I understand Him, but not as Jamieson does. It is not his prerogative to dispute my claim until he shall have proven my understanding to be wrong and his right; and this he might find a task not easily performed. "The natural man," says Paul, "receiveth not the things of the spirit of God, for they are foolishness to him; neither can he know them because they are spiritually discerned." —(1 Cor., chap. 2, 5, 14.) Our critic seems to be of the class here referred to, as he is able to see little else than foolishness in Christ's teachings. He will pardon our classifying him. But in regard to the contradictory character of Jesus' teachings, I fear not to affirm that by comparison and a rational exegesis the contradictory features will mostly, if not all, disappear. Allow me to take one of his most prominent examples, and one of the most difficult to reconcile. Christ teaches us to love all, hate none, honor parents, to do good for evil, even to bless our persecutors and love our enemies. It is thought that His commanding or making it a condition of discipleship, and consequent happiness, that the husband and wife, and partial relations, must not only be forsaken but hated, is contravening the direct command to love all; and hence, our critic avers, if we take one position, it is impossible to take the other. I must be excused for taking a different view. That they do not antagonize, and that they are all in support of the pure, sweet, loving and unselfish life which the blessed man taught and practiced during His earthly pilgrimage, I shall proceed to show.

It is well known that Christ was a celibate, Spiritualist and communist, possessing a heart overflowing with the milk of human kindness, charity and love for humanity; and who taught that whatever antagonized with these should be hated and forsaken. Now, selfhood and selfish property must exist in the procreative and generative world, all of which are at variance with the equal spiritual communism of Christ, and consequently must be forsaken in coming into the Christ-life. The husband and wife who may desire to come into Christ's spiritual community would at once perceive that the relation of husband and wife, private property and generation, were incompatible with the Christ-life conditions, and must be forsaken. The woman could now very consistently say to her husband · "I love you, William; but the husband of it I despise—that is what has brought on ' all our woes ; ' and now if you will permit me to hate the husband and allow me to remain your sister in Christ, I will love and respect the brother better and more than ever I did the husband." The husband could consistently say the same to the wife, and love the sister while hating the wife. Hence it is clear that the wife and husband may be hated, according to the command of Christ, while all mankind are loved. Thus this stumbling paradox is found to be no contradiction at all ; and thus it is with all our critic has set before us.

He complains, and says Christ "commands us to cultivate poverty in order to secure bliss," and adds, "let him keep his bliss." I will certainly be enlightened if he will point out a single instance in the history of the world where riches have produced bliss. Riches and bliss are incompatible with each other. I would almost go as far as a certain great teacher who said : "Every rich man is either himself dishonest or the son of dishonest parents ; " and dishonesty and bliss cannot occupy the same berth. Solomon's experiment might satisfy any one on this point. He says : " I made me great works, builded me houses, planted vineyards, made pools of water, got me servants and maidens and greater possessions than all that were before me. Whatsoever mine eyes desired I kept not from them. I withheld not my heart from any joy, etc., and behold all was vanity and vexation of spirit." All men naturally would do the same if they could, and find the same result.

Thus we see that there is nothing in riches to satisfy the spirit Natural riches can satisfy in some measure the natural desires of the animal body ; but it takes spiritual riches to satisfy the immortal or spiritual man and woman.

Our critic, after placing Christ below the heathen, tells what He (Christ) would have done had He been equal with some of them. He says if Christ had been sensible, He would not have requested others to follow Him, but, instead, would simply have enjoined on all—" Be thyself." He consoles himself however "thus : " " There is none to do Jesus honor, none whose common sense will permit him to keep *His* sayings. No one believes on Jesus ! None follow Him ! " Now, I would just here beg him to make one or two exceptions, if he pleases. We will admit that we do not follow Him as friend Jamieson understands Him ; but we *do follow Him as we understand Him*. Hence I here confront him by asserting that there are still some to " do Jesus honor," " whose common sense permits them to keep His sayings," " who believe on Him and follow Him." So, right here, we and our critic are at swords' points. If he sustains himself in the position assumed, he must show that we are not Christ's followers by putting his finger on facts.

But before I close, at the risk of being thought invidious, I would beg leave to institute a short comparison between the wisdom of what Christ *did* and the wisdom of doing what our critic says He should have done. Christ's doctrine, carried out in His life, was to love and do good to all ; boundless in forgiving, charity unto death, from the prostitute to the thief on the cross. Such love hath no man ever had, and such a life was never before exhibited. But now for the application of our critic's wisdom,—" Be thyself : " Gambler, be thyself ; drunkard, be thyself ; thief, be thyself ; master, be thyself ; slave, be thyself ; whoremonger, be thyself ; prostitute, be thyself—don't listen to Jesus' advice, " go and sin no more ; " ravisher, be thyself ; ravished, be thyself—don't cry, because *he* was *being himself !* Thus we see what a world J. would have—passion let loose with no restraining influence—who would wish to be a denizen thereof ? His doctrine, carried out, would make a world of devils incarnate, instead of saints. But Jesus, the " Blessed Jesus," has followers.

ANOTHER DANIEL.

A certain individual, Billings by name, has found materialized fingers of a man's hand to write on the walls of the Shaker Church, or Christ's Kingdom on earth, the ominous words, " *Mene, Mene, Tekel, Upharsin*," himself being the diviner to give the " interpretation thereof," which, in short, is the calamity of decay and extinction, together with the loss of exclusive ownership of Ann Lee, unless important concessions and changes be soon made. The first is to do away with the destructive element of centralized power which was engrafted upon the body of the order by Ann Lee; who, when under the divine afflatus, was more than human, and by her great gift of spiritual discernment caused her followers to become as little children in her hands. This is the way he avers the centralized power, of which he now so bitterly complains, was established in the order; if so, it must have been of God divine, and not of men; consequently it would be a sacrilegious act to disturb it. But we shall not clothe said Billings in scarlet for his divination, nor make him ruler in the kingdom. But we deny the charge of having become unworthy of Ann Lee, and will battle to the death against any power that may try to remove her from the regenerative and transplant her into the generative order. It would be nothing less than an effort at abduction, prompted by lustful covetousness on his part, to try to win Ann Lee by over-wrought flattery, and thus rob the children of their Mother. He essays to give a reason why, what was good and proper in her day is evil in this day, and that is because she had a power of discernment then that is wanting now. Pitiful reason! It is no reason at all why a lead was necessary then and unnecessary now, and should be obeyed then and not now. But this leadership began with Jesus, not with Ann, and our sole prosperity depends upon our strict adherence to their teachings and example, and to the counsel of their appointees; utterly and wholly ignoring all Anithopelic counsels whatever.

In the face of their teachings Billings makes the astounding declaration that "It cost more to become a Shaker 100 years ago than now, but more was received in return then than now for the sacrifice," thus showing remarkable ignorance of the teachings of our leaders It costs now precisely what it did 100 years ago, or 1800 years ago—no more—no less. It cost a man then just "all that he had," including "his own will and his life" It costs just the same now. It is a fatal mistake to suppose that any thing can be reserved in this day that had to be sacrificed in that. This reservation, keeping back part of the price—reserving a few sheep and oxen (1st Sam. 15), forgetting that "obedience is better than sacrifice, and to hearken than the fat of rams,"—was the cause of his failure to receive the promised reward—salvation and redemption from sin and a "life hid with Christ in God." Any reserve whatsoever will defeat this end, and it is only by receiving those sent of Christ, in childlike simplicity and confidence, that we can receive Him. Our critic next speaks of the "inexorable law of compensation that cannot be set at naught nor avoided." Law of compensation! What can he mean? The compensation in Christ's Kingdom is the same to all literally. Spiritually it is a justified conscience, with the bliss occasioned by it, and freedom from the bondage of the world, together with increasing power over evil. In these things he talks like a stranger. But the leadership seems to trouble his spirit like a nightmare. He says: "The absolute, unquestioned dictatorship of the lead in the Shaker order was the child of the wonderful inspirational character of Ann Lee." If so why should he wish to slay the child and then lay claim to the mother who bore it? There is a strange inconsistency here. To pour out his affections on the mother and then slay her offspring—"even the little child that must forever lead them." He continues: "The wisdom of the spiritual agents may be questioned by those who judge from a natural stand-point." Just so. The wisdom of both Jesus and Ann was questioned from the material stand-point, as much as their followers are now; but such materialists "cannot discern spiritual things—they are foolishness to them."

Our critic doubtless became weary of being controlled by the child spirit, and "looking through a glass darkly," from a material stand-point, supposed he discovered a great lack of wisdom in the spiritual leaders. But he exaggerates largely when he says: "The authority of the elder is the entire control of the individual under him, body, soul, and mind; the member must act through the elder in all things, even in the occupation of his mind." There is such a mixture of truth and falsehood in this that a special analysis becomes necessary. The Elder's rule, over the subject's mind, extends no farther than to determine the kind of business he or she is to pursue for the time being, for the benefit of themselves and the community. I will illustrate by my own experience I was requested in times past to work at various branches of business, mechanical and otherwise, and thereby learned several trades, in all of which I had the freest possible exercise of all my faculties to develop my mechanical genius; my mind was entirely untrammeled by the elder's mind, and was brought as fully and freely into exercise as if I had appointed myself to the several callings It was the same with my studies — Philosophy, Logic, Language, History, Mathematics, Theology, Physics, or Metaphysics, etc., save I was not permitted the use of novels, sensual nor amative works; but my mind was as distinct and free as is possible for other minds to be under any circumstances

It is nonsense to speak of our order as a "crystallized body" with no room for the mind's expansion. So, also, the charge of mental and physical bondage among the Shakers has not an inch of solid ground to rest on Having been brought up from babyhood within the pale of the institution, I am satisfied that in no condition of life could my mind have been freer to expand in every thing good and valuable than here, the line alone of expansion having been directed by elders and others, just as any father or mother would do for their son. Thus the fog and smoke are brushed away from our critics' Elder-bondage statement, and the conditions made truthful and clear It is the duty of every person on earth to follow any light, or copy any example above them, and there is neither slavery nor bondage in so doing; and if he should perceive, as Billings did, "more of Christ among the Shakers than is to be found elsewhere," it is not only a privilege but a duty to close in with it and obey its behests, and not set oneself up to judge it and pronounce upon it condemnation and extinction. The fact is, the true-souled and obedient Shaker is the freest person on the foot-stool of God, because all his bonds are self-imposed, whereas all others have bonds imposed on them

24

against their will which they would gladly throw off but cannot. The bondage that Billings suffered, was that he could not be free to subvert the order with his "angel forces," and fix it to suit his own materialistic ideas. But he should remember that

> "Order is Heaven's first law and this confessed,
> Some are and must be placed above the rest,"

else all would be chaos and confusion. Other complaints of little family rules seem hardly worth notice ; yet, I will offer a few remarks concerning them.

I The authorities must see the letter correspondence of members with the outside world. None but false-hearted persons could, and ever did complain of this rule

II. Members are not to absent themselves without the knowledge and permission of the elders A child can see the necessity of this

III Whistling. While we have no absolute rule forbidding it, it is not a commendable practice ; still, I would not object against the whole community whistling even Yankee Doodle in concert, and blessing God for the liberty of conscience which was obtained under its martial strains

IV. Sexes talking together. I presume any restriction in this quarter would interfere with his sense of gallantry. But the sexes conversing with each other is not prohibited except it be two alone in closed apartments; hence three or more are recommended in such cases. Billings seems to be well posted in Shaker Spiritualism, and must have been a member during the great outpouring between the years 1837 and 1844, as he tells us what he heard himself. But I cannot fully determine what he means by the " new angel forces " then introduced, unless it was the inspiration of " babes and sucklings," or the false and deceptive spirits that come to make inroads on what Ann Lee had established, but which were exorcised by the discerning lead. But true mediums then told us, the time would come when some in the outside world would try to claim Ann Lee. This prediction seems now to be somewhat fulfilled, but we object to her abduction.

He goes on to say: " In those days the Shakers were prosperous ; " that is, in the days when the lead was respected and obeyed by all; and this condition, let me say, when once more fully restored, will bring equal, if not greater prosperity than we ever enjoyed But so long as a majority of the members allow them-

selves to occupy the judgment seat, and obey and disobey at
pleasure, prosperity will remain among the impossibilities. God
cannot bless and prosper such conditions. In fact, such are not
Shakers at all. But again he says: " It was human to reject the
new angel forces, but in that a birthright was forfeited " I would
ask, what birthright? The right for every one to do as he listed?
Or to change the government from a Theocracy to that of a Democracy? Something of this sort, it seems. was what the expelled
spirits wished to introduce Then Christ's prayer should read ·
Thy Democracy come, instead of "Thy Kingdom come." He
speaks truly when he says: "We were told by the spirits that
they would leave us for a season, and turn their attention to the
world, but it was not because we cast out the evil spirits with their
" new forces." But they having strengthened and established us
on the foundation which was laid by Christ and Ann Lee — they
could now depart for a season , still they have at times visited us
to this day, and their power and influence are not yet reduced to
the "unknown quantity." The true spirits informed us at the
time when we were looking for a great increase, that, instead of
this, our numbers would be reduced, and that " a great flood
would be poured out from the mouth of the Dragon to destroy
the woman (Ann Lee) and the remnant of her seed. (Rev. xii,
. 15, 16,) but the earth would swallow the flood," and Zion would
thereafter flourish and grow like a " well-watered garden," and
her testimony would spread to the ends of the earth. This was
then, and is now our hope and consolation We next have his
" experience as to the spiritual discernment which was manifest
in so high a degree among the old time Shakers." He now finds
a total inability of the lead to " discern the thoughts and intents
of the heart."

Admitting this, in part, to be true, it still affords no reason for
the curtailment of the power of the lead. This gift is not so
necessary now, where an organized order exists, as it was in the
beginning, when all were strangers and no order existed Still
there is much more of this discernment in the church than is apparent to an outside materialist. Greater purification in the body,
I admit, is necessary, and a more close union and dependence in
the gift of the lead, and a greater separation from the world and
worldly kin, to insure the coveted blessing. I am not prepared
to dispute the disreputable circumstances alluded to, but rather
suppose them to be substantially true, and have been mortified

that any Shakers should betake themselves to the dark seances of flesh-loving mediums in quest of purely virgin, Shaker spirits who had left the form. Over this I would throw a veil.

Billings' remarks about fire, and protection therefrom by spirits, is far from truth. Destructive fires began with the founding of the institution. If I am correctly informed, Ann Lee had a house burned. We had our first grain barn burned here on Oct. 6, 1810, and the Ohio Society had theirs burned the 29th of Nov., 1807; all the work of incendiaries, and this, too, when we were on the tip-toe of expectation, and all aglow with the spirit, and we have had our constantly repeated cautions from the elders about fire ever since. So there never has been a time, with the thoughtful portion of our community, when no fears were indulged about fire. The true gift of healing has never left the Shakers. "If any are sick (of sin) and will call for their elders, if they have committed sins (and will confess and repent,) they shall be forgiven them" (and be healed,) — James. v, 16. Lastly, our critic confesses honestly, if reluctantly, that there is "still much genuine spirituality among the calm, quiet, self-denying brother and sister Shaker, whose chief end and aim seems to be how they can do the most to bring sunshine and joy to those around them," and adds: "More of *Christ on earth I never have seen than I found among this people.*" Then I would ask; Why, under high heaven, did you not stay with them? Was there too much of Christ to suit you? Did you wish to be where there was less of Christ, and so retreat to Ancora? Was the atmosphere in Shakerdom too pure and rare for your weak lungs? Please rise and explain.

GOD'S WORD.

Notwithstanding the subject of what constitutes God's word has perplexed the world for ages and been widely discussed and much befogged by writers, so that agreement has hitherto seemed impossible, still, I think, it can be made plain to the common mind. This is the task I have now proposed for myself It will first be necessary to state what we are to understand by the term God. It is hardly sufficient to say the "Supreme Being," as a finite being may be supreme over all other finite beings Such was Christ; but Christ was not God, only as God-man, the Son of God. We understand the term God in its highest sense to mean, *Infinite Spirit, omniscient and omnipresent.* Then to speak of more than one Infinite God is childish, equal to declaring there is no infinite God; but being infinite in his presence, as well as in His power, in all worlds and places, in all humans and all things, at all times, makes all works His own except that which is changed, obstructed or counteracted by *free agents,* and for which the free agents are themselves accountable. We admit that the doctrine of free agency is disputed by some philosophers of note, and although we are conscious of this freedom, it is difficult of demonstration in the face of *necessity*

The non-acceptance of this doctrine is where the honest Hebrew philosopher, Benedict De Spinoza, missed the mark, who, in his "Ethics," throws all acts, causes and effects back to infinity, making them rest with God, disagreeing with Locke, who thus manfully comes to the rescue · "Whatever *necessity* determines in the pursuit of real bliss, the same necessity with the same force establishes suspense, deliberation and scrutiny of each successive desire, whether the gratification of it does not interfere with our true happiness and mislead us from it. The government of the passions is the right improvement of this liberty, " etc

Now the word of God to free agents is the operation of the ever-present Infinite Spirit on the higher consciousness of their unfolding. God does not impress His word on any above and beyond the condition to which He has unfolded them, else His word to them would be incomprehensible and therefore void ; hence it is not unreasonable to affirm that it was the same God or ever-present Infinite Spirit operating upon the higher consciousness and highest unfolded condition of Moses, when the utterance was made of " an eye for an eye, " that operated upon the still higher unfoldment of Christ, when the utterance was made to " love your enemies. "   To affirm that both were equally God's word, affords no evidence of contradiction nor change in the mind of God ; it only shows that the latter had attained to a higher state of development than the former, comprehending the attributes of love and mercy, in a degree which the former had not reached ; thus doing away with the subterfuge that one God directed Moses, and another Christ, and another the Quakers and Shakers, and so on, losing sight of the omnipresence of God altogether, and concealing the grand truth that the word of God to all humans, heathens, Protestants, Catholics, Oneidians, Quakers or Shakers, is the operation of the Infinite on their higher consciousness, which if obeyed brings present justification to each class.   But justification is not salvation nor redemption.   These are attainable only through Christ ; that is, by seeking until we find Him, where He has " placed His name for salvation, " and then by " walking as He walked and overcoming as He overcame. "

But we say *God is dual.* Very well ; but this, properly understood, does not destroy His unity.   He is dual only in the subordinate sense.   He exists equally in both male and female ; He is therefore male in the masculine, and female in the feminine.   The everpresent Infinite Spirit speaking by the organs of the man is the Father ; the same spirit speaking by the woman is the Mother—His unity remaining inviolate ; and unity and duality are thus reconciled.

All anti-Christian notions about a fixed throne located in space somewhere " twixt earth, sea and skies, " are pure fiction, chimera, with no rational basis, as such an idea destroys the thought of His infinity.   This, however, does not conflict with the idea of His kingdom in heaven, where Christ is the visible head, who is still directed and controlled by the operation of the Divine Essence on his higher consciousness, and to whom all must bow, angels or men.   But the God that can go and come from one part of space to another is finite and must be some subordinate creature to whom the term God is applied. Moses and Jesus were God to the people in a subordinate sense, they being the highest unfolded of the race One under the natural law, the other under the spiritual. The idea of the Infinite focalizing his whole self in either, is very absurd and finds no support in reason nor revelation ; because whilst operating on their consciousness, He was at the same time operating, holding and guiding millions of worlds and all within them If the affirmation that "God cannot possibly be in any evil work " be construed to deny the eternal presence. then the affirmation is at fault, because God is either omnipresent, or He is not. If He is not, He is circumscribed. If He is circumscribed, He is finite, and can be measured, when infinity disappears. But God is ever present, in the cyclone, in the fire that warms, or that which reduces cities to ashes He is equally in the flint of the winged and quivering arrow of the wild Indian on its errand of death, as in His heart to condemn or approve, or in that of angels, or men on errands of mercy and love That it has been His will to impart free agency to man, who may do evil or good at pleasure, does not deny in the least degree the ever-existing Eternal Presence But to further elucidate, we return to Gospel ministers. Being appointed from above, and moved in obedience to the Infinite Spirit operating upon their higher consciousness, or in obedience to the more highly unfolded ministers or agents before them. when they speak or act free from every earthly bias or passional influence, either in or out of themselves, they simply are agents or tools in the hands of God, and what they say is the word of God. and what they do is the act of God, which would be sin for them to withhold or to change, and which should be freely accepted by all under them, notwithstanding such ministers or appointed agents may have many imperfections to contend with in common with the rest of their brethren and sisters Christ Himself was tempted in all things like His brethren. No excuse for disobedience to the law of Christ, or God through Him, or His appointees, should be made in consequence of this. Now of appointments : Some one or ones must be appointed to lead in every department of Christ's kingdom, either in heaven or on earth. To make it a God-appointment, the appointing power must be freed from selfishness and passional bias. Then such appointments should be acquiesced in by all Because some such fail to properly fulfill the call, is no argument against this conclusion. One of Christ's was a failure. The false but popular democratic cry of " *Vox populi*, *Vox Dei*," is at variance with the whole genius, tenor, structure and very existence of Christ's kingdom, which is a Theocracy pure and simple, and every iota of democracy that finds lodgment therein only has a tendency to lower its status and cause it to interblend with the kingdoms and communities of the world, and make it both " common and unclean. " Ours is the antipode of democracy—the one being the government of God, the other of men ; the heads of one being appointed by God above them, the heads of the other by men below them. The one is from above, the other from beneath.

When Christ said to the Pharisees in the temple, " Ye are from beneath, I am from above," He did not mean that they came from some nether world up through a hole in the ground any more than He did that He came down from some supernal world through a hole in the sky. He simply meant to convey to them that they were actuated from the lower regions and impulses, whilst His promptings were from the higher — theirs from beneath, His from above. But they were natural and carnal and could not understand Him. " You have not chosen me, but I have chosen you," said Christ, and so it must remain in solid contrast with all other communities of earth. We are not chosen by the world, but chosen out of the world.

All the external gazing and clatter about this great day of scientific progress which is attempting to make of Christ a myth, and to shun His cross ; and all the twaddle about more elbow room, throwing off priestly shackles, and asserting personal rights and removing necessary restrictions within the kingdom, comes from an overweening conceit and a restless, worldly, animal nature that is ever pleading for more indulgence. It never comes from the truly spiritual side of their being. This, under all circumstances, is ever childlike, simple, unobtrusive, thankful, prayerful, meek, loving, good, forbearing, forgiving, unretaliating, holy, happy and angelic. Who would not choose this state at the expense of fettering and crucifying the world within ?

LITERAL RESURRECTION.

TEXT.—*Now this I say, brethren, that flesh and blood cannot inherit the kingdom of God, neither doth corruption inherit incorruption.*—1 Col. xv, 50.

When such a prominent individual as the Rev. Dr. Talmage can stand up in the latter half of the nineteenth century, before an audience of intellectual men and women in one of our most populous cities, with a display of rhetoric seldom equaled, and advocate the literal resurrection of the animal body, and his ecstatic rhapsodies be received with approval, it would seem that the wheel of progress had rolled back two hundred years in the ages, and that there was little place in the world for the unfoldment of truth. But while the world seems thus floating away on the tide of error, it becomes the duty of all who see it, especially every minister, to do all that is in his power to check its downward course. It is no time for any such one to stand idle. In the case under consideration, there is so much spread-eagleism and that which is merely sensational, together with much sophistry and unsound reasoning and mystery, all covered up by fine drapery, and made so fascinating, that people seem little inclined to go behind the tinsel and outside glitter in quest of truth. For this reason I feel it a duty to review a portion of the Doctor's Easter discourse, at least sufficient to show the sandy foundation on which it rests. I feel some diffidence in doing this because of his many good labors, but this being a matter of *grave* importance, I shrink not from duty.

THE SEED OF REPRODUCTION.

FIRST—He says: " If God had not kept on creating men, the world, fifty times over, would have swung lifeless through the air; not a foot stirring, not a heart beating, a ship without a helmsman, etc." This is a mistake When God created the

25

heavens and the earth and all therein, He left every thing with "seed within itself" and laws for its reproduction, "each to propagate after its kind;" and nothing could be spoken more derogatory to the character of God than to affirm that He created and was still creating all the thieves, murderers, whoremasters and adulterers that now disgrace the planet on which they are permitted to dwell.

THE UNION OF BODY AND SOUL

SECONDLY—"Heathen philosophers," he says, "guessed at the immortality of the soul, but never dreamed that the body would get up and join it," and adds, "this idea is scriptural and beyond reasoning." He afterward says, though it is beyond reason it is "nevertheless reasonable." But, having pronounced it beyond reason, he should have informed his audience by what process of induction, or deduction, he found it to be in accordance with reason But, having thus pronounced it. he gives us the liberty of trying it in that crucible. Law and order are essential attributes of Deity; hence he has not made laws for the purpose of showing us how often and how easily he could violate them. All deviations from the laws of God are the works of man. God is not chargeable with them. There is no regression in Him who is Himself law and that law is eternal and unchangeable. He said of man: "Dust thou art, and to dust shalt thou return," and since then He has not changed His mind. The scriptures, properly understood, are reasonable, but they cannot be saddled with the story which "philosophers had not dreamed of," that the body, after having returned to dust—gone to gases and isolated molecules — would on some certain day, when an angel would blow a big trumpet in the upper air, burst up through holes in the ground, and first call back the molecules and gases, though millions of miles away, to take their respective places and positions in order to re-form the original bodies of babies, boys, girls, women and men; then after their bodies were made by the action of the particles themselves, the air would be filled with spirits flying hither and thither in quest of the bodies they formerly occupied! It is no wonder that this had not entered the dreamy heads of heathen philosophers, and I would very respectfully inform the reverend divine that the Bible nowhere, properly understood, sustains the ludicrous statement.

AS TO BODIES EATEN BY CANNIBALS

THIRDLY—In his remarks regarding bodies eaten by cannibals he simply begs the question by asserting, "There is no proof that the earth part of the human body can ever be absorbed in another body," when there is the same evidence for this that there is for any other substance. Such subterfuges do any thing but honor those who resort to them. The fact is, he saw that if it went to form a part of the cannibal's body there would be no possibility of deciding to which body it belonged in the resurrection, well knowing that God Himself could not make the same particle of matter occupy two points in space at the same time. Thus his whole theory would be spoiled beyond restoration, and the material resurrection of the same bodies become an impossibility But he thinks he found a hole to crawl out at by asking: "Could not God make a substitute for the part absorbed by the cannibal?" That is to say: Could not God make a law and then break it? He then adds: "For the *good* resurrected man would rather not have the part of his body returned which the cannibal had eaten and digested." But he makes no provision for the bad boys and girls eaten by cannibals I presume they have no choice in the matter and are left to fight over it in the great day of the resurrection. But this is just another thing that philosophers had not thought of. Now, if by far the larger portion of all animal bodies is *water*, and especially that of man, then in the great day of resurrection the larger half of all that were ever on the earth's surface will be floating in rain clouds or in rivers, or boiling and tumbling in tidal waves in lakes, seas and oceans; the other half in building up trees, grass, flowers, shrubs, animals and man How are they to be separated and brought back to the first human body of which they formed a part, as they have since formed a part of myriads of other bodies? Again: Has God so far violated His laws as to give thought to matter, to dust, to thus reform itself? Or does the spirit go in search for its matter? and, when found, how can it know its own molecules and gases, when Omnipotence Himself can find no difference in them? Oxygen and hydrogen are the same in both beasts and men. Oxygen is oxygen and hydrogen is hydrogen wherever found— nothing more, nothing less. What avails it, then, if the resurrected body has for its largest half the oxygen and hydrogen that were in a buffalo or bear, seeing there is not an iota of difference between what the bear contained and what the man contained. These are not pictures, but facts.

PHYSICAL CHANGES.

FOURTHLY — He further says: "Objectors say a man's body changes every ten years, so that a man of seventy years old has had seven distinct bodies." This is true, but his conclusion does not follow that such changes of the matter of the body gave him a plurality of heads and also fourteen feet. The fact is indisputable that the body changes from childhood to old age, but it no more gives seven distinct heads than the shedding of leaves and bark of a tree would make of it seven distinct trees. The Doctor cannot be serious. This is only a subtile evasion to support a false theory at the expense of truth.

"PURELY SENSATIONAL."

FIFTHLY — The Doctor informs us that the Bible distinctly states "that it is the body that goes down to the grave that will come up again." I will inform him that the Bible makes no such distinct statement; and further, it makes no statement touching the resurrection but what may be shown to appertain to the resurrection of the spirit without reference to the body. Whereas there are many texts that cannot be tortured into the sense of a resurrected corpse. Witness: "The time is coming and *now is;*" "I am the resurrection and the life;" "Flesh and blood *cannot* inherit the kingdom of God." But if the identical body that is buried is to rise, then we had all better die in youth, so as to have the better body. But just here the speaker seems to be tangled in his own skein, and tosses it off, saying: "Let us get out of this." And suddenly he sails off to the top of the Catskill Mountains, and here gives us a grand panorama of the resurrection scene as follows: " The arrows of light shot from heaven; the mists went skurring up and down like horsemen in wild retreat. The fogs were lifted, and dashed and whirled, when the whole valley became a grand illumination and there were horses of fire, and chariots of fire, and thrones of fire, and flapping of wings, and angels of fire — gradually, without sound of trumpet or roll of wheels, they moved off, and the green valley looked up, " etc. Grand as this is, it is purely sensational, with little sense and little bearings on the subject under consideration.

RESURRECTION OF THE SPIRIT

SIXTHLY — He continues: "Various Scripture accounts say the work of grave-breaking will begin with the blasts of trumpets and shouting." * * "Millions flying toward the tomb, crying, Make way, O grave! Give us back our body!" The Scriptures nowhere give any such account of shouting and trumpets at grave-breaking. He must have known his audience did not spend their Sundays reading them. Christ says: "The hour is coming, and *now is the hour,* when the dead (in sin) shall hear the voice of the Son of God, and they that hear shall live." John, v. 25. This gives the key to unlock the text quoted by the Doctor himself. "They that are in the graves of sin, or are now buried in sin, shall come forth," etc. This is doubtless the true exegesis, as it then conflicts with no other scripture. The Bible nowhere unequivocally says that the material body of any one shall be raised up from the earth and taken into heaven. Such idea is wholly at variance with the whole tenor of the New Testament scriptures when properly and harmoniously understood. The saying of the apostle that it is sown in corruption and raised in incorruption inevitably has reference to *it,* the body, sown in corruption, and *it,* the spirit, raised in incorruption. The expression is similar to Christ's, where he says: "He that would save his life shall lose it," etc., meaning he that will save the carnal life shall lose the spiritual life. And further: If the body sown was corrupt, and the one raised incorrupt, they could not be the same body. Were this not so, then the body would have the preference over the spirit, and what would be done with the corrupt spirit that inherited the corrupt body? When will its time come to be resurrected from its dead estate? Nay, my friends, the immortal spirit is all the part that is a subject of the resurrection. The material form when once put off is no more a part of the man nor woman than any other dead matter, but simply "dust returned to dust," as God has decreed. The body is only a clog to the soul before it is put off, and would be no less so if returned. I here repeat the declaration of the beloved apostle: "Flesh and blood cannot inherit the kingdom of God, neither doth corruption inherit incorruption." From this it is impossible that the corrupt body can inherit incorruption. Besides, the corpse or body that goes to the earthly grave is flesh and blood which cannot inherit the kingdom of God. So, in order to enter the kingdom, the flesh and blood must be removed, the bare bones only remaining to enter the kingdom, which would cut a rather ghastly figure in heaven among saints and archangels.

MATTER AND SPIRIT.

SEVENTHLY — The Doctor further pictures the scene as follows. At the great trumpet's blast "thousands of spirits arise from the fields of Waterloo, Gettysburg, South Mountain Pass, etc.," all hunting up their old bodies! "The whole air full of spirits — spirits flying north, south, east and west. Crash goes the Westminster Abbey, as all the dead Kings, orators and poets get up searching among the rooms — William Wilberforce, the good, Queen Elizabeth, the bad! Crash! go the pyramids, and monarchs of Egypt rise out of the desert Snap! go the iron gates of modern vaults. All kings of the earth, all the great men, all the beggars, all the victors, all the vanquished, all the infants, all the octogenarians. All! All! Not one straggler left behind. All! All! And now the air is darkened with the fragments of bodies that are coming together from the four corners of the earth; lost limbs finding their mates, bone to bone, sinew to sinew, till every bone finds its socket, etc." One can scarcely believe the Doctor to be sincere. He seems to forget, as I have shown, that ninety-nine hundredths of the mortal bodies that have passed from earth, even within the last 6,000 years, have been in their turn grass, tree, animal, man, etc, and are still swinging around the circle of vegetable and animal life, and that, before these amputated limbs and fingers could get wings to fly through and darken the air, the properties to make up these limbs would have to come from the bottom of the ocean and other remote distances, and out of living structures; the oxygen, hydrogen, nitrogen, carbon, electricity and finest molecules of matter must be by affinitive attraction drawn together to form the bone of such arm, such finger, and that, after the bone particles had found their mates, and bone formed, then would flesh and blood, etc., commingle, and attach to it, when the work would be complete To accomplish this, God would have a more impossible work to perform than He had in creating the universe, and a far more inconsistent one; and as all this would be in

VIOLATION OF HIS OWN LAWS

and edicts, it becomes evident that no such thing as physical resurrection of the same body is possible. But the Doctor further says, that God would supply those who died with a limb or an eye lacking, and would also re-form the crooked, lame and humpbacked. This would do away with the necessity of extra limbs being made of their former materials somewhere in the woods, and then setting off on a flying journey in quest of the body to which they were formerly attached. But the further I pursue the subject the more ludicrous, silly and senseless it appears ; and the wonderment is, that any man in this age of the world, with the brain and talent of the Doctor, could be induced to publicly advocate so great an absurdity as that of the material resurrection of the same bodies that had been put off and returned to dust, as he could not help knowing that in order to get the same body that went into the grave he must of necessity get the identical particles that went down, and the very same gases, the same electricity, the same particles of salt, of sulphur, of lime, of iron, and all others that it contained ; and, as before shown, he must have known that the same atoms of matter, or by far the larger half of all the dead, had been incorporated in building other bodies scores of times. He must have known this, and at once seen that the thing would be impossible to the Infinite, let alone the possibility of dead matter searching for dead matter, as though it had thought and understanding. I say he must, with his capacious brain, have known these things, which are indisputable ; and how he could make the utterance of its possibility is beyond my comprehension. Beside, if distinct matter had to be supplied to re-form all the living bodies that have ever existed or may exist on the earth's bosom, it would be a question whether our planet could supply the demand ! I can conceive of many questions that might be propounded on scriptural grounds that may be construed to support the Doctor's position, but none that give him support when properly understood. To name and explain them all would detain you too long. At present I would call your attention to one or two subjects of importance: "And they came and held Him by the feet;" "And while they yet believed not for joy and wondered, He (Christ) said unto them : Have ye here any meat? and they gave Him a piece of broiled fish and an honeycomb." — Luke xxiv, 41–43. This is taken as positive evidence that Christ was there in the resurrected material body,

AS SPIRIT CANNOT EAT MATTER.

This was doubtless done to substantiate their belief, quiet their minds, and make them familiar and conversable. What became of the body, if it did not rise into life? I answer by asking, what became of the body of Moses? If it was necessary to conceal it to prevent idolatry, it was more necessary in the case of Christ's body, and, as stated, His body was flesh and blood, and could not enter God's kingdom. Besides, the Scriptures plainly declare that the same "that descended, ascended." — Eph. iv, 10. We know the body did not come down from heaven, consequently did not ascend. "As they thus spake Jesus himself stood in the midst of them, and saith, Peace be unto you. But they were terrified and affrighted, supposing they had seen a spirit; and He said unto them, Why are ye troubled? Behold my hands, my feet, that it is I, myself; handle me and see; for a spirit hath not flesh and bones as ye see me have. And when He had spoken He showed them His hands and His side."— Luke xxiv, 36–40. "The same day in the evening He appeared in the midst of them when the doors were shut," and so on various occasions. It is argued that

MATTER CANNOT SEE SPIRIT.

But the disciples saw Jesus, therefore it was the natural body they saw. This is sound reason. That matter cannot see spirit is granted, but the person may be spiritually conditioned to see and handle and feel spirit, just as the apostles did the feet of the Saviour. The representation of the side, hands and feet at once got their sympathy and rendered them familiar. For this it was surely and wisely done; but that the stone had to be rolled away from the mouth of the sepulchre to admit the egress of the material body shows clearly that it was a different body that entered while the doors were shut. Hence, it is clear that it was spiritual, and that the disciples were conditioned by spirit influence and power to enable them to see, feel and converse with their Lord. Christ's work was spiritual and His kingdom spiritual. And as spirit cannot become matter, nor matter become spirit, and our work is spiritual, for spirit redemption, we may let the old body alone when once put off, not forgetting by any means the significant, true and weighty words of the Apostle John: "All shall come forth; they that have done good, unto the resurrection of life, and they that have done evil, unto the resurrection of damnation." — John v, 29.

THE JUDGMENT OF SIN.

NO TUTELARY DEITIES

TEXT.—*For the Son of Man shall come in the glory of the Father, with His angels, and then He shall reward every man according to his works* —Matt. xvi, 27.

Before entering on the main subject of my discourse, I will offer, by way of prelude, a few remarks concerning tutelary deities It would seem that some minds of ordinary intelligence have imbibed the idea that there are grades of deities in the spirit world who are sent to this planet as occasion requires, to occupy God's place in certain emergencies, while the Almighty absents Himself; that is to say, when God finds His people too rebellious to be guided by Him, He retires after appointing a tutelary deity to occupy His place for the time being! Such ones cannot see how imperfect counsels can come from Deity, and think in this way to exculpate Him Hence we hear it said that the God of Israel was not the God of the universe, because we now see that some of those counsels were not up with our present standard of perfection, by which rule of judgment, if carried out, we should have a different God for all denominations of people and exclude Deity from our planet! Each denomination, however would claim theirs to be the true God and consider all others substituted, while it is the same God for each and all, operating on their present unfolded conditions It is even so in the smallest animalcule, the lowest savage up to the highest archangel There are some things which are impossible to the Infinite, and one is, He cannot absent Himself from any point in space without losing His infinity Even Mahomet spoke truly when he said· "There is no God but God Will they give to God companion deities?"

The idea is heathenish and came from heathen land There can exist no such beings as tutelary deities in an independent sense. A tutelary is a guardian, and it is unwarrantable to apply the term Deity to such, as Deity signifies the attributes that con-

26

stitute the Supreme Being It is wholly unnecessary, as some have contended, to have recourse to what they term tutelary deities, or God-appointed Gods, to account for erroneous commands, passional display or defective counsels to God's people. These can be accounted for in a much more reasonable way It should be remembered that the infinite God of the universe does not operate retroactively upon any object, spiritual nor material. He does not, as Professor Bush says, "roll up planets like balls [I quote from memory] and toss them from himself as the child does his football." God is not dependent on any thing to make known His will ; He has but one mode of operation. He *evolves, unfolds*, within—speaks within the soul of man. The proof of this rests on the fact that any other mode would involve retroaction and make Him a dependent being. It discovers

NO INCONSISTENCY IN DEITY ;

that what is given with the unfoldment of to-day may be superseded to-morrow; or that what is sinless with the light of to-day may be sinful with the light of to-morrow. If we are faithful to listen to and obey the monitions within, ours will be a perpetual increase in the light and knowledge of God, because He operates on the unfolding of every day, every hour, every minute and every second of our existence, so that in the passing of one moment it may be sinful to repeat what was sinless a moment before In this consists spiritual progression. To-day, if your highest light directs you to engage in generation, it were sinless to obey. If at this instant your light increases, by the unfoldment of God's evoluting power, or by the teaching of His agents, enabling you to see the beauties of the Christ-life of regeneration, that it is a higher, more angelic and more godly condition, your duty then calls you out of the world and former life into the new and superior condition, because now to practice the old would be sinful, bring compunction and God's displeasure. If not, why should the higher light be given ? It is then clear that what may be sinless and right for one person, or a body of persons, to-day, may at the same time be sinful to another person or body of persons, without involving change, vacillation, or any inconsistency in Deity Finite beings only operate externally to, on and with each other. All words or sounds that are, have been, or ever will be conveyed externally on waves of the vibrating atmosphere to human ear, come, came, and will come from finite

agencies of matter in motion. Who ever hears spirit voices or
sees spirit forms must first be spiritually conditioned to enable
them to do so. But spirits do speak by the organs of conditioned
mediums and give us news from beyond the vale. Normally the
minds most unfolded in the body speak the more perfect word to
the less unfolded, while God is within them both. Hence by
God's unfolding the normal mind, and by inspirations from
angels above, He has established His order, by obedience to
which

ALL ARE BROUGHT INTO HARMONY

with Him exactly in proportion as they conform to it. Thus we
see He has law and order in all things—order in the universe,
order in creation, order in the human race—which order is His
judgment seat, and by which tribunal all have to be tried, judged
and condemned, or acquitted. This has been the case in all past
history, from Adam to Noah, to Abraham, to Moses, to John the
Baptist, to Jesus, to Ann Lee, in His second appearing. So that
all the teachings of God's appointed agents, which have been and
are uninfluenced by the selfish animal or passional nature, have
been and are from God, and adapted to the state and unfolded
condition of the race, which to obey in the day and time given is
to obey God and insure present harmony with Him, consequently
present peace and happiness. In the advanced stage of humanity
many things would be defects now that were not defects then,
and many things that now seem perfect and are best for the present conditions may, in the future, be quite imperfect and even
sinful. I repeat that God cannot withdraw from any point in
space at any moment. To say that a man or woman, or a people,
is or are God-forsaken, does not mean that Deity is absent, but
God, for the time being, ceases to strive with those who persist in
disobedience—disregarding the monitions of conscience. It may
be said of such that God has withdrawn or left such ones to reap
the reward of their disobedience. Still "God is present every-
where, beholding the evil and the good."

> "He warms in the sun, refreshes in the breeze,
> Glows in the stars and blossoms in the trees,
> Lives thro' all life, extends thro' all extent,
> Spreads undivided and operates unspent."

Should we deny, as some do, that the God of the universe was
the God of typical Israel, we in the same breath and for the

same reason, deny that He is the God of the Shakers, or that He has been at work in man from Adam to our day, or is at work in His Zion now. On the same grounds He is denied of one, He is denied of all.. If our God is the God of the universe, and Israel's God was not, there could be no agreement between law and gospel—type and antitype, and we should thus limit Him, who is unconditioned as to space, and therefrom omnipresent, and unconditioned as to time, and therefore eternal and unchangeable.

THAT GOD IS OMNIPRESENT

and unchangeable, all philosophers of note affirm. Locke says: "Motion cannot be attributed to God, because He is infinite spirit." But all nations and all peoples, by their greatest minds, unite on one invisible, omnipotent, omnipresent and unchangeable Deity, and, how much soever atheistic infidels strive to doubt, there is a force and power that make them realize the fact that there is a cause of their being and of their intelligence and for the existence of the harmonious universe ; and the power within that forces this confession must be the operation of that inexplicable something that the world calls God. If then we predicate, as we are forced to do, unchangeability of this ever present Deity operating *within*, it becomes impossible for Him to operate directly on objects from *without*. *Without* and *within* are contradictory. This, then, being impossible, it follows that He cannot focalize Himself external to man, ascend a great white throne and occupy a judgment seat, hear evidence for and against and acquit or condemn the human race. Hence the great day of judgment so much spoken of by pulpit orators, at which time the infinite God is to sit as Judge, becomes an impossibility. But "the Son of Man shall come with His angels" for this purpose. Christ Himself gave us the key to unlock the mystery of the judgment when He said to His disciples: "Whosoever sins ye remit, they are remitted unto them ; and whosoever sins ye retain, they are retained." —John xx, 23. This, then, was God's judgment seat, and verifies God's order, before spoken of. It is *now* His judgment seat, for God will not have two judgment seats, and the great judgment day will come to each one "in the twinkling of an eye." It follows from this that Deity alone cannot forgive sin. Why ? Don't be startled. Because He has established an order among finite beings for that purpose, and, being changeless, He will not disestablish it. Hence no souls can be fully and finally forgiven until they have found God's order and come to His judgment there. It becomes a matter of importance, then, to each and all to seek until they find this order, if such order has an existence. But this does not deny

THE PRESENCE OF THE SAME GOD

in all sects and denominations to whom invocations are made and worship is given. But their name is legion who "ask and receive not, because they ask amiss that they may consume it upon their lusts." — James iv, 3. If sin can be forgiven as well and as fully by God without His order as with it, the order would then be useless; but all history shows that God has ever had His order for the time being among men. His final order for full restoration is in Christ, both in His first and second appearing. To this order and seat of judgment all must bow, of angels or men. Here, at this throne of judgment, all mountains sink and valleys rise (the high and low are brought on a level), forming, " as it were, a sea of glass mingled with fire, and them that had gotten the victory over the beast and over his image, and over his mark, and over the number of his name stand on the sea of glass (all on a perfect level), having the harps of God " — Rev xv, 2. This order of God was the sign seen in Heaven by the revelator, when all the high and lofty, the Kings, Queens, lords, ladies and gentlemen, stand on a level with the lowest peasant All such as come to this seat of judgment in time " their sins go beforehand into judgment" and "their sins and iniquities, saith God, will I remember no more." — Heb. x, 17. How merciful is God! But I hear it said: If I cease from disobeying God and of committing sins which I have been guilty of, what good can it do for me to make them known to another? Answer: It is impossible for them to be forgiven until the forgiving power knows what they are God has established the seat of judgment and appointed the Judge, who is the light of the world, to whom the deeds must be brought, and your disturbed harmony can never be restored without doing so. Still, if you so elect, you may cease committing certain sins and carry them concealed in your bosom for years, employ your talents in God's service, be respected and loved, yet to this light they must finally be exposed, or complete salvation will be unattainable God has settled this question The truth of this is based not only on the Scriptures, but on the predicate acknowledged by all of the stability and unchangeability of God, and there is

NO WAY OF EVADING IT

any more than there is of dodging the tomb. Black as are your sins, to this light they must finally be exposed, and, though we cease to commit them, those that remain unconfessed will be leaden weights on the soul; besides, " He that covereth his sins shall not prosper, but whoso confesseth and forsaketh them shall find mercy." (Prov. xxviii, 13.) If covered sin in one individual prevents his prosperity, what will it be to a family or body where there are ten, twenty, fifty or one hundred and fifty out of two hundred that have sins of any kind willfully covered? They may mingle together and come and go and walk and talk and sing and pray and work and play and eat and sleep, but spiritual prosperity for such family is impossible. To prosper such body spiritually is an impossibility with God. But if they confess and forsake they shall find mercy, they shall find prosperity. Now, I defy the whole world of religion, philosophy, reason or logic to disprove the conclusion arrived at on the judgment seat of God, while admitting Deity to be omnipresent and changeless. I do not say it boastingly, but to fasten it as with steel rivets on the mind. Let me still make it plainer. Any sin committed by an individual, secret or otherwise, destroys the harmony between him and God, his maker. Heaven is lost; but a merciful God has established the plan by which this harmony can be restored. If, through weakness or want of watchfulness, a sin should be committed, compunction follows. If God without, in the visible order, be ignorant of the transgression, God within knoweth and reproacheth, and the soul finds no abiding peace until repentance is found and confession is made in God's appointed order — restoration made and satisfaction given to an injured party, if any. When this is done, forgiveness and acceptance are obtained, and the broken harmony is again restored, both in the visible and invisible relation, because they are blended — "their wings touch each other." When the soul has done this, God Himself, and heaven, and angels can require no more. The sin is forgiven.

THESE VISIBLE AGENTS OF GOD,

perfect in one sense, imperfect in another, always teaching as they are taught of God, according to their unfoldment and powers of receptivity, do administer to those below them; thus, what the finite does, the infinite does — simply because it is His operation on their highest unfoldment So it has been, so it is now, and so it ever will be through all time and eternity — men and angels always approximating, but never reaching, the entirety of the infinite; ever having the great God to worship and adore; themselves changing from bad to good, to better, while God remains changeless Thus agent after agent, in all the cycles of time, with greater unfoldment of additional light, will teach as they are taught of God; and thus, instead of having God absent, we do away with independent tutelaries and foreign Christs, and so preserve reason, consistency and truth. It is improper to say God permeates all things as light permeates glass This would imply change and retroaction, which are denied; but He is in all things, "as perfect in a hair as heart." But should it be insisted that God operates from without externally on objects, like men and angels do, by sound or otherwise, this would place Him under necessity. He would then have need of atmospheric air or other medium to convey His word and will, and His infinity would thus be destroyed. Again, if He has the external action and is omnipotent, this would obviate the necessity of any agent or order either with men or angels on earth or in heaven. He would be all-sufficient. But that such external order and agents do exist and have existed — are and have been appointed and commissioned from the earliest history of the world — is proof positive that God does not operate externally, and since He does not, herein lies the absolute necessity of a visible order and seat of judgment, and confirms the declaration that all external operations are those of finite agencies, either spirit or mortal This point then, I think, is proved I am still asked, how are we to know that such and such agents are God-appointed? That is just what cavilers said to Christ — " Is not this Jesus, whose father and mother we know?"—John vi, 42, and "Master, we would have a sign from Thee." But He answered and said: " An evil and adulterous generation seeketh after a sign, and there shall no sign be given it " I would say, let their life and testimony be the sign. If they ask you to vary from the life of Christ, you need not obey; but if they ask you to live the Christ life, and you will do it, you will not want a sign Persons finding the visible order of God, and seeing

His attributes externally manifested by finite agents to them and to the world in a higher degree than they have attained to, who, through pride or any of the lower impulses, refuse to acknowledge, yield to and be led by it, are foolish indeed. This would be trifling away their day, call and opportunity. But still more foolish are those who, having seen, blended with and "tasted of the good things of God and the powers of the world to come" [Heb. vi, 4], revealed to them in and through the visible order, turn their backs upon it because their ideal of perfection is not found in it, constitute themselves judges, and say: "Who is Moses? Are not all God's people holy?"

The same that existed in the type appears in the substance, as some even of authority say of the anointed Lead: "Who are they more than others? Are not others as good as they? Does not the Christ-spirit dwell in and administer to all the good? I do not believe in one worm of the dust bowing before another worm of the dust"—forgetting the gracious words of Mother Ann Lee, who, when some would do her reverence, said: "It is not *me* you love, but God in me." The mere persons of the anointed first Lead neither want nor deserve more reverence than other persons equally good. But God, in His order *visible* must be reverenced, or the *invisible* God will not accept your reverence. So it will be wasted adoration. The Apostle Paul says it is impossible to renew such to repentance, because they have crucified to themselves the Son of God afresh and put Him to open shame. Heb. vi, 6. Such ones, at least, prepare themselves for the earth (earthly nature) to open her mouth and swallow them up, though in tears and mourning, as was done in the type. They seem not to realize the fact that to reject the visible is also to reject the invisible and leave them without hope in this or any other world ! They may look up and strive to see the great God in whom they trust, but this sight is only

RESERVED FOR THE PURE IN HEART,

few as they are, and these can only see Him in the spirit faces and life of His order of appointed agents and people. So, let the "exalted imagination" come down and look for God where He may be seen — where He is pleased to manifest Himself. I repeat again, here is His judgment seat before which all must bow, of angels or men — for it is impossible that a changeless God should establish an order of judgment with exceptions to it.

So, then, it follows that obedience to this order when found is man's only chance for full redemption   I cannot too often repeat that it is impossible for a changeless Infinite Being to focalize and show Himself external to man, only as He is pleased to reveal Himself through the finite.   " They that have seen Me," said Christ, " have seen the Father " — seen the attributes of the Father manifested to them.

By seeing Christ they did not see the Infinite wholeness.   This, Christ Himself never saw, nor ever will see   " No man hath seen God at any time, the only begotten Son, who is in the bosom of the Father, He hath declared Him." — John i, 18. But Christ was His judgment seat; after Him His disciples were — " All that my Father hath given me have I given them ; " next, " The saints shall judge the world " — 1 Cor. i, 2 ; " For behold the Lord cometh in myriads of His saints to execute judgment upon all, and to convince all that are ungodly among them of all their ungodly deeds which they have ungodly committed, and of all their hard speeches which ungodly sinners have spoken " — Jude 14 and 15 ; " and the kingdom and dominion and the greatness of the kingdom under the whole heaven shall be given to the people of the saints of the Most High ; " "and the judgment was set and the books were opened." — Dan. vii, 10 and 27.   Do not now, with Pope, begin to doubt, saying :

> ——— " I know
> The saints must merit God's peculiar care,
> But whom but God can tell us who they are ! "

" Seek and ye shall find ; knock and it shall be opened unto you." — Matt. vii, 7.

" For the time is come that judgment must begin at the house of God, and if it first begin at us, what shall be the end of them that obey not the gospel of God ? " — 1 Peter iv, 17.

Thus have I shown you from sacred writ what the judgment is, and what its purposes are.   I have also shown you that it accords with philosophy, reason, logic and sound sense — have made it plain to the common and uncommon understanding.   I have shown that God cannot forgive your sins without confession, and that to His visible order.   Then, as you value your soul, hesitate not, but come at once to the judgment, that your " sins may be blotted out," and the angel life attained to in this world. Lo, then, let all who hear — let all who read this in any part of the world, of any nation, kindred or tongue — consider them-

27

selves invited to come, with a life insurance in God's kingdom on earth. All that are sick of the world and world of sin, all who desire a higher and better life than the world affords, all who feel that they have a soul to be saved or lost, all, *all* may consider themselves invited. Are you a King, or are you a Queen? Consider yourselves invited. Are you Emperor or Empress, or President, statesman or lawyer, doctor or religionist of any denomination? You are invited. Are you rich, or are you poor? Are you male or female, white, black or yellow? You are invited to come. The gates stand ajar waiting your arrival. Come to a merciful judgment, and it will soon be known whether you are a fit subject for a seat in the kingdom. "Come now, let us reason together," saith the Lord. "Though your sins be as scarlet, they shall be white as snow; though they be red like crimson, they shall be white as wool. If ye be *willing* and *obedient*, ye shall eat the good of the land." — Isa. i, 18, 19. Come now, "consult not with flesh and blood." Are you married? · "Come, let your eyes be made single that your bodies may be full of light, for while it is evil (double), the body is full of darkness." — Luke xii, 34. Are you single? Come, that you may be married to Christ. Are you athirst? Come, partake of the waters of life freely and live. Come, I say again, to God's merciful judgment, for know ye of a certainty that at some time every one of you must be judged for the "deeds done in the body, whether they be good or whether they be evil." "For the Son of Man shall come in the glory of the Father with His angels, and then He will reward every man according to his works." Amen!

INFIDEL MISTAKES.

TEXT. — *For the natural man receiveth not the things of the spirit of God, for they are foolishness to him ; neither can he know them, because they are spiritually discerned.* — [First Cor. ii, 14.

Every honest man will, while commenting on the writings of another, give them a rational construction when it is possible to do so. The Bible, which the Colonel assails with such vehement vituperation and sarcastic epithets, he may find is not so easily demolished as he has supposed. A book which contains ages in a chapter, and a book in a verse, needs the most profound study to be even partially understood. He informs us that this book was made from a jumble of unpunctuated Hebrew consonants. That such a book could be produced of such material speaks much in its praise, and affords much evidence of its original inspiration. We find it to be a book speaking of three worlds — the macrocosm, the microcosm and the spiritual — sometimes of one, sometimes of another, and sometimes of all three in very close connection. We find it also abounding, besides its history, in metaphor, parable, allegory and beautiful tropes and figures of speech much of which the unspiritual mind cannot readily understand. "For the natural mind receiveth not the things of the spirit of God, for they are foolishness to him ; neither can he know them, because they are spiritually discerned." But the Bible, so much ridiculed by skeptics, does not need defense half so much as it needs to be understood, which is almost a hopeless task to the natural and carnal mind. There is no perfect book ; absolute perfection exists nowhere, only in Deity. The Colonel, in portraying the mistakes of Moses, not only mistakes Moses but makes mistakes himself, some of which I shall endeavor to point out to you to-day. While assuring us of his entire sincerity, he exhibits much that is disingenuous. He says : "They say the book is inspired. I do not care whether it is or not. The question is, is it true ? If true, it does not need to be inspired ; nothing needs inspiration but a falsehood or mistake." If this is true, the Colonel needs inspiration badly himself, for we find both in his eloquent diatribes ; but this is mere play upon words. Inspiration makes nothing either true or false, and may itself be either one or the other.   He continues: " The gentleman who wrote the Bible begins by telling us that God made the universe out of nothing. " Right here, according to the Colonel, is where inspiration ought to come in, because the gentleman he speaks of tells us no such thing ; and, as the Colonel says, " a lie will not fit any thing except another lie made for the express purpose, " we must be on the lookout to see where the fittings take place. There is little apology for this mistake, as he has education enough to know that something cannot be made out of nothing. It is disingenuous to make the Book say what it does not.   He also knows that to change or invest with a new character is to create, and this is just what is said in the Book. and no more.

THE TERM NOTHING

was not found there, and was doubtless absent from the thoughts of the sacred penman.   The next thing he proceeds to tell us is " that God divided the darkness from the light, and there may be in immensity some Being whose wing in the universe exists, whose every thought is a glittering star, but I know nothing about Him, not the slightest," thus proving the text to be true ; but, by dividing the light from the darkness, he may come to agree with SPENCER and TYNDALL. The former says we cannot help knowing that such power exists, and the latter admits an inscrutable power behind nature, confirming SPENCER. As the Colonel questions us freely, we shall take with him the same liberty, and ask: Has ordinary matter, such as the accidents of tree, rock, etc., the power of thought ? You will say no.   Then I ask: What is it that thinks ? You may reply, as some do, and say: It is the action of the gray matter of the brain. We know the properties of this gray matter, it is mostly phosphorus and electricity.   I then ask: Did these think before forming the gray matter ? You will say no.   I will then ask, how it came to form this gray matter, since it could not think how to do it ? You can only say, I don't know.   Well, you know there was a cause of its so forming.   Yes, because it is an effect, and there cannot be an effect without a cause.   It follows, then, that this cause was something besides matter.   I ask, then, what was it ?   You may say an inscrutable force in nature. You agree, then, that this force is not matter, for matter itself could not think how to make matter think? Well, yes. Well, then, seeing it is not matter, it must be a distinct substance from matter, and as it is cause underlying all causes, what better name can it have than God? Perhaps none. And as this intelligent force, or God, is also called Spirit, you must agree that it is not only distinct from matter, inscrutable, but all-powerful and unchangeable; hence, we are bound to admit that it is the cause of causes and the power of thought, which power, together with reason, He has delegated to man. Now, as you can know this as well as any one, and cannot escape from it, then "come up to the rack like a man," and agree that it is the Infinite God, the fountain of intelligence to whom His creatures are accountable. This, then, is the God the Bible speaks of, which the Colonel so ignorantly ridicules. But it also speaks of God in the subordinate sense, as that of Moses, Elijah and Christ, whom the Colonel says he hates, but why should he hate poor mortals because they spake from their highest unfolding, or because they were in advance of others and were called God? No good reason can be given why such should be hated, nor for hating the Infinite because He did not give other inspirations. Now, as we have made him know that God exists, we shall undertake to show how much he is mistaken in his warfare upon the little gods. Before too much side-splitting laughter about God dividing the darkness from the light, we should be certain as to which world was meant. All will acknowledge that it is

MIGHTILY MIXED

in the microcosmic world, and in no one part is the mixture more complete than it is in the Colonel's own little microcosm If God can separate it there, the Bible statement will be confirmed — and the "gentleman who saw God dividing the light from the darkness" was not so far wrong as the Colonel imagined But he goes on with false charges, and says: "The gods came down to make love to the daughters of men " This mistake is made to "fit in" with the others. The Colonel read too hastily. It reads: "The sons of God saw the daughters of men; that they were fair, and they took wives of whom they chose " The sons of God were those who were called into the Adamic Gospel The daughters of men were outsiders So their lusts caused them to violate Gospel rules; excluding God's hand in the matter, they went outside and chose wives for themselves. Again he says : " The children of men built a tower to reach the abode of the gods. " It seems the Colonel is at the same folly now, which must end just as disastrously as theirs did, in great confusion of tongues, with all the Infidel tower-builders, of whom the Colonel seems to be master mason. They will fail to understand each other. Won't that be sad ? He also found that " the sun and moon were stopped a whole day to give a certain general more time to kill Amalekites. " It was the general himself that performed this feat. This is a true story. Now, let the Colonel answer me " without looking around for pictures or poetry. " Where were the sun and moon that were addressed by Joshua ? Were they up in the blue sky ? The book says they were on Gibeon and in the valley of Ajalon. He says he read the book for a purpose. Was it for the purpose of warping the language and making it say what it does not ? Is this fair ? If the sun and moon were where the book says they were, why should he place them elsewhere ? What was it that was on Gibeon and in the valley ? Answer: Two great Gentile armies, whose assistance Joshua refused. They obeyed Joshua and stood still in the midst of heaven or happiness for the space of a whole day, to see Joshua discomfit their enemies without their assistance. The Colonel is not to be blamed for his unbelief here, for he is a natural man and cannot yet " receive the things nor workings of the spirit of God. They are yet foolishness to him, " but he will neither be " roasted nor damned for it. " He is now a star of the first magnitude in the infidel constellation, which may yet be (using his own metaphor) " a glittering thought of the Infinite. " It is not objectionable that God first made man male and female and afterward made him or them man and wife. If the first man was made with intellect and reason from the ground on which the animal creation stood, the second was made a spiritual man or " living soul " from the dust of the ground on which the animo-intellectual man stood, for now God " breathed into him the breath of spiritual life and man became a living soul. " This is progress from the animal to the intellectual, and from the intellectual to the spiritual. The Colonel has taken the first degree, but not the second ; that is the reason he " cannot receive the things of the Spirit of God. " He sadly needs the spiritual inbreathing so that he may be made a living soul, and be in the image of God. He facetiously asks us if we " believe in the

rib-story in getting a wife for Adam?" We answer we do, but
do not expect to get the "harp" for this belief. We believe it
because it is every way consistent and rational. The Colonel has
education enough to know that the word Adam may mean the
race or an individual thereof. So while Adam or Adam-kind
slept, God took therefrom a rib, binder or wife for Adam, and
closed up the flesh or flesh relation thereof as daughter, and took
her to Adam for his wife. She coming from the same place that
Adam did, and being made of the same material, she was bone of
his bone, and flesh of his flesh — "the twain were one flesh!"
"Don't you see?" But he further mistakes when he says:
"You will see by reading the second chapter that God tried to
palm off on Adam a beast for a helpmeet." We find no such
proposition hinted at. The Colonel has need to come to the confessional. He says: "I am probably the only man in the United
States who has read the Bible through this year." "Jus' so,'
old Si would say; "I'se jist done readin'

DE ELEMENTS OB EUCLID,

an' I is de only man in de U. S. dat has red 'em thro' dis yeah.
I can see all dem marks an' angles an' pints as well as da can, an'
da all 'mounts to nuffin', caze dese geometrics tells us dat three
angles of a plain triangle is ekal to two, dat is, two is ekal to
three. My son Bob knows better 'an dat. I 'monstrates de
'surdity ob it in dis way: I takes three dollars and lays 'em down
on de points of de triangle, den I takes two dollars an' lays 'em
down on de two angles, and I says, sonny, is dese ekal? 'No,
sah, de three is de most.' 'You's right, sonny; rake 'em off.'
So de 'surdity is 'monstrated." It seems to have been just so
with the Colonel. He read the Bible all through, and thought
he saw all the points and absurdities, and could knock it into
smithereens and satisfy the world that it was one general, pro-
longed hoax and fish story, and unworthy of credence, and he
succeeded just as well as did old Si in solving the problems of
Euclid, and but very little better. He seemed not to realize the
magnitude of the task before him, and that it required far more
labor and study to comprehend it than is required to comprehend
Euclid. He should have known that no man with prepossession
against a book is fit to examine it. Such cannot do it justice.
He goes on in his simple way to say: "God having used up the
nothing in making Adam, he was compelled to take one of his

ribs with which to make him a wife." This has been explained.
I cannot notice all the good points in the Colonel's two discourses
before me, but will say his remarks regarding the census or numbering the children of Israel are correct, and to the point. Right
here the Hebrew consonants must have been misplaced. Will
add further, that the Colonel has said many things good and true,
for which I give him thanks. But he mistakes the hornets when
he says: "Do you believe that God Almighty ever went into
partnership with hornets?" A good deal of his irony will be
moonshine when I-inform him that the hornets had just as many
legs as had our Louisiana Tigers in the late war, and the snakes
the same as the Copperheads. The Colonel himself makes use of
such metaphor when he says: "Slimy snakes of lust and hatred."
Must we consider them to be rattlesnakes? Be consistent, Colonel.
But I pass on. The jugglery spoken of is easily explained. The
rods that were thrown down becoming serpents, were the tortuous
arguments *pro* and *con*. Moses had the best of the argument;
the consequence was, his swallowed the others. So all the Colonel's
"wit and fun fire" are spoiled on this branch of the subject. The
Colonel, I must say, shows much ignorance of Bible language in
the latter half of His discourse. He may say I am not warranted
in thus metaphorizing — but a cunning, crooked argument may
be called a serpent, just as well as the lust he spoke of can be
called slimy snakes. He seems not to be able to think of God
only as some being external to man, perhaps fifty feet high.
While the Infinite always speaks within, He never did nor ever
will speak externally to His creatures. If man speaks God's word
to another it is modified to his highest unfoldment, except it may
be a medium under spirit control using human organs; then it is
the highest unfoldment of such spirit. Part of his discourse, I
am compelled to say, is silly clap-trap, and undeserving the trouble
of reply, as he asks many times why did not God do so and so
and so and so? He may as well have asked why did God not do
every thing as *I* think it should have been done? But again, to
his credit I must say, his head sometimes gets quite level. That
is, when he gets the "light and darkness partially divided." He
is truthful and right in what he says of the atonement doctrine of
one man dying for the sins of another; of the literal blood of
Christ cleansing any soul. He says his reason for attacking the
Book is because it teaches this infamous doctrine, and says, "I
deny it." So do I deny it, and also deny that the Book teaches

any such doctrine when properly understood   In this the clergy preach

WHAT THE BOOK DOES NOT TEACH

The book is right and teaches the very reverse of this.   The way Christ died for the sins of the world was by dying to sin Himself, setting the world an example to follow Him in dying the same death.   It teaches "the soul that sinneth it shall die; every man shall be rewarded according to his works, not his beliefs, but his works: they that have done good shall come forth to the resurrection of life; he that committeth sin is of the devil; be ye doers of the work and not idle hearers of the word," and much more to the same purpose.   It was in bad taste, to say the least, for the Colonel to throw a stone at the Saviour for saying "Depart from Me ye cursed," etc.   Matthew goes on to tell what these fellows on the left hand were guilty of   The Colonel himself would hardly be willing to keep the company of such. See Matt. xxiv, 41.

The Colonel is to be thanked for admitting that all is not literal: and the fact that it was not printed till the year 1448, and suffered by the hands of translators, should make us the more careful to get its true meaning.   The prophet's ravens were doubtless of the species homo as well as Sampson's foxes.   With all its apparent failings the Bible was acknowledged by Daniel Webster, Dr Franklin, and many others of the greatest minds of this or any other age, to be the Book of Books, nowhere equaled in its sublime eloquence, poetry and inspiration; some of it so grand and inspiring it would seem to have been sung out from the rolling spheres   O! nay, Colonel, you need not try to equal it   It must be, especially the New Testament, the pole-star of the world for at least many thousands years   Though I'm becoming tedious, I need not apologize for reading an extract or two from an article just from the pen of the unostentatious, but able founder and leader of the Oneida community, Jno. H Noyes, confirmatory of what I have said.   *   *   *
"From Judea the Bible went forth into the Gentile world and overturned the idolatrous systems of Rome and the whole Roman Empire.   *   *   The breaking up of the central power of heathenism is fairly attributed to it.   *   *   *
It is the very heart of all the free movement that is now going on in this country   *   *   It is now the best friend of

28

the future and truest opponent of the dead past.   *   *
It has proved itself the mightiest enemy of all those systems
and institutions that have abused mankind.   *   *   *
Any who will look at its central doctrine will see that nothing
can satisfy the demand of Bible radicalism short of destroying all
sin and selfishness and the actual establishment of heaven on
earth." — [American Socialist, page 244.] No one can successfully gainsay these truths. But the Colonel, being yet a "natural
man, cannot receive them." He speaks of the children mocking
a gentleman with short hair, and ridicules the idea of God sending two she-bears to stop their clatter. It is an easy thing to be
torn in pieces, while the body is left intact. The tongues of
those two-legged she-bears doubtless did the tearing in pieces of
these saucy children, and who does not know how quickly two
earnest women could settle up with naughty boys? They were
doubtless God-directed. The Colonel says he can neither "injure
nor help God." Now, God is love and goodness in the human
heart; it is each one's part so to speak of the infinite: to help
increase these in any soul is to help God; to decrease them is to
injure God in them, not in His wholeness, but in the individual;
as the good book says, it is

"FIGHTING AGAINST GOD."

So I would say for the Colonel, instead of closing his discourse
with a quotation from Burns, it would have been more to the
purpose to have quoted from Moody and Sankey:

    'The mistakes of my life have been many."

In a subsequent discourse the Colonel has the boldness to say:
"The reason I say the Bible is not written by any God is because
I can write a better book myself." Take up the pen, Colonel. If
true, there's millions in it. The difference between God's and
man's work, I repeat, is this: Whatever is done, man being the
instrument, which is untainted by any of the lower, animal impulses, is the work of God, by the influence of his spirit. But the
contrary is the work of man. So if the penman of the sacred
volume, in any part thereof, was actuated or influenced by any of
the lower animal passions or impulses, this part was man's work.
On the contrary, it was God's.

Christ spake from the operation of God's spirit acting on the
higher consciousness; hence His word was the word of God. A great
many foolish questions may be asked, such as "Why did not God,
the Infinite, give a perfect word through an imperfect unfolding?"

Had he done so, progression would have been at an end. Why did He not make man impeccable? Why did not the Infinite Himself write it? Why did not God create man as perfect as Himself? That is, to inquire why man was created at all? Any creature from the hand of God must be less perfect than Himself; then there is a road of progression open to him All the multitudinous questions asked by the Colonel, why God did not do so and so instead of what He did, exhibit his ignorance of Him and establish the truth of the text that "The natural man receiveth not the things of the spirit of God, because they are foolishness to him." I am compelled, however, to admit that the most of the criticisms of the Chicagoan clergy fell still-born. All their flung javelins only

> "Played durl upon the bone
> And did no more,"

while their antagonist walked off with the belt But all the questions put to these clergymen are answerable; but I must content myself with a few which may answer for the rest. He says. "I want these ministers to say it, and to say it without evasion or any pious construction, whether they believe the Eternal God of the Universe ever upheld the crime of polygamy?" I answer yea. Why? because polygamy was progress in the right direction. It was one step forward from animal promiscuity where the beast with the longest horns took the prey. All those who came into this regulation obeyed God in so doing. When light is insufficient to bind men to one wife, it were better to be bound to three than to be led by unrestrained passion bound to none; but to go back from one wife to three is progress in the wrong direction. One wife was the next step upward, and no wife with a perfect restraint of the animal which was introduced by Christ when the angel life began, was and is the highest So, Colonel, "if thou wouldst be perfect go sell that thou hast and give to the poor, and come take up the cross and follow me." Then we might expect the Colonel, instead of telling what he hated, to tell his audience to "love their enemies, to do good for evil, and when smitten on one cheek to turn the other, to resist not evil, to love and do good to those who hate you and despitefully use you," etc, etc. Then his happiness would be of the angel kind, instead of the animal, with which he now seems content. The same may be said of slavery as of polygamy. No part of the world has yet been freed from it. The United States has many thousands in her jails and penitentiaries, and still more, soldiers who are the most abject slaves, and the white slavery at the North under a cloak of pretended freedom is but little less odious than was the black slavery in the South, and the Colonel himself is a slaveholder if he has a waiting maid to do his bidding, and the only hope of deliverance is that some time in the long ages the whole world may be gathered into grand communities of equal members and equal rights and obligations, natural and spiritual — one the order of nature — lower-floor — one the order of grace — upper-floor — one for generation freed from its common abuses — the other for regeneration to wholly spiritualize and complete the happiness that was barely begun below. But now, any one holding another in any of these phases of slavery who is wholly actuated by philanthropic motives is God-directed. Now I have answered the Colonel on the square without " going off into any rhetoric or fire works." But the Colonel, in his maidenish simplicity, still harps about God outside of his creatures, whom he saddles with all that he now conceives to be wrong, and whom he hates inveterately, when none such exists only in his fancy. But he mounts the tower which he has builded, and dares and

DEFIES ALL THE GODS,

little and big, and tells them to their faces how much he hates them for ordering men to kill the babies of their enemies and old men and women, and saving the maids to satisfy their animal passions. In this he reminds me of a noted darkey when the lightning killed his little daughter. He carried her into his cabin and mourned over her, but got madder and madder at the thunder god, finally threw off his coat, bared his head and walked out into the storm, and looking up at the clouds he told God how cowardly it was to " come down and kill dat little lamb," and added, " You think you done a great thing in doin' dat. Now I dar's you, jis come down and try your han' on old Sam." After waiting a reasonable time, and God didn't come, he went back into his cabin to his lubbin wife, one whom, like the Colonel, he lubbed better than any God, and said : " Kate, I dar'd God, but he wouldn't come ; da all knows da ar' gettin' into business when da tackles old Sam." I presume the Colonel felt himself quite as much of a hero after defying all the gods of the universe, and none came to defend themselves. But this hating either Deity or His instruments for any thing that now seems wrong to us is folly. The Colonel himself, when he speaks from the highest instead of the lower impulse, speaks God's word to him. as imperfect as it is. Should we hate either him or God in consequence of it? Not at all. What is applicable to him is applicable to others. He accuses the Bible of teaching witchcraft, and says that "God made a trade with the devil, and sent evil spirits out of men into pigs, and then drowned the pigs! God got a corner on that" I would inform him that the swinish multitude that were too much of hogs to hear the Saviour into whom the evil spirits entered, on hearing his testimony, fled and ran down the precipice of vice and was drowned in the great sea of humanity. That's the corner that God got in this transaction. If the Colonel would subdue his irony and strive as hard to make people serious as he does to make them laugh, he might do great good in the world, for many fine talents are given him. Equally mistaken is he in regard to Jephtha's daughter, whose vow was to give to the Lord and not to man. His great regret was that she could not have offspring, but had to remain a virgin unto the Lord, and as the book says, "Jephtha did according to his vow, and she knew no man." This is fire enough, and this only was the burnt offering and the sadness of the story all told. So we think well of the man who was true to his vow, and also well of the Lord who accepted the offering. But we cannot follow the Colonel through all his questions, but enough have been answered to satisfy the general demand. He seems to be partially insane on the woman subject. He says· "If there is a pure thing on earth — a picture of infinite purity — it is

A MOTHER WITH A CHILD

in her arms." A baboon would think the identical same thing, and with as good a show of reason. Would he say a harlot, who had conceived and had a child in her arms, was the picture of infinite purity? She is a woman and had her babe by the same process of all others. What can the Colonel say about that? Is that a purifying process or a contaminating one? Come, Colonel, yes or no. Don't run off into pictures of woman's love and beauty. Answer square. Is the harlot's a purifying, angel-like process? "Honor bright," say. Pure and holy or sensual and animal? No grunting; "walk up to the rack and answer on the square." He objects strongly that the Jews considered it impure. But I think the Jews have "a corner on this." Bruin thinks just as highly of it as the Colonel possibly can. He seems to have no more idea that any impurity attends any part of the process of generation than a tom-cat "Yes," he exultingly says, "I think more of a good woman with a child (I presume he hates a virgin) than I do of all the gods I have heard the people tell about." I do not doubt the truth of this assertion, because he is a natural man only, and "receiveth not the things of the Spirit of God"—can see nothing above the animal plane. But we neither blame nor hate him for it; all he needs is a higher unfolding of Spirit with his brilliant intellect. Then he will learn that he himself was "conceived in sin and brought forth in iniquity." He badly needs an Adamic creation, and that God should breathe into his soul the breath of spiritual life, so that he, like Adam, may become a living soul. To this end we pray the Father.

ESSENTIAL POINTS.

FIRST. It is thought by many that we, the Shakers, are but natural co-operative communities, than which there can be no greater mistake. Jesus Christ, the head of the first Shaker community, said : " My kingdom is not of this world." John, xviii, 36. This is Christ's kingdom, therefore it is not of this world ; neither are we one or more of the *communities* of this world — nor are we of the reformers of this world, but are reapers to gather in and harvest the ripened grain, and let the prophet's word be fulfilled. Micah, iv, 2. " The law (spiritual) shall go forth from Zion and rebuke strong nations," etc , while at the same time it is for Zion's inhabitants to watch lest the prophet's further inspirations come upon her " They shall also look upon Zion and say, let her be defiled." Than which nothing could please them better. To avoid this we should not descend from the higher and trail our skirts in the mire of the lower law, nor give our spiritual substance to rudimental man to enable him to better enjoy the generative conditions We should not become common and unclean by blending with them and voting in their assemblies on worldly matters, or their ends will be accomplished and our defilement certain ,Reformers are called to labor in the old earth and heavens, while Zion's inhabitants are called into the new. Theirs natural, ours spiritual. If duty calls us there, it is not to talk of homestead laws, nor how to circumvent the wealthy, and relieve physical oppression, and devise some decent mode of generation, but to gather the lost sheep into Christ's fold.

SECOND. It is also thought by many that mere celibacy or abstinence from sexuality is fulfilling the law of Christ. Such are blind indeed. Many worldings, Catholics and others, have lived

CELIBATE LIVES,

but except they find God's order and there become engrafted into the vine — enter the furnace and become purified by its fire — they will never reflect the image of the refiner, but will still remain

with and be one of the world unsaved Any respectable world-
ling can realize more happiness in the aggregate, by living the
life of external celibacy than the opposite; but *internal* celibacy
is a different thing — for which the proper term is *continence.*
Those who really live continent lives and keep all the lusts of
their lower nature under the control of the higher impulses,
have found a new country — entered into a world of bliss and
enjoy a felicity, of which those who do not are in total ignorance,
and to which they are entire strangers The external may be
lived, while the heart is corrupt. But chastity alone, although
indispensable to the

CHRIST LIFE,

will save no one. Much beside this is requisite. Persons may
thus live and still retain so much of their antagonizing natures,
that half a dozen cannot domicile together in peace; whilst they
may be beset with

" DIVERS LUSTS,"

which wholly disqualify them from being "heirs and joint heirs"
with and of our heavenly parents. At the same time such feel
themselves to be on a higher plane than the world, when the difference between them is this: the latter trim off the outer
branches and cultivate the main stem, while the former cut down
the trunk but permit rank suckers to grow up from the roots,
such as

First.— *Self-will* and self-importance, which sprouts, some say,
are harder to conquer than the main stem.

Second.— *Disobedience* and judging the order before them,
saying. "Shall I blindly submit to an order that is imperfect, be
a machine, and lose my identity and individuality ? What did
God give us reason and judgment and faculties for if we are not
to use them? I can't be a mule for anybody." All such have
need to be informed that

ABSOLUTE PERFECTION

is nowhere only in Deity, and in His kingdom it is for the less
perfect to submit to the more perfect — the less spiritual to the
more spiritual — the less capable to the more capable — all in
childlike simplicity to their appointed lead, otherwise harmony
cannot be had in our Mother's household. They should further
learn that they can be identified as well *in* obedience as *out* of it,
and employ all their faculties, judgment, reason, art, ingenuity

and skill, as fully in doing what some one lays out for them as in what they lay out for themselves — their individuality being left intact, though cemented in the body No excuse whatever for disobedience. It is only the *obedient* that have the right to eat the good of the land.

Third.— *Importunate lust.* Herein we have the paradox of being obedient and disobedient at the same time. We want our own will but dare not assert it, but by incessant importunity it is reluctantly granted, or by pressing demand it may be granted; then, it not working well, as it seldom does, the importuner very innocently says: "I did it in obedience." This is a hateful lust.

Fourth.— *Partial lust.* Whoever does a kind office or gives a present from partial motives to one individual over others equally needy and worthy, and such person receives it in the same partial spirit, who can say they have not gratified their lusts together — their partial lusts? which if continued will work irreparable mischief.

Fifth — *Worldly kin* The lust of holding to worldly kin, or blood kin, within the household, is like Lot's wife looking back to Sodom, it will petrify the soul.

Sixth — *Complaining*, grumbling, taunting, fault-finding, censorious, teasing, revengeful, selfish, unthankful, uncharitable, unforgiving, jealous, gluttonous and many others unsubdued All or any of them habitually indulged in unfit the possessors for the Master's use. What kind of adornment could such be to our Mother's spirit home, even though they had lived strict celibates during their whole earth life? Troublesome and pestiferous here, they would be the same there: hence will doubtless be excluded.

Third. Many come, not comprehending the loss they are under, nor the spiritual conditions which are necessary for a full union with Christ's body, and being full of intellectual and worldly knowledge, suppose they see many defects, and, with good intentions, begin to teach, forgetting that they came to be taught the way to overcome in themselves the lusts of the world with its partialities. Their zeal is commendable — but they should let "patience have her perfect work, and be slow in demanding changes in a system that has stood midst all vicissitudes for more than a hundred years." Though faults it may have, and perhaps many, yet, in

29

OUR FATHER'S AND MOTHER'S KINGDOM

is an awe-inspiring world's wonder; a standing miracle of the age ; persons with soul and body consecrated to God, filled with quiet, unpretending goodness and unselfish love, a divine con-tentment resting on each countenance; an inward peace that nothing can destroy ; an indescribable, ineffable sweetness per-vading them, exhibiting a heaven-born greatness and grandeur, which the world of science can neither comprehend nor imitate. Ah ! why should it be wasted "on the desert air " by seeking worldly association, worldly knowledge or applause, or be spent in a strife to comprehend their mysteries ?

We are, to all intents and purposes, a *theocracy ;* the govern-ment of God, by His appointed order among men. It is there-fore sheerest presumption in any member of this body, to try to assume their prerogative, and to seek for spiritual truth and light, around, independent of, and not in union with this order. For God, having an order, must of necessity work in, through and by that order; if not, then His order becomes a useless excres-cence, and the whole pretension *ab initio* null.

It is wrong to entertain a *feeling* to go counter to the head of God's order; and, to carry such feeling out in word or action, with the knowledge, or even the supposition that it is contrary to the leading gift, it becomes a crime to be confessed and repented of ; because, to admit it to be right in *one* case, we may in one hundred or one thousand, or, as a principle, which would utterly destroy that which we are laboring to uphold; so

THIS IS A LICENSE

that no sub-Minister, nor Elder, nor any member should ever allow themselves to indulge in, for if they do, it will prove fatal to such one's prosperity.

FOURTH. Numbers come to this order who belong to some secret organization, such as Masons, Odd Fellows and others, who feel bound to keep the secrets of that lower floor order hid-den from the order of God. None can succeed to a full resur-rection and oneness in Christ who do so.

In coming up to this higher order, every breast should be, as it were, of glass, so that by this order, and this alone, may be seen every throb of the beating heart, from which no secret should be willfully concealed. To come, as some do, to half ex-pose and half conceal, is trifling with the greatest privilege that is possible to sinning mortals — far better be dumb — cover the whole and withdraw, than to do so   Still I am asked, perhaps for the hundredth time, what good does it do to confess before a mortal?   How is forgiveness thus obtained?   Answer.   First know that you are in the presence of God in His order   Second, that the confessor has been purified by the same mortifying process — the same by which Christ himself was purified when John was the confessor.   It is God operating in the sinner, bringing him to repentance and honesty, and God in the saint, filling him or her with love and charity, when the spirit blending takes place   In no other way can the sins be removed.   God has not two ways to do the same thing   " What is thus remitted on earth is remitted in heaven." John, xx, 23.   We now become a branch of Christ the vine, and receive strength and nourishment from Him.

It was not the Infinite God, outside of His order, who said : " I never knew you; depart from me ye worker of iniquity " Matt vii, 23; also, " There will be weeping when ye see others in the kingdom and yourself thrust out " Luke, xiii, 28.   And remember, " There is nothing covered that shall not be revealed, neither hid that shall not be known " Luke, xii, 2   As it was then, so it is now.   It will be God in His order, on earth or in heaven, who will say to the unfaithful, " I never knew you ; " for you refused to make yourself known, therefore, *depart!*

The unconditional obedience that Christ required in His first, is no less requisite in His second appearing.   The chain runs thus :

1st. He obeyed God.

2d   His vicegerents obeyed him.

3d. Sub-ministers obey them.

4th. Elders obey the ministry.

5th. Officers — deacons and others, obey the ministry and elders.

6th. Members obey the elders and deacons.

7th. Children obey the elders and caretakers.

It is disastrous to break a link in this chain of obedience   No church nor society can prosper under two or more heads, that feel at liberty to act independently of the order before them, even with the very best intentions: A willful independence must result fatally to any who persist in it

It is where *true spirituality* reigns that no one need say to another, " Know ye the Lord," — and it is only the want of this that necessitates external law and arbitrary rule;—precisely in proportion as the former is wanting, the latter must remain in force for protection. If we " first make clean the inside of the platter," the outside will become so as a consequence. It is a very great mistake, and unchristlike, to begin on *externals* as *causes* to produce *spiritual* results. A perfect inward spirituality will make every external thing right, without force, grating, infringing or abrasion; with this, the same harmony would exist in God's kingdom that is in the spheres and rolling worlds. Reasoner or not as I may be, I am compelled to admit that one ounce of *true* spirituality is of more value than a pound of reasoning; because the former is always right, while one missing link in the latter renders the whole worthless. The phases of the world to be left behind are,

1st. Promiscuous, animal man.

2d. The Adamic gospel of marriage.

3d. The Abrahamic and patriarchal.

4th. The Mosaic laws and ritual.

5th. Judges, kings and prophets, until John.

6th. The external Baptism, which brings us to the

7th phase — To Christ and his gospel, which we have received — and which is the highest phase possible to man, translating him from the natural to the spiritual, wherein he gives not only his property, but his soul and body away: To speak of another phase seems simple, because more than this cannot be. This is the maximum of all possibilities either of men or angels. We have no power of thought to enable us to reach a higher, a better, a holier or more advanced or happy condition, than to be *unitized, and " hid with Christ in God ;"* therefore, it were folly to expect some great manifestation among men of something better. Then let us herein perfect ourselves, seeing it is now made possible, and a better is impossible — as herein we may become " as perfect as our Father in heaven is perfect." Thus have the seven thunders uttered their voices. The seven seals are broken, and the seventh vial is being poured out on the world, whereby the existence of wholly spiritual men and women is made possible, and complete salvation and redemption attainable, by living the life and dying the death of our Lord and Saviour Jesus Christ in His first and second appearing.

SPIRITUAL MATERIALIZATION.

On this subject, it seems more need to be said, as many seem to be misled by it. If it be true that spirits can materialize so as to become visible to the normal eye, and then dematerialize at pleasure, as claimed by the lower floorists or denizens of the wonder-world, they are in advance of those on the upper floor. But such is not the fact, both are impossible, as I will proceed to show.

None of the external senses are reliable in abnormal conditions, as persons can be made to see white to be red and black to be white, to hear sounds when none reach the external ear, to taste food when none is present, to feel when no substance of matter is near, etc   It is not strange, however, that the simple are misled. No reason whatever is appealed to to sustain the theory. Its devotees seem to rise on the wings of the wind and by imagination, and a love of the marvelous, and are carried away to the supersensuous and still find no solid resting place.

That there is more than one substance, and not more than two in existence, I think, is self-evident. These are *matter* and *spirit*, and that one of these cannot become the other is also evident, but as others think differently, I propose to offer some reasons on the subject :

First — If there are two distinct substances they cannot be alike in any particular, else they would be but partially distinct — a mixture which would prove them to be the same.

Second — If they are not alike in any particular, they are contradictory. If they are contradictory, it is impossible for them to affiliate, or for one to become the other. Oh, nay; this must be set down among the things which are impossible. Two substances that are in no respect similar are neither interchangeable nor interblendable. The conditioned cannot become the unconditioned; nor the extended the unextended, nor *vice versa*. To admit this would be equal to asserting that a thing could be made to exist, and not exist at the same time, which, with bowed head, I must say is impossible with God. Thus we cannot fail to perceive the impossibility of spirit materialization; but if one can become the other, the one substance theory is proven to be true. Let this be granted, see what follows:

First.....Sumption......... There is but one substance.
          Sub-sumption...... But God is one substance.
          Ergo .... The one substance is God.
Second...Sumption.......... The one substance is matter or nature.
          Sub-sumption...... But God is one substance.
          Ergo .... God is matter or nature.

Hence we have no God but nature, and to nature only are we accountable. Shall we become Atheists?

The foregoing conclusions cannot be avoided admitting the one substance doctrine. And this admission is all that *can* make spirit materialization possible.

LOCKE

reasons thus: "If matter were the external first cogitative being, there would not be one infinite cogitative being, but an infinite number of cogitative beings of limited force and distinct thoughts, independent of each other, etc. But unthinking particles of matter, however put together, can have nothing thereby added to them but a new relation of position, which it is impossible should give thought and knowledge to them." Thus the two substances are proved to exist, which at the same time proves also the impossibility of spirit materialization. What then do we have from the foregoing corollary?

First.....Sumption.......... Matter cannot think.
          Sub-sumption...... But there is a substance that thinks.
          Ergo .... This substance is not matter.
Second...Sumption.......... God is either matter or spirit.
          Sub-sumption...... But God is not matter.
          Ergo .... God is spirit.
Third....Sumption.......... The spirit of man is either of the substance of God or matter.
          Sub-sumption...... But the spirit of man is of God.
          Ergo .... The spirit of man is not matter.

And I think the impossibility for it to become so is proved to a demonstration.

BROTHER PEEBLES

seems to have still a different theory — three substances instead
of one or two. He says: "There are three substances: essential
spirit, spiritual substance and physical matter. These three are
factors that constitute actual being" This theory, though erroneous, is preferable to the one substance. If these three factors constitute all being, they constitute God. But the brother
does not inform us what the spiritual substance is, only that it is
a microcosmal entity. It would seem to be Bearing-Gould's axle
that connects the antinomies of matter and spirit. But this axle
must be either spirit or matter, and hence stand itself in need of
a medium to connect with spirit Brother P. says: "Essential
spirit is as indefinable as it is indestructible, and that the soul is
allied to the over-soul," but as his spirit substance is a microcosmal entity, this would seem to make the over-soul a microcosmal
entity also! a God of matter! Thus the three substance doctrine
seems to defeat itself.

See Prof. Mapes, p. 140.

Then I would say let not the elect be deceived by the weird,
phosphorescent, moonshine ghosts and hob-goblins, manufactured
by spirit tricksters and jugglers in both worlds to make money
and deceive the race. Just take all the money away from this
spirit circus, and it would die in a fortnight. I am asked if I
would not believe were I to see them myself? I answer, not at
all. It would be impossible for me to believe, until I should be
first convinced of the truth of the one substance theory, and that
God and the thinking principle within me were matter and that
I was not possessed of a spirit substance distinct from matter.
Prof. Mapes says the senses are unreliable

In order to make spirit materialization possible its advocates
are driven to the point of denying spirit existence altogether,
hence leaving no spirit to materialize (!) and thus knock out their
own underpinning, they make it only the disappearance and reappearance of matter, as that of water and vapor, and seem too
obtuse to know they have stultified themselves. When we take a
rational view we know matter is unintelligent — we look into
nature and find it not — but continue our mental vision up
"through nature to nature's God." We behold the two sub-

stances in bold relief, and are compelled to exclaim, in spite of every effort at unbelief: "Spirit exists distinct from, and with power over matter."

The highest phase of spirit action from the spirit world in this sphere is that of their using the material organs of living human beings to convey their thoughts to us. This was mercifully bestowed upon believers in every branch of Zion long before their thumping began at Rochester, N. Y. They can never improve on what was given to us. This thing of the

EXUDATION OF MOLECULES

of matter from the pores of a groaning medium, being spiritualized and becoming the spirit form of one's deceased brother, sister, wife or child, is one of the sheerest humbugs and grandest impositions on human credulity with which the gullible can be gulled. It is far worse than the Keeley motor deception, which it is said proposes to run a train of cars across the continent with a half-pint of water! And this latter is more possible than the former. And, strange to say, there are many in the simplicity of their innocent natures that believe in the possibility of both. Every one, or every thousand, who see, hear, feel, taste or smell departed spirits, are abnormal and conditioned for the purpose. No person while in their normal condition ever saw a spirit, or ever will. Spirit seeth spirit — matter seeth matter. We may become abnormal, and be so conditioned by spirit power as to see, hear, converse with, feel and handle them; but on returning to our normal condition they disappear, and we know not whither they have fled. Spirit cannot reflect the sun's rays to the pupil of the normal eye, neither can they speak a word as we speak it, so as to be carried on the atmospheric wave to the drum of the normal ear, only through and by the medium of the organs of a material being which for the moment they can control. This they can do and they frequently avail themselves of this auxiliary. The famous seer,

A. J. DAVIS,

has given the clue to this mystery. When on a certain occasion while he and Swedenborg were walking together, Swedenborg disappeared. On their next meeting, the seer asked Swedenborg why he left him at a certain point? Swedenborg replied, "I did

' not leave you; you left me; your condition changed, and you knew not that I accompanied you home " Some are more easily conditioned than others, not that they are more worthy. Spirits choose those organs that are most easily conditioned Not content with this the highest phase and most reliable spirit action, some, in their great anxiety for the marvelous, visit worldly cabinets in the shades of even, and pay their money to be deceived, and get what they go for. Brother H., in his ecstatic fervor, believes, like the unbelieving Thomas. without putting his finger in the pie, says: "*Thoughtless* people are gazing heavenward with wonder-struck eyes." If he had used the term *thoughtless,* would it not have been more to the point? He hails materialization and scouts materialism, without realizing the fact, that the latter is the parent of the former — anticipates the skeptic's sneer, but thinks any of us would believe our eyes enough to get out of the way of

A MAD BULL

So we would; because we should feel a strong suspicion that he was *matter;* and when matter meets matter the weaker must give way, but we should not get out of the way of a mad ghost It is the ghosts that do all the running and hiding now-a-days They seem to be remarkably careful to keep out of the clutches of skeptics, though they do not always succeed. Brother H., just bring on your ghost; we should be glad to lock horns with him. * ∗ * We seem to be madly floating away at sea. When we return to the *New Testament,* with

CHRIST JESUS AND MOTHER ANN LEE

for our pole-star. Leave the world's reformers to work out their *own* problems, and "*We preach Christ crucified to the world,*" with no dodging around this order, to find a male and female God half as big as the moon, behind and above them, to whom we expect to appeal; then we will again have struck the rock foundation on which we can safely stand and build, and against which all the storms "and gates of hell can never prevail." These we can easily defend against all religionists, dogmatists, scientists, spiritualists, materialists or infidels, with no fears of suffering a single defeat. Thus is my mind freely spoken on these important matters; submitted, however, in the fullest manner, and in every particular to the head of the body.

UNITY OF FAITH.

TEXT.—*And Jesus answered and said unto them : Take heed that no man deceive you.*— Matt. xxiv, 4.

It is not necessary in order to become a member of Christ's body, that every one should have the same identical belief in the meaning of every text of Scripture, such as : Whether the death of Lazarus was a bodily or a spiritual death, and his resurrection from spiritual death to life, or was it a bodily resurrection. Or whether Ananias and Sapphira were struck dead to the animal, or the spiritual life of the body of Christ Or whether other texts should be literally or metaphorically construed Or whether it is in the power of departed spirits to return and construct a temporary body of the escaping dead matter from the body of a medium, as is claimed, and also construct in such body a material diaphragm, trachea, tongue, lips, etc., so as to enable it to convey its thoughts by sound to mortal ear, and at the same time and of the same dead matter weave and make a temporary suit of clothes, of silk, cotton or wool with which to clothe said body. Or whether said spirits can change their spiritual bodies into matter for the time being and weave and make up fitting garments of the surrounding matter wherewith to clothe themselves.(?') Or, whether the individual only has to be spiritually conditioned in order to converse with spirits. I say, these and such like things are measurably unimportant. But, in order to form a successful union with Christ's body and become a living member of the living Vine, it is absolutely necessary that all should receive a baptism into the higher Christ life, with continued obedience to his teachings, both in his first and second appearing, and all be united in this *one faith, one Lord* and *one baptism*, unmixed with any of the elements of the under-world or generative life, even in its highest, most refined and modified form. It is a matter of the utmost astonishment that any one who has been, even but a short time, connected with Christ's body, should for a mo-

ment entertain the false and absurd idea, that "the higher laws
of the natural, pertaining to earth, to generation," etc., "was to
be embodied in Christ's spiritual kingdom," and that any but his
spiritual law was to go forth from Zion to the children of men.
The purity, the oneness of faith in Christ's life and teachings
wholly excludes any such idea   Generation cannot blend with
regeneration, neither can any law but the spiritual go forth from
a spiritual Kingdom, and whosoever would mar this unity of faith
in Christ, or in his order, either in the dread of popery or any
thing else, would inflict an injury in Zion hard to be atoned for
The lack of this unity of faith is, to some extent, already apparent; and to aid in its restoration shall be the burden of this discourse.   Then permit me to ask : Is there any point or example
to which all mankind may look and follow with perfect safety ?
Or is there none ?   I answer there is : It is faith in Christ, both
in his first and second appearing.   First in his order, in his
appointees or vicegerents, in following and obeying them, as they
obey and follow Christ, and whosoever obeys them obeys Christ,
obeys God ; and whosoever rejects them rejects Christ, rejects
God, and fails of salvation.   I ask · Is there perfect safety in
thus believing and thus walking ?   I hear the responsive *Yea*,
because all are saved that do so.   I ask further : Is there perfect
safety in deviating from this and looking elsewhere for light and
truth by which to be guided ?   *Answer.* There is not.   But one
replies : "No one or ones have the key to unlock all truth "
This is true in material things, but not in things spiritual   Christ
and his appointees hold the key to this door ; but one continues :
"I believe with Christ, that in *truth* are hid all wisdom and
knowledge."   But it so happens that Christ never said so, and
this is misleading.   Christ said · *I* am the *way*, the *truth* and the
life, and *no man cometh unto the Father but by me.*" John, xiv, 6,
And also, said the Apostle · "In Christ are hid all the treasures
of wisdom and knowledge, and this I say lest any man should
beguile you with enticing words."   Col. ii, 34.   If this be true.
that the truth, the wisdom and knowledge in Christ are sufficient
for the redemption of the race, it would seem unnecessary to go
a-gleaning in the generative world for materialistic truths which
are unmixable, inapplicable and unnecessary adjuncts to spirit
growth and progression.   It were simple folly and waste of pre-

cious time to do so, as by this course we add nothing to our spiritual light, but turn the sense to unnecessary objects, take it from the real to the perishable and gain nothing by it but division, dissension and disorder. Whenever we go in quest of truths elsewhere, indifferent to God's order, we are apt to eagerly clutch every apparent truth that conflicts with the truths in Christ, especially such as will relieve us of the shackles of self-denial which the truths of Christ have imposed. It is then we begin to think Christ's way is too narrow — his yoke too galling — feel the need of more elbow room, etc. A persistence in this course will finally relieve the soul of all self-denial — when it will feel free. Then such ones will think they have progressed, and many small things that previously brought compunction, now trouble them no more — they have outgrown them, and rejoice that they can now think for themselves, independently of Christ or his order or any one else. But the sadness and truth of the case is, their "Light has become darkness, and how great is their darkness." Many are the souls that have lost their relation to Christ and his people by this line of truth-seeking. But such seem not to know that there are only two roads of progression open to them: The one is *toward* Christ and his perfections, which none of us have yet reached; the other is *from* Christ to the world, with its conceits, its vanities, its freedom from restraint, its pleasures and seeming greatness, and thence into its sins and iniquities. One course or the other is open to all mankind, and happy are those who accept Christ as the way of the truth and the life, and are content to follow him as he is manifested in his order. Some quote Christ's words to justify themselves in not following him, saying: "He that believeth on me, the works that I do shall he do and greater works." This is true, but it only means a more extended work, but not a different kind of work. All who ignore Christ in his first and second appearing and range the universe in quest of new truths leave the substance and grasp at the shadows, while among them all there is no agreement except in one thing, and that is for each and all to think and act for themselves. But Christ says: "*I am the way and the truth,*" etc. "My words they are spirit and they are life," and more of the same sort. When each of these would-be progressionists finds a new truth to suit himself, he soon learns that it suits but few others and harmony becomes an impossibility, and when they cannot agree, what is their freedom worth? Look at the boasted free thinkers the world over, and the spiritualists as well. All is confusion and jargon. A very prominent and good man among them writes: "There is no harmony existing amongst us. The very hells are loose," and so it will be in Zion if their line of truth-seeking should be adopted. But if Christ, as the fountain of spiritual truth, is accepted, and his order as the manifestor of the same, then unity of faith is attainable and prosperity possible. God has not given his order to be ignored without the severest penalties attending. By going on the independent line, the conclusion is easily reached that "Jesus was not the Christ, only an elder brother," and it must have been a foreign angel that entered and controlled him, whom none can see, nor hear nor follow. All this notwithstanding his affirmation, "*I am the Christ.*" I am aware that I am tedious, but the subject is too important to be passed over lightly. Again, I say, the truths of Christ as made known in his order are sufficient for our redemption, or they are not. If they are sufficient for all who enter the fold, I would ask, why addle our brains or vex our spirits in seeking for something to add to this sufficiency? and that of a materialistic nature, which in striving to connect with the spiritual, only makes confusion. For instance — the subject of diet, or the matter that goes into the man's body, these should be discussed from a scientific standpoint, disconnected entirely from the spiritual This is the Christ of it, and very sensible too, for, he says, it "is not that which entereth in the man that defileth him" Matter and spirit are contradictory substances, and 'tis folly in the extreme to try to mix or blend them. The truths of one can be found with a yard-stick and intellectual effort. But the salvatory truths of the other are the gifts of God, and only obtained by obedience to him who is the "light of the world" and to his established order. This, then, is authority for truth, badly as we may hate to acknowledge it. But we are told "The world has progressed since Christ's day," and that "Jesus and Mother Ann are only two stones in the building. The one an elder brother and the other an elder sister." "But they did their duty grandly and faithfully," etc.— did well in their day and time. This apology for Christ and Mother reminds me of a dusky African brother, who, when I was a boy, went, with some white brethren, flat-boating down the rivers to New Orleans and returned home by steamboat. He became so inflated by the world's progress and greatness he concluded to leave us and go to it. As the society had bought him and paid for him, I thought him ungrateful to leave as soon as he got his emancipation papers, so I took him to task and preached Christ to him as well as I could. He listened attentively, but to my surprise replied, saying : "Dat was all well enough in its day; but de worl' knows a heap more now than Christ did den. Why, I tells you, my boy, Jesus Christ nebber saw a steamboat." So after thus flooring me he turned on his heel and majestically walked off. But the poor fellow was after-ward kidnapped, taken south and sold into perpetual slavery. I never learned whether his ideas of Christ underwent any change. Just in keeping with this is all the cant about the ignorance of our gospel parents; their light being insufficient for this day, simply because the world is more intellectually advanced now than it was then. So far the negro was right, and only so far are all others right who produce the same arguments to justify either an amendment to their doctrine and life, or a departure from the narrow path marked out by them and supported by their vice-gerents or successors. When, as has been said, our glorious Bridegroom and Bride — the King and Queen of Zion — are only so and so, even though not intended, it goes to lessen the respect and veneration due to them and their order, and while we are "building story on story" above their heads, let us try to keep on the foundation pillars. Look not to those without on the lower plane for guiding maxims and spiritual truths. We should not forget that ours is a coming down work. It is easy to rise, but very hard to come down and clothe ourselves with the child spirit, without which we cannot enter the kingdom and occupy a "Mansion in our Father's and Mother's house." The lack of veneration for the established order of God is one of the crying evils of the day and shuts out many blessings. The present visible head of Christ's Kingdom on earth. The *Order* is holy and sacred, to be looked to, venerated and obeyed. To criticise or reject it, as before said, is to criticise and reject God who es-tablished it. Christ says: "If a man love me he will keep my words." "I am the vine, ye are the branches." "Ye are my

friends if ye do whatsoever I command you." John, xv, 14
But Matthew, xiii, 11, is quoted: " He that is greatest among
you shall be your servant " This scripture is verily fulfilled to-
day. The head — the order are truly the servants of all. They
are flayed all the day long. Their labors, their sorrows and toils
to serve all Zion, none outside the order can ever realize. Their
whole life is one of toil, of watching and prayer, and few seem
to have mercy on them and pity for them, and still they cheer-
fully serve as servants they are. Their greatest solace is in knowing they have served faithfully and have done their duty But
their heart-bleeding anxiety for Zion's prosperity and the redemption of the race, few seem to know. But, if there *is* a holy
thing on earth, it is this order, by so many unthanked for their
sacrificial lives. Objections are ignorantly raised against the title
of the " Holy Anointed." But it is the holy anointed order of
God, because he established it. To venerate it is to venerate God.
To slight it is to slight the Eternal, because it is the work of his
hands and not the work of man. Before closing, I will say further, the belittling, criticising and unholy handling of this order
is as much of a curse to-day as it was in the type of the unholy
handling of the ark of the covenant, and, here I predict, and you
that are young mark the prediction, that God will never prosper
his Zion as of yore, until she return to her respect, reverence and
obedience to this holy order and the holy laws by them given
forth. The sooner we learn this truth and come to it, the sooner
will God's full blessing return to Zion. How could our sins be
forgiven without it? Go tell them to the howling winds. Go
tell them to the moon and stars Go tell them to the seas, the
oceans, the rivers and running brooks Go tell them to the for-
ests Go and pour them out to a foreign deity in the darkness of
night. Go tell them to the fields and the flowers, the vines and
the wild grass, and mourn and lament, and still they remain un-
moved from the soul. Then in despair call on the rocks and the
mountains to fall upon us, cover us and hide us from him that
sitteth upon the throne. Still they are neither banished nor ob-
literated. At last, in faith, look up and appeal to the order that
God in his infinite goodness, wisdom and mercy hath established.
Then with repentance and confidence on our part the mountains

will be removed, the shackles broken and the spirit set free!
Who, then, would not venerate it? even worship God therein,
not the human vessels, but as Mother Ann said, "God in me,"
God in Christ, God in his order, God in the saints. If we over-
look all these and call to God in the skies, he will be too far off
to hear or answer. But, as before said, if you come into his
order, confess and repent, your sins shall be blotted out to be remembered no more.

REPLY TO AN INFIDEL QUAKERESS.

RESPECTED FRIEND: — You say, "I have read thy book," but you have need to read it again. Your not understanding it compels me, although I regret it, to speak more plainly You should have quoted the parts from which your opinions were drawn. As it is, I will have to follow thee as the hunter would by tracks left in the snow.

The most of your reasons for preferring indefinable infidelity to definable Shakerism are mine for preferring the latter. "It believes in truth wherever found (either natural or spiritual :) It binds no one to follow gods or christs or man or woman. It does not say believe this, that or the other on pain of damnation It does not scorn any innocent pleasure of body or soul: It is true, liberal, generous, considerate and reasonable." All this the book teaches which you have "carefully read" But infidelity itself seems to be "creed-born." It does not allow its adherents to touch the realm spiritual. If they do, they are pronounced fanatics and excluded from the brotherhood! If not so, why is it fighting every thing spiritual the whole world over?

It is not so comprehensive as Shakerism, which embraces both the natural and spiritual, allowing to each its appropriate place. It leaves all to be free, to believe and to do as they may elect, admitting all to be justified before God who act up to their highest light. This also the book teaches. But it cannot change fixed and unalterable law. It cannot cause a particle of matter to occupy two points in space at the same time; but it could do this just as easily as it could cause any one to occupy the generative and regenerative plane at the same time.

Can we be censured for not doing impossible things? It seems because we cannot alter this law, which stands philosophically in the fixedness of things, positively unalterable by any power in heaven or earth, we are to be considered fanatical and "creed-

31

bound." The two planes and orders are as distinct and separate as things can be. They are illustrated in the book by lower and upper floor. One plane for generation, the other for regeneration. Now generation means to procreate as animals do — regeneration means to create anew, that is to take the procreated and make them new creatures: Create in them different, nobler and higher impulses and aspirations, and giving the soul the entire ascendancy over, and control of the creature, which is not the case on the plane below, where the passions control and run riot in spite of internal remonstrance. Who then can consistently blame us for not admitting that generators occupy as high a plane as do the regenerators. Shakerism leaves all free to accept the guidance of any person or body of persons and does not consider them "slaves and fanatics" for the exercise of this freedom. Christ is the Shaker's pattern, but they condemn no one for choosing another or for choosing blind nature. Is infidelity more liberal than this? *It* reaches not above matter, saying "look to nature and not to God the cause of nature. We are here without our consent — let us take all the pleasure and enjoyment that our natures crave." "One world at a time, ladies and gentlemen." "Follow no one, be your own judges, be free, any other course is slavery and fanaticism. You need not trouble yourselves about laying up treasures in heaven where thieves cannot steal, till you get there." "A bird in the hand is worth two in the bush," "enjoy yourselves here, let the future take care of itself, if there is any future — go it while you're young, etc."

This is infidelity "defined." But after all this, it turns preacher, dons the sacerdotal robe and really gives some good advice. "Be kind, be charitable, be generous—help the poor and needy, etc." This the Shakers have been doing the last hundred years and more. It continues: "Why follow Christ when the all-powerful voice of nature demands the union of sex?" "But be careful, don't indulge too much," keep it on the "honor line." This is good lower floor advice; but does the priest himself keep it on the honor line? You ask: "who are Christ and Paul that they should judge for you and me? Is not nature the better guide?" When you tell me what nature is, I will then answer the question. You say: "please do not take me for a sensualist in the exaggerated sense, but let me plead for a pure and temperate

gratification of all innocent pleasures." I would be most happy
indeed if I could avoid considering you to be a sensualist even
moderately—but Shakers claim for themselves the enjoyment of
all pure and innocent pleasures The difference between us
would be in classifying them. The sensualist is one who is devoted to sensual pleasures; you take and advocate this position,
saying: " I go for the present and its possibilities " The restraints
you recommend are only to heighten their enjoyments, not for
any higher or spiritual purpose. So then your happiness is merely
animal, just such as animals enjoy, the acme of which is the association of the sexes, but even this leaves its sting behind. You
are in consequence wholly ignorant of the higher happiness
which the unsensual and spiritual minded enjoy and which is
imperishable

I very freely admit that the union of sex in love-marriage
which you speak of would be irresistible were it eternal. The
nuptial hour---the vows—the priestly ceremony—the thrilling
touch—the feast—the flowers—the music and the dance—the
five senses in bewildering and dazzling blazes, form a perfect
oriflamme, even with the golden spear through the heart. But
from this very hour the blaze diminishes, grows less and less as
beauty fades and trials come, till it flickers and disappears, which
all the kindling-wood brought to the altar fails to renew. We
despairingly stir the coals and the embers again and again, producing some warmth ; but colder, *colder* and COLDER it grows
until nothing is left but cinders and ashes. It is DEAD ! But
the spiritual, regenerative increases, grows brighter and stronger,
time without end. Its life is eternal. Now which ? The true
follower of Christ occupies this higher ground. Am I now
understood ? You ask " Are not body, soul and mind so closely
related that what benefits and pleases one just as surely affects the
other in the same degree ?" I answer, by no means. All philosophers agree that spirit and body are distinct and contradictory
substances. The body loves the excesses that disgust the spirit—
the body has the pleasures, the spirit the pain, the body may be
sick and the spirit well, the body may be burned at the stake and
the spirit rejoice ; all these are undeniable.

If Epicurus meant what his language conveys, I indorse the
most of what you have quoted ; but the difference between us is

this, that while we quiet the passions by subduing them, you subdue them by gratifying them. So you should not have quoted Epicurus to sustain yourself. But you further say : " It is not for Shakers to purify the race by regeneration." How do you know? If purified at all, it must be done either by generation or by regeneration. Generation has been trying its hand " fast and loose " for some thousands of years, and has proved an utter failure. Suppose we now agree to try regeneration; should it fail, then our case will be hopeless. You add : " A few reformed drunk-ards will never make a temperate world." What then ? Will the moderate drinkers do it ? Or, must we depend on the drunk-ards to do it ? You propose to get all the passions " on the honor line " by moderate usage ; but you will find that there is no cure for drunkenness occasioned by the wine of the grape or the wine of fornication, but total abstinence. It is just so of the other passions. No sensualist can be reformed by a moderate sensual-ity. Badly as we may hate it, total abstinence and separation from the companionship of such is the only sure remedy.

Shakerism does not say no marriage and no children ; but says marriage and children for those who desire them. But in order to escape the stigma of sensualism, they must be as orderly at least as are the birds of the forest. I mean no offense, please permit me to be plain : Any contact of the sexes, married or unmarried, for mere pleasure, is sensuality. Who then on the lower plane is clear ? Shakers contend that marriage is not Christian because its founder was not a generator, but a regenerator. The work of the former is below, and is performed in the dark — the work of the latter is above, and is performed in the light. The one is absolutely the work of darkness — the other of light.

Now please do not call us creed-bound because we cannot blend the two into one. This would be as impossible as to blend light and darkness together. Persons coming up, standing and walk-ing in this light, it is impossible for them to do any thing in the dark, for there is no darkness there to do it in. I am wondering now if I am plain enough to be understood. You think and say : " Shakers must marry or come to nothing." But they could not marry without coming to nothing. This has often been predicted by moderate drinkers in the last hundred years. But marriage unshakerizes and unchristianizes all who engage in it. There is nothing to hinder any from marrying who so desire. But there is no element up in the regenerative world of light adapted to it —nothing in harmony with, or congenial to it.

Therefore, as the door is open and the stair-way clear, all such go below of choice, excepting the regenerators. Who can blame them for looking upon such with the eyes of the good apostle, who, in his coarse language, compared them to the "dog returning to his vomit and the sow that was washed to her wallowing in the mire?" I trust you will have charity for this plainness of speech, as it seems I cannot be understood without it, as all I have here said is contained in substance in the book which you say you have carefully read. That the Greek philosophers and Stoics avoided sexual indulgence to promote vigor and bodily health is true, and a strong argument in its favor; and that the idea took visible form in our evoluting world and was taught and lived by the Essenes and others and failed, is no evidence of its not being elevating to its devotees. In all history the virgin state has stood high, if not above every other condition. Witness the virgins who watched in turns by night and day, the sacred fire on the Altar of Vesta. But I need not cite cases, history is replete with them. It is by no means a marvel that Christ took this highest ground, not for the body but the soul. he is the first in our world's history that touched bottom. Leaving the body he comes directly to spirit elevation and says: "Whosoever *looketh* upon a woman (married or unmarried) to lust after her hath committed adultery in heart." Not one before him ever touched this ground. If the thought, motive, look and action are the same in the married as in the unmarried, the sensuality and adultery are the same. So all the efforts on the part of scribblers, to place Jesus on a level or a little lower than "fifteen other crucified saviors" in order to save their lusts, are futile, as none who preceded him ever entered the soul world as did Jesus. His acceptance of all that was good and true before him, which his followers now do, goes to his credit instead of disparagement. You say: "A marriage of one man to one woman seems to be the highest outgrowth of our civilization;" this is true of the generative and rudimental plane. The only advantage man, on this plane, can have over the birds is, he can build a finer nest, that's all. As to his "honor line" being equal to the birds, we dare not affirm. The birds obey the law of nature, but of the species homo, where is the pair on the rolling planet that so govern themselves? It is a shame to say it, but they cannot be found. Oh! would I not be thankful to be able to make one exception! But none are so temperate, none so self-governed. None! no, not one! You ask: Offer your young men and maidens a good home, love and marriage, and how many would refuse them? Of this I cannot say; but I have known fortunes offered and refused. You say: "Knowledge alone has the key to the door that must be opened for the entrance of the goddess of love and purity." By your speaking of the physiological only, you seem to recognize no other. There are two distinct kinds of knowledge, intellectual and spiritual. It is improper to apply physiological knowledge to the spirit — this pertains to the body. The difference between animals and men is this; the former are animo-intellectual — the latter besides the animal, are intellecto-spiritual.

All humans who have no spiritual knowledge are directly on the line of intellectual animals. The infidel who recognizes this has put one foot at least on the round of the spiritual ladder, making further ascension possible. You think I "over do till the good becomes evil." Good cannot become evil. But you go on and say you are so bound up by creed.

Why, sister, we have no creed, unless it be to vie with each other in doing good. But we must have order in the regenerative, as you must in the generative — without order the celestial heavens would become a bedlam; but we are the freest of the free, as all our bonds are self-imposed, bringing a happiness which the world of generators know nothing of: While below, they are fettered and bound by unbreakable chains imposed on them, for which all their pleasures are not *quid pro quo*. Their very souls are paralyzed by the deadening stroke of that "triple bolt, the world, flesh, and devil," to whom life, vigor and true happiness cannot be restored until they "pant for the higher state of righteousness as the hart for the water brook." Then if they will hold up their beseeching hands they will find angels on the stairway to keep them up, saying: Come up hither, and when rescued, the tongues of angels cannot express the joy they will feel at their souls' deliverance.

This is no fiction but a reality now attested by a cloud of witnesses, in whom Christ has appeared for the redemption of the world.

INFIDEL SOPHISTRY REBUKED.

" The fool hath said in his heart there is no God " — Psalm 53, 1

FRIEND · — It seems there were plenty of infidels in the days of the Psalmist, as he complains often and mournfully of being perplexed by the taunted question · "Where is thy God?" I had thought I would not trouble you further, until I saw Underwood's argument, which he used in the Scranton debate Yours and his being so far short of sound reason, and so misleading, I have concluded to briefly notice them You think I have "not made a point for Shaker celibacy." I admit the impossibility of making a favorable point for any who are swallowed up in sexual animalism, as most of the world now are. They are like moles working away under ground, and know nothing of the bright sunshine above them. My first duty to you is not to make a point for celibacy, but to convince you of an immortal part and immortal life; failing in this, I know, so far as you are concerned, all my efforts will be labor lost; but I trust it may save others from being drawn into the maelstrom in which you seem to be engulfed. I think you honest, but lacking in education This is strikingly manifest in your asserting that the thinking being within you is merely a portion of your body, though you afterward contradict this by saying your thinking being was not in a tub-mixture. You say that "thought is the result of certain organic combinations of matter and molecular action." If these molecules were not in the tub-mixture, whence came they? You are very correct in saying the power of thought was not in the tub-mixture of which your body is composed, because in its formation no other matter was added, but there was a thinking power added which was not in the tub of matter. If you had known that it was the uniform testimony of all the great philosophers and deep thinkers that ever lived, that thought was the attribute of spirit, but not of matter, your cool, self-assuring positivity would have yielded to a modest doubt respecting the truth of your position in saying dogmatically, that "thought is merely a movement of the molecules of the brain." Now, remember these atoms were in the tub-mixture — why did they not think then? Did a mere change of position give them the power of thought? Do these molecules move upward to have high thoughts, and downward to have low thoughts, and backward to think wrong, and forward to think right? Further, do the molecules act of themselves, or is there some other power which causes them to think? Were you a logician, I would call you back to a reconsideration of most of your postulates, which are as defective as the one under consideration. Does your intelligence and knowledge increase by the tumbling together of a thimbleful of molecules? Are the little corpuscles or atoms of matter which form the molecules independent in their actions when they take a notion to think? When passion demands and your judgment objects, saying no, on which side are the molecules? Are they both objecting and agreeing, saying, "I will not consent, consented?" Or is there not a judge within to approve or condemn, besides the passions or atoms? What is it that causes compunction? Is it the liver, stomach, lungs or heart, or is it a little phosphorous or electricity? You surely can now see that your position is untenable. You confess this by saying, "It is true mind was not in the tub-mixture." You acknowledge you have a mind. Whence came it? I pass over all your hads and ifs as containing nothing germane to the subject of mind, as you now cannot fail to see the dilemma in which you have placed yourself. You say "If there is an existence superior to man I am ready to believe. If you or any person will give me a single proof of it." I gave you proof *a posteriori*, which is the most sure and correct mode of reasoning, but it seems you did not comprehend it. I will try to make it more clear before I get through. You say, "I am not too proud to be converted." Will you compel me to think you are too dull? You say, "I feel accountable to myself." Which part of you is it that feels accountable to some other part?

What part? Now look at it: Is it not the animal material part that is accountable to the mental or spiritual being within?

Or do the eyes feel accountable to the ears? How must we under stand you, if it is not the outer self that is accountable to the inner self. You cannot help seeing and knowing that matter cannot be accountable to matter, hence you have acknowledged your spiritual being in saying ·you are accountable to yourself. Again, you are mistaken in saying that animals think as we do. The difference is this: The former act without deliberation or reason, being governed by the laws of instinct. All they learn from man is from the external, while man deliberates, reasons and learns almost wholly from within by the operation of the infinite mind on his intellect and higher consciousness; from this source comes his increased intelligence, while animals progress not. The magpie builds her nest now just as the first magpie did. Fixed laws govern all but men, who alone is a progressive creature. You say you want proof. Are these evidences insufficient? But you believe particles of matter think without a particle of proof. Of this, proof is impossible in any direction — *a posteriori* or *a priori*. Still you believe this easily, while you "fight shy" of all evidence going to prove mental, soul or spiritual existence. You should strive to be consistent. Now please stand up while I again give you my proofs of a higher existence than man. Listen attentively, *a priori* reasoning is from cause to effect, while *a posteriori* reasoning is from effect to cause. In either case the judgments must be palpable and indisputable or the reasoning will be vain. Assertion is at no time reason. Yours is incumbered with too many of these. First, let me question you. Will you agree that no effect can equal the cause? Yes. Is man, as we find him, body and mind, an effect? Yes; he did not cause his existence. Then if he did not cause his existence, that cause was greater than man? Yes. Now, is there any thing in the arcanum of nature greater than man? No. Well, then, it logically follows beyond cavil that there is an intelligent cause of his existence above and distinct from nature. I call that cause by the name God; you may call it by what name you please. Still unsatisfied, you ask me, did not man arise out of nature? Answer: His body is of nature; his mind of God. If it did arise, the cause of the rising was God. You can now be seated. Was not the Psalmist right in saying: "The fool sayeth in his heart there is no God?" I now

32

with you stop abruptly, as I wish to show up the sophistry of
Brother Underwood's reasoning. He and Evans, his antagonist,
both seem drifted out to sea without chart or compass. Persons
who both affirm and deny the same thing of a proposition vitiate
their whole line of argument. This is more particularly the case
with Underwood than with his opponent. He starts well by the
enunciation of a Spencerian truth : "All change is due to an absolute self-existent substance, the nature of which is inscrutable."
He could not mean matter, for matter is not inscrutable. He
must have reference to Spencer's and Tyndall's unknowable force
or power behind nature, which we call God.

But he goes on and affirms that "matter and force are not two
separate entities, but are simply two aspects of the same thing."
This postulate violates the canon of logic which demands that
"every proposition which is not self-evident be analyzed and reduced to its simplest elements, and made clear before the syn-
thetic process begins." Both of these gentlemen frequently violate this, with other canons of logic in their arguments, which
render them unreliable. Now if matter and force are only different aspects of the same thing — he must mean matter at rest
and matter in motion — hence we have no use for the term
"force," but herein is involved a contradiction ; for he has told
us that all change in matter was due to an inscrutable substance
in nature which must be different from matter. His adding, "No
force without matter — no matter without force," is, according to
his own definition, simply saying, no matter without matter.
But he blunders along, as one false position requires another false
position to sustain it. Not recognizing mind force, he goes on
to affirm that "intelligence is a form of force." Thus runs his
logic :

First sumption — Force is an aspect of matter.

Second sumption — Intelligence is a form of force.

Ergo — Intelligence is a form of the aspect of matter. Such
logic for a teacher ! But any thing to deny an intelligent power
above nature. Now, Underwood, please stand up till I question
you. First — What kind of matter is force ? Answer — I said
it was an aspect of matter. Well, then, it is an appearance of
matter ; that is, matter and force are two appearances of the same
thing ! Well, then, if matter is rough or smooth, or black or

white, it is different aspects of the same thing. Then intelligence is a form of the same thing. When an otherwise intelligent mind is driven to such a corner in defending the no-God idea one cannot help exclaiming that the Psalmist spoke a high truth when he said : "The fool sayeth in his heart there is no God." Now let us return to the "inscrutable substance" that causes all change in matter. I ask, Is that inscrutable substance intelligent ? Yes. Is the matter which it changes intelligent ? No. Well then that inscrutable substance is not matter. It follows then that nature or matter is subordinate to this changing power which you call cause, and we call God. So then confess that God exists, seeing your arguments establish the fact contrary to what you intended Now it is evident and not to be disputed that this infinite intelligent force operates on the mind and consciousness of man, increasing his knowledge and giving mind power, and this power which fills immensity we most properly call God. This conclusion, it seems to me, is irresistible. Again you say : " Mind is disappearing." How ? It is reappearing much faster than it is disappearing. Please tell me what mind is, as you acknowledge a distinction between it and matter ? Is it conditioned or unconditioned, an extended or unextended substance ? Answer — Well, I hardly know ; to be honest, I cannot tell. Can *you?* Certainly It is the spirit entity that inhabits your clay house. You ask : Can this be demonstrated ? Certainly. Matter we have agreed cannot think. Mind thinks within you, therefore it is a distinct entity from matter. This entity we call spirit. To concede, as we do, that mind is greater than matter, and then say it was the product of nature, would be making the effect greater than the cause, which is impossible ; and as this cannot be, it follows that a greater cause than either nature or man gave mind to him ; as said, this cause we call God. There is no escaping this conclusion. Again, Underwood says, after portraying the evils that are in the world · "Infinite power could remove evil. Infinite goodness would do it, but evil exists ; then there is a lack of either goodness or power, therefore an infinite God cannot exist." Thus he supposes he has proved the non-existence of God to a demonstration. But the sophistry is easily exposed. It is simply saying that if God does not remove or retain what I think should be removed or retained, then there is no God. Ignorant presumption! As though his finite sense of right and wrong, good and evil, should be the rule for the infinite mind of the universe! All evil originates with man, who, in order to progression, is created with free agency. If he could not deviate from the breath of goodness, he could no more progress than a block of wood or stone. If all mankind would so govern themselves as to be moved only by the attribute of goodness, there would be no suffering in any quarter of the globe. Why did he not say at once, if God is good and all-powerful, why did He not make me a perfect and good man? Why did He not make me God, equal in goodness with Himself? And why does He allow me to stump my toe, or cheat my neighbor, or go astray in any thing? If He does not do all this, but leaves me to take care of myself, then " an infinite God cannot exist." Is it not the fool that sayeth in his heart "there is no God?" The Fetish who bows down before the orb of day in worshipful veneration, with his mind extended beyond to the Author and Cause of the luminary, acts with much more sense and wisdom than the learned infidel who denies the existence of such cause. Let it be noted that I am not contending for an anthropomorphic Deity, not for one who would require a hole like the Mammoth Cave for an entrance, nor for the pantheist's personal infinite — a personal infinite is a contradiction — a personal infinity is impossible. The pantheist is as senseless as the atheist, and much more so than the theist who gives a human form to the Deity. He mistakes the shadow for the substance. And while he can easily perceive that his finite mind is distinct from the matter of his body, he is inconsistent and foolish enough to affirm that the shadow is a component part of the infinite mind, when he denies the same of his own mind and body! It is no more the case with the infinite mind than his own shadow is a part of his body; but thus the pantheist lives all his life in a contradiction. Could he look upon all matter as a mere shadow, which it is, when compared with mind, his difficulties would all be removed. For when this fleeting shadow passes from us, and the soul is free, it is not then a world of matter we shall live in, but a world of mind, for matter is no more obstruction to spirit movement than a shadow is to our bodily movement. Then we shall have exchanged the shadow for the substance. Whoever claims that a part of the infinite mind is insensate matter is as insane as the man who would say his nose or great toe was a part of the finite intelligent Ego within him, or that the spittle from his mouth had been a part of his soul which he was now spitting out! If we know, as I contend we do, and as I have demonstrated, that we have a spirit entity or Ego within us, which is distinct from the matter of our body, we may then know that the universal over-soul, or Ego of the universe, the infinite mind is distinct from matter, and by law directs and governs it, as he, by our finite spirit, directs us It is not rational nor sensible to declare that matter is a part of the infinite mind because we cannot see how infinity can be infinity without including the shadow with the substance. I repeat, matter cannot be a part of the infinite mind any more than our fingers and toes can be a part of the finite mind. The two are distinct, matter is ever changing, but the infinite mind is changeless, always existing from everlasting and always perfect It is said by a late writer that the Bible teaches a personal God. It also teaches an infinite God. The personal God is simply a person through and by whom the attributes of Deity are most conspicuously manifested to the world This is " God manifest in the flesh," and it is, then, both safe and our duty to look to this light and obey it, because he will never see the infinite wholeness, neither in time nor eternity. The finite will never comprehend the infinite. Among all who ever walked on the planet, Christ was the person who manifested the greatest fulness of the attributes of Deity — was the first to call him *Father* He was the manifestation of God to the world To him, then, we may safely look, and if the infinite mind has through and by him established an order whereby we may likewise be brought into the same harmony and relation to God that He attained to, then we should look to that order, and blend with it. Any other course is senseless and suicidal.

SHAKER AND CATHOLIC.

The nameless C. has again appeared in the columns of the *Courier Journal* of the 9th inst., and as he says he has come to a stopping place, I would no further intrude only for the purpose of enlightening him. While our hands are in, it might be well to continue long enough to bring Catholicism and Shakerism into juxtaposition, and let the good as well as the bad of each be laid before the world, so that we may profit by the one and be enabled to shun the other. He opens by saying: "The little book must correct Rev. Eads, who pretends that lying is allowable when in the interest of the Church." I affirmed that a certain chapter in their writings had such heading, and when and where it might be done was therein specified. This remains uncontradicted. Instead of denying it, he quotes from a certain little book, not that it is wrong to lie for the benefit of the Church, but simply says: "Cursed is he who teaches it to be lawful to do any wicked thing though it be for the interest of the Church." We must infer from this that there are wicked things which it might be to the interest of the Church to perform. It is evident that the Church does not consider it wicked to lie under certain circumstances, and to swear to it. This is not claimed to be among the things that are wicked. The liberties given in the chapter referred to have never been condemned. We have in Peter Den's and Bishop Kenrick's moral theology this: "What answer ought a confessor to give when questioned concerning the confessional? He ought to answer he does not know it, and if it be necessary, confirm it with an oath." This is in force and practice to-day, as shown in Bishop Kenrick's work, vol. iii, page 172. Again: "A man is brought as a witness, only as a man, and therefore, without injury to conscience, he can swear he does not know these things," etc. So if C.'s little book considers this to be wicked it is in conflict with the Church, past and present.

His next effort is to get Mary out of the God-head by invalidating the testimony of M. Renan, his evidence being that of the editor of a French paper, and he states that Pope Pio Nono sided with the editor, at least enough to praise what he had written. If the Pope had so felt, it was his duty to issue a papal bull of excommunication. It may be said he severed himself from the Church. If he did, and was as wicked as reported by the editor, the papal curses would then have been in order, which are usual on such occasions. I will give a part of the text of one as a sample of all : " By the authority of God Almighty, the Father, Son and Holy Ghost, and the undefiled Virgin Mary, mother and patroness of our Saviour, and of all celestial virtue, angel, archangel, thrones, dominions, powers, cherubim and seraphim, and of all of the apostles and evangelists, of the Holy Innocents, who in the sight of the Holy Lamb are found worthy to sing the new song of the Holy Martyrs and Holy Confessors, and all the Holy Virgins, and of all the Saints, together with the Holy Elect of God may he be damned ! * * * May the Father who creates men curse him ! May the Son who suffered for us curse him ! May the Holy Ghost who is poured out in baptism curse him ! * * * May the Holy Mary, ever virgin and mother of God, curse him ! * * * May he be damned wherever he be, whether in the house or in the alley, in the woods or in the water or in the church ! May he be cursed in living and dying. * * * May he be cursed inwardly and outwardly, in his hair, in his brain, his temples, eyebrows, nostrils, grinders, lips, arms and fingers. May he be damned in his mouth, breast, heart, down to the very stomach * * * etc." How is that for a little madness of God's Vicegerent ? Shakers would not do so. Any one who would thus curse and swear would find himself turned out of the Church. But so far the renegade, M. Renan, has escaped the curse, which is evidence that both Catholic and editor are mistaken. I can but thank Reverend C. for his good wishes that I might with him be one of the God family. I do not doubt his honesty, and he only wants a little more enlightenment and firmness of purpose to follow it independent of Catholic dogma to bring about the desired result, which would be as agreeable to me as pleasing to him, but he seems " joined to his idols," and I fear I will have to " let him alone." I think he could scarcely say Sweet Holy Ghost as pathetically as he says "Sweet Mother," and Renan is right in saying "the forgotten one without lovers or adorers" was eclipsed by a woman. Reverend C. says " where is the lover, be he peasant or prince, who, if he be so favored as to have a sweetheart, does not worship her, aye, adore the sweet picture of that thrice worshiped, thrice adored face?" If one would worship a sweetheart, how much more the sainted mother of God. This I take as an honest confession, and confirms Renan's statement of saint worship in the Church. I'll venture to assert that the little book he speaks of has the following which is included in the layman's oath: "I most firmly assert that the images of Christ, of the mother of God, ever virgin [two lies], and also of other saints ought to be had and retained, and that true honor and veneration [worship] are to be given them." C. reasons thus: If because the Virgin Mary is immaculate, she is, therefore, equal to the Son and member of the God-head. Then Adam and Eve before their fall being immaculate were entitled to the same rank! That is if they were immaculate; but they were not. Reverend C. goes upon the principle that Adam and Eve were the first of the species *homo* on this planet. They were not the first of the species, but they were the first pair. The Catholic idea is different from the Shaker. They believe that God made use of some anæsthetic agent — put the man Adam to sleep and cut out a rib bone, of which he made him a sweetheart; and who can help worshiping a sweetheart, says C.? I presume they went to worshiping each other instead of worshiping God, and, being tempted by their serpentine natures, partook of fruit that was forbidden. But C. would doubtless make the fruit a peach, pear or something of the kind, among the limbs of which a big black snake had coiled himself, who talked down to Eve and gave the fruit. The great-learned Bossuet said, two hundred years ago: "We see already appear in the world the half of our hope — the new Eve. There will presently come the new Adam to accomplish with Mary the chaste and divine generation of the new alliance." I doubt not the learned Doctor's sincerity, but it was a display of learned ignorance. It seems he would have the new Eve come before the new Adam, spoiling the types completely. Not only so, but the new Adam, Mary's Son, to be the Bridegoom to accomplish with his mother a chaste and divine generation! Is this the kind of source we are to look to for light? If so, the "blind lead the blind" sure enough. Not so, Reverend C. Christ Jesus was the new man, the second Adam. The first man was a natural man, the second a Spiritual man. The first the type, the second the antetype. Ann Lee has the honor of being the new woman, the second Eve. She was the very first person to whom the life and testimony of Christ was exhibited to the world; hence was manifested the second appearing, under which the Shakers now live, bearing the same testimony and living the same life that Christ, our exemplar, did. Can Catholics say so much? Mary could not be the antetype of Eve, because she lived and remained under the type dispensation a natural generative woman, just as was her mother, Eve, both alike, while she rose above the generative a spiritual woman. The type natural, the antetype spiritual. Bossuet further says: "No, no; believe not, Christians, that the corruption common to our nature had ever violated the purity of the mother whom God destined for His holy son [that is, according to C., He had destined to be His own mother]; you willingly believe that original sin has not touched Mary." I presume it was Bossuet that opened Pio's eyes on the subject. C. says, "the fact that the blessed virgin complied with the Jewish ordinance of purification is no proof she had any taint." If this is no proof, the baby was. It is truly astonishing how blind people can become in a determination to support a cause to which they are attached, or in defense of a creed; so blind as to assert that a woman is a virgin with her own babe in her arms to give it the lie! Again he says Elder Eads will hardly affirm that our Saviour needed to be purified or regenerated because he submitted to the baptism of John. But this is just what Eads affirms. He was generated once like "His brethren," of course needed regeneration the same. Eads throws overboard that "heavenly mystery" as a spurious interpolation. Jesus was the son of a carpenter, worked at the trade under his father, and stuck by him until he was nearly thirty years old — a good example for boys to follow now. On hearing of God's work by John, he went, and, for the same reason that others did, was baptized, confessing his sins like others did. There can be no doubt but what he was the best of his class, and was, therefore, chosen of God to supersede John in the higher work of regenera-

33

tion. Were he any thing else he could not have been the second Adam and antetype of the first. Reverend C. wishes Elder Eads to explain how it was that Epiphanius should say: "The Virgin stands before all saints on account of the heavenly mystery accomplished in her."

Eads rises to explain. He acknowledges his oversight in the use of the term "first." He should have said Epiphanius was one of the number who at one time threw cold water on the "heavenly mystery." C. is correct in his quotation of St. Epiphanius. But this was an afterthought. I consider him to have been a wire-pulling hypocrite; that he was justly accused of heresy. He was a secret enemy of St. Chrysostom, one of the best men that ever lived, not second to St. Peter himself. Epiphanius doubtless felt the force of his scathing rebukes of the general looseness and worldly pride of the priesthood. Hence he was banished and hounded to death, but his bones were brought back and fairly worshiped. Oh, nay! I have no defense for Epiphanius. C. goes on to say that Adam and Eve were immaculate, while their progenitors were animal men and women. Were they immaculate? It is entirely too late in the day to talk about God being a prestidigitator — of his taking a few ounces of bone matter from the body of a man and making of it a grown woman, when it did not contain enough of the proper material to make a baby's nose. But, then, the Pope says so, and that's enough for Reverend C., whom I would take the liberty to advise to use the brain and power of reason that God has given him and obey the monitions within, as did St. Chrysostom, though excommunication should be the consequence. Of course Christ became immaculate after passing through the order of God in John, but that the boy and youth of the young man Jesus was innocent previous thereto wants proof. The apostle says "He died to sin" — to the sin of his youth. It is impossible for a person to die to a thing or condition to which he had not been alive. And we must all die to these sins as he did before we can become immaculate. But C. adds: "To complete the mystic renewal of the pristine innocence of the race, is the second Eve immaculate?" Thus argues natural reason, and thus the heart, left to its own promptings, wells up in unison toward the new mother of mankind, who is half of earth and half of heaven!" C.'s reasoning would be acceptable were his predicates true; but unfortunately none of them are self-evidently true, or proved to be true. So all his "natural reason" falls to the ground. This new mother who was "half earth and half heaven" had earthly, carnal parents. How then can she who was "conceived in sin and brought forth in iniquity" be any more half heaven than her sisters who had their being precisely as she had hers? Can the Rev. C. explain this? He cannot put the miraculous story into St. Peter's mouth. Neither he nor any of the apostles can fairly be made to indorse it. But as before said, we freely admit that Jesus lived free from sin after He became the Christ; but St. Peter shows plainly that he was not previous to that time. He says: "For as much then as Christ hath suffered for us in the flesh, arm yourselves with the same mind that Christ did, for He (Christ) that hath suffered for us in the flesh hath ceased from sin, that He should no longer live the rest of His time (as He had done part of His time), to the lusts of men, but to the will of God." 1 Pet. iv, 1, 2. None of the apostles, at any time, have stated that Jesus was miraculously begotten, and even the interpolated chapters contradict themselves. Rev. C. tells us that "the Shakers need have no fear that any thing can be brought against them in the long past ages, seeing they have only existed one hundred years." I would be glad if nothing could be said against the Catholics during their first hundred years. But Gibbons tells of their devilment beginning even before the death of the apostle John. They became so worldly proud that they (the popular party) denied their Lord, saying that Jesus was not the Christ, but that the Christ descended from the great pleroma and took possession of Jesus, but forsook him just before his crucifixion, and ascended to sit at the right hand of God. The good aged apostle met this heresy and denounced those who promulgated it as liars. But he passed off, and all those that clung to Matthew's Hebrew gospel rejected the miraculous story and clung to Jesus as the Christ, were driven to the wall; were forced to leave the city of Jerusalem; were literally driven out to a small town called Pella, where they continued some three centuries before they became entirely extinct, which event was the entire downfall of the true Apostolic Church; and — must I say it? — the Beast has had at least partial dominion ever since. This is not denying that there are good men and women in the Catholic church. No one can visit their self-sacrificing sisterhood and charitable institutions and not prize their honest labors for the good of their race, and must bless them for their integrity of purpose in doing what they believe to be right in this the greatest of lower-floor churches. Rev. C. himself, I have no reason to doubt, is an honest man; honestly bound in Catholic fetters and chains from which he is unable to extricate himself. This he shows by his firm adherence to whatever the Pope says, be it intrinsically true or false. Rev. C. is mistaken in saying Ann Lee called herself a divine person any more than any other follower of Christ may be divine. She was simply the first person in whom the life and testimony of Christ appeared. Hence was the Bride, the Lamb's wife — the new Eve — Jesus Christ being the Bridegroom. These are the two pillars on which the Shaker Church now rests, but, having charged the Rev. C.'s church with changing from the Trinity to a quadruple God, it is but fair that I should produce some of my reasons for making the charge. No one can read carefully the history of the church without realizing the fact that it blows hot and cold to suit Conditions, but my charges were not against the fathers but against the present generation. Still there is enough at hand against them to damn a nation. The most senseless wranglings, strifes, contentions, as it were, about nothing; cruel and bloody wars among themselves, even drenching in blood the sepulcher of Christ on account of a little difference of opinion about two natures in him, venting the most relentless fury upon others; racks, tortures, dungeons, fagots and flames, all lie at the door of the Church unatoned for, and even to-day we have evidence of latent fire beneath her smoldering embers. But I am happy to say there has been great improvement upon old conditions.

It was a marvel to me at the time of Pio's council, while he was stealthily getting Mary into the God-head, that even my good and intelligent friend, Bishop Purcell, could not see that Mary could no more be free from taint while her parents were tainted than that Jesus could be free while Mary was tainted. The declaration of the Pope aforesaid, that she was free, did not make her so. Thus, my good reviewing Catholic, the Pope lied, and you are compelled to say you believe the lie, on pain of being counted heretical, if not of being excommunicated. Although the Pope did not issue a papal bull declarative of the fact, still this was equal to such declaration, as she was made immaculate and equal with the Son; and why not, since she was the mother of God? The mother of God certainly has a right to be one of the God-family; and Pio Nino had with his Council as much right to install Mary as the Nicene Council had to install the Son or that of Constantinople had to include the Holy Ghost. But I have evidence from the very hot-bed of the Church corroborating the view I took of the matter. John Ernest Renan, a born Catholic and an able and truthful defender, says in his Relig. Hist and Criticism, page 223: "St. Peter, a fisherman of Galilee, has ruled the world for a thousand years; Mary, an humble woman of Nazareth, has ascended through successive and continually enhancing hyperbole of generations till she has reached the bosom of the Trinity! Nevertheless, we say it boldly, it is never chance that singles out an individual to be idealized" And further, pages 334 and 335. "On what has the meditation of Christian piety, the imagination of enthusiasts, preferred to exercise itself? Is it on the Trinity, on the Holy Spirit, on the controversial dogmas which are received as a sealed formula? No; it is on the little child, *Santa Bambino*, in his manger ⁘ ⁘ It is on Mary. Mary has sufficed to satisfy the craving for love in ten centuries of ascetics; *Mary has entered by full title into the Trinity* (Italics mine.) She far excels that third forgotten person, the Holy Spirit, with neither lovers nor adorers She completes the divine family, for it would have been a marvel if the feminine element, in its triumph, had not succeeded in reaching even the bosom of God, and between the Father and Son introducing the mother." Thus making Mary the wife of God No 1, and the Holy Spirit the wife of God No 2, all in keeping with lower-floor church practices. If the Councils of Nice and Constantinople had only had Pio there to introduce Mary, it would have prevented weeks of squabbling about the sex of the Holy Spirit and whose wife she should be. They had no alternative but to change her to the masculine gender. Now they can give back her gender as God No. 1 is supplied But Renan goes further He says: "By its varied mysteries, and *especially by its worship of the Virgin and the saints*, Catholicism meets that need of outward demonstration and of plastic art which is so strong in the South of Europe" (R. Hist p. 316.)

I would now ask whom should I believe — one without a name who denies the godship of Mary and the worship of saints, or a man of uncommon ability, who publishes a book and gives his name to the world and risks his honor for veracity and truth. On which side does the greatest amount of evidence lie? Who now is the false witness? I plead justification for my declaration on the grounds above stated. Nay, my good Catholic, acknowledge your mistake or give us your name. I can but admire the ingenuity of Pope Pio, even though it detract from his truthfulness. I cannot think it possible that so enlightened and able a writer as Renan, and one so well posted in Catholicism, can be mistaken. He could have no cause to misrepresent any thing he seemed to love so well, and since he is so open and above-board, I am bound to believe he has told us the truth. My reviewer says he "fails to see wherein it concerns the 'lower-floor churches' — the question of two infinite beings." It should have occurred to him that the question was intended only for those who differed from him in not believing that God made the devil, but that he was a self-existence independent of God. Their name is legion who so believe both in and out of his Church. The postulate of my friend that God had created Spirit Angels in the spirit world previous to the formation of this, who turned into devils, and whose Captain, through his wiles (by the assistance of a snake), accomplished the fall of Adam and Eve, stands greatly in need of proof. If the devil and his angels could not have accomplished it without the assistance of a snake three, six or twenty feet long, the whole host of them are not very dangerous. I must, before closing, return my thanks to "Catholic" for his suggestion to consult those two primers and the children's catechism in order to become fully posted in regard to the faith and belief of the Church, so that I may not hereafter be liable to the charge of bearing false witness against my neighbor

RELIGION AND SCIENCE.

The subject to which I wish now to call attention, has been brought to my notice by a late writer, who bases pure religion on a knowledge of the sciences, and, as some seem to swallow it with gusto, I feel it my duty to at least make an effort to disabuse their minds on the subject. Not satisfied with the seven sciences of the ancients, he has given us nearly seven times seven, to be comprehended and unfolded to the senses in order to form in us the basis of pure and abiding religion, thus making true religion impossible to the human race ; for no mortal can master them all so as to have the " combined effect of these unfolded powers, in these grand departments of our being, on which to form the basis to sustain the temple of pure and abiding religion." (!) But none of them, nor all of them combined, can give internal religious light. It was St. Chrysostom who said : " We should study philosophy in order to contemn it." But I do not agree with him, as all truth should be received and revered wherever found. The study of philosophy, logic, etc., enables us to meet those who stand on that ground ; but a life-time is insufficient for any one to master the occult sciences, though his years should outnumber those of Methuselah. The simple one — the physical — so easily handled, still has doubts hanging over it, after the labors of physiologists for thousands of years. So dark and obscure it still is, that none of them have been able to tell us, with any thing like a certainty, what is the office or function of the milt, or spleen in the human body ; and, if so simple a thing is beyond our reach, would not the man be a maniac who would undertake to master them all in one hundred years ? The same may be said of nearly all the divisions and sub-divisions presented to us. It would be better to never have learned our a, b, abs, than to endanger the intellect in such a strife   Yet I would not be understood as undervaluing a literary education. All that is said on this subject may be well enough for the denizens of the underworld, as well as the religions based upon them, as it is all theologica-moral, or a simple belief, without the corresponding works demanded by Christ, who said : " If any man will come after me, let him deny himself," etc. " Seek first the kingdom," not seek first a collegiate education, but " seek first the kingdom," and all necessary things (education included) will be given you. It is unphilosophical to say that the sciences are illustrative of the objective and subjective worlds. In fact, it is a contradiction; because the objective and subjective are not tactual. One is spiritual, the other material ; and just as erroneous is it to use the terms "spiritual " and " intuitional" as synonyms. Spiritual pertains to the soul, touching not matter ; intuitional is human instinct, differing from the animal, in that it may reach the intangible as well as the tangible, while the animal reaches the tangible only. The intellect being a faculty, and not a system, is for objective, and not subjective purposes. It takes cognizance of morality, but not of spirituality or religion, only in an external sense, not in *essentia*. Morality is not religion.

The external law may compel a man to be moral, but it cannot compel him to be religious. Environment and neighborly conditions may induce one to live morally who does not believe in a future life ; but such one must be pronounced a moral man in the absence of every religious feeling. Every word in a discourse should have a distinct signification and application to prevent misunderstanding. Then, what are spirit and intellect? To speak philosophically and truly, the spirit is an entity. The *ego*, the inner and real person ; the subjective *me*, in which the intellect is not seated. The intellect is not an entity but a faculty, seated in the brain of the objective me, which is only a little barque for the spirit to guide on the ocean of life. The intellect perceives by brain power, while the spirit perceives by the unfolding power of God in the soul. The province of the intellect is to judge, to know, invent, look into, and see to the fitting and fitness of material things. The province of the spirit is to scan the motive of the fitting, but not to judge of the material fitness. Thus we see their functions are as different and distinct as things can be, and it is obvious that the one cannot be made to do the work of the other. And any one who does not go behind or beyond the intellect is, to all intents and purposes, a materialist, and knows nothing about pure religion ; for, practical religion is obedience to the

inward monitor, and this inward monitor is not the intellect.
When this speaks, saying: " Think, or think not, on this or that;
speak, or speak not; do, or do not;" then pause, give heed;
listen not to passion, but *obey*.   For it is the voice of the infinite
God in the soul, who " cometh quickly, whose reward is with
him, to give to every man as his works shall be." Rev. 22-12
But I am still asked: " If the intellect does not aid the spirit,
why do you preach ? Or why are books written ?" Answer: All
that ever may, or ever can be spoken or written, to be effective
must meet in harmonious rapport with the inner, spiritual unfolding, or it will pass as so much idle wind   How many millions hear incontrovertible truths who honestly see no necessity
of their application to themselves.   So the light without and the
light within must harmonize, or all preaching is vain   Thus, I
think, the functions of the two are made plain.   If we look within,
the spirit speaks; if we look without, the intellect responds

It is in this way the world strove to get religion, and failed
until the illiterate Jesus, from teachings within, " brought life
and immortality to light, and introduced to the scientific world,
and world at large, the only true, pure and abiding religion that
the world ever saw, or ever will see.   And it is worthy of remark
that he selected not followers from the scientific circles, nor
courted, nor recommended science in any shape, for the simple
reason that the sciences do not contain one iota of spiritual and
pure religion.   The same has been now re-introduced to the
world by an illiterate woman — Ann Lee — and I doubt not but
all Zion would be far better off to-day, being in possession of her
spirit, with the absence of all literary education, than to be master
of all the sciences with her spirit and example ignored.   God did
not choose the learned to give the gospel to the world   But He
" hid these things from the wise and prudent and revealed them
unto babes "   These facts should be enough to satisfy every
inquiring and discerning mind that the "grand departments"
introduced to our notice have nothing at all to do with the " basis
of the temple of pure and undefiled religion."   But I would not
disparage a literary, philological or other intellectual education:
but I again deny that they contain even the germ of pure religion
Pope said: " A little learning is a dangerous thing;" and so is
much learning to the self-conceited and aspiring mind; but no

34

amount, be it little or much, is dangerous to the meek, modest and unobtrusive mind. But as nothing merely intellectual can benefit the spirit, the scientific study of music, poetry, analogy, psychometry, etc., must be ruled out. Had they been absolutely necessary to spirit culture, Christ would not have neglected them, innocent and harmless though they may be; but devotion, revelation, contemplation and prayer, were the constant companions and very essence of His God-serving life. While it is admitted that extreme and constant study in any direction may be injurious, I would say the spiritual was the least dangerous, and I would by no means discourage spiritual study on account of its dangerous tendency. I doubt much if any person ever became a maniac by this study who maintained the Christ-like and child-like spirit. It is only those who are puffed up with self-conceit, and aspire to be something more than mortal, that are in danger of becoming maniacs; but many have had their reason dethroned by undue excitement caused by the pictures given of a world of hell-fire, with devils for firemen, and such like, presented by fanatical pulpiteers and others. All such things should be avoided and discountenanced.

It is to be hoped that none will be afraid to let the mind run on spiritual things. We may do the best we can in this direction and still find it difficult to prevent worldly things from entering in at times and occupying a seat where they should not Hence, says Christ, "Watch ye, therefore, and pray always." Luke, 21, 36. The more we study spiritual things, and put them into practice, the more happy, angelic and useful we will be. The maniac will not touch us while possessing the obedient, child-like spirit of Christ, who said : "Whosoever shall not receive the kingdom of God as a little child, he shall not enter therein." Mark 10, 15. In order to succeed we are required to give to God the "whole mind, might and strength," without reserve, every moment of our existence. All such God will direct, protect and prosper. Such one, or ones, can be relied on and followed with more safety than all the wise-acres of the earth blended together. "But to this man will I look, even to him that is poor and of a contrite spirit, and trembleth at my word." Isa. 66, 2. Even so God has always looked and blest, and ever will. Therefore would I say to all who enter his kingdom on earth, cease to look after, or covet the intellectual and mechanical greatness of the world, which is the apocalyptic beast, whose tail of pictured pleasures has "drawn down the stars of heaven;" and, alas! is yet but too successful. The only safe and sure way for all, is to look to God in the order of His appointing. Any one who rejects the gift of God there, because of a lack of scientific knowledge, will find some day the great mistake he has made, and learn the fact, that " to be carnally minded is death; but to be spiritually minded is life and peace."

Finally: Let me add a last and parting word, and tell, without the charge of egotism, vanity or dogmatism, what we, the followers of Christ know, that others may be benefited by the same. We know that God has set up his kingdom on earth We know that we and all who live the Christ life are in it " We know (don't think us vain), with the Apostle John, that we are of God and the whole world lieth in wickedness." 1 Jno 5 : 19. We know this, because we have consecrated soul and body to His service, and are not moved by any selfish purpose. The unselfish is of God — the selfish is of man. We know the world is *diseased* and " full of wounds, and bruises, and putrefying sores from its crown to the soles of its feet." We know there is a place where all can be healed and purified, and this is within God's kingdom ; and so we say : " Ho! every one that thirsteth come." But come not for a *material*, but for a *spiritual* union and joining with the body of Christ ; for those who have only a *material* joining are in danger of falling away every day that this condition continues There is no real safety for any soul, until such become quickened into spiritual life. One more word, I say it humbly, and I am done. In order to have God's blessing rest upon us, all must respect and give heed to His Order ; for God, though of long forbearance, will not be trifled with. No branch, division or family can prosper and have His blessing, whose leaders possess not the child-spirit of perfect dependence upon it, and keep a close union and connection with it. The taking our own judgment independently thereof, or concealing from it in any way, presages decadence and makes prosperity impossible. " By humility and the fear of the Lord are riches and honor and life." Prov. 22 . 4. This being true makes the contrary — poverty, dishonor and death.

TWO POEMS.

[These poems, added to the second edition, are in time, always — these same questions and answers ever coming up — and more particularly now, because they give to the reader the first literary efforts of the author. They were first presented as being written by his good mother — who was a clean, dutiful and beautifull Shakeress — and the two last lines lead to this thinking; but our author wrote the same; and now, forty-eight years after, we spoil the *novel* and give the *real* — H. L. Eads — as the author. Young men, take notice — " go thou and do likewise — and remember you always had and ever will have a beautiful, sympathetic friend, in him who wrote the foregoing pages. — EDITOR.]

Lines,

Suggested by a Visit to the Shakers, near Albany.

BY CHARLOTTE CUSHMAN.

1.

Mysterious worshippers !
Are ye indeed the things ye seem to be,
Of earth, yet of its iron influence free;
    From all that stirs
Our being's pulse, and gives to fleeting life
What well the Hun hath termed, " the rapture of the strife ? "

2.

Are the gay visions gone —
Those day dreams of the mind, by fate there flung,
And the fair hopes to which the soul once clung,
    And battled on ?
Have ye outlived them ? All that must have sprung
And quickened into life when ye were young ?

3.

Does memory never roam
To ties, that grown with years, ye idly sever,
To the old haunts, that ye have left forever —
    Your early homes,
Your ancient creed, once faith's sustaining lever,
The loved, who erst prayed with you — now may never ?

4.

Has not ambition's pæan,
Some power within your hearts to wake anew
To deeds of higher emprise — worthier you
    Ye monkish men —
Than may be reaped from fields ? — do ye not rue
The drone-like course of life ye now pursue ?

5

The camp, the council, all
That woos the soldier to the field of fame --
That gives the sage his meed — the bard his name,
    And coronal —
Bidding a people's voice their praise proclaim —
Can ye forego the strife nor own your shame ?

6

Have ye forgot your youth,
When expectations soared on pinions high,
And hope shone out in boyhood's cloudless sky,
    Seeming all truth —
When all looked fair to fancy's ardent eye,
And pleasure wore an air of sorcery ?

7.

You, too ' what early blight
Has withered your fond hopes, that ye thus stand,
A group of sisters 'mong this monkish band ?
    Ye creatures bright ' ' (?)
Has sorrow scored your brows with demon hand,
And o'er your hopes passed treachery's burning brand ?

8

Ye would have graced right well
The bridal scene, — the banquet or the bowers,
Where mirth and revelry usurp the hours --
    Where, like a spell,
Beauty is sovereign, where man owns its powers,
And woman's tread is o'er a path of flowers

9.

Yet seem ye not as those
Within whose bosoms memory's vigils keep,
Beneath your drooping lids no passions sleep,
    And your pale brows
Bear not the tracery of emotions deep —
Ye seem too cold and passionless to weep '

Answer : —

To Lines by Charlotte Cushman.

We are "indeed the things we seem to be,
Of earth, and from its iron influence free ;"
For we are they, or halt, or lame, or dumb,
" On whom the ends of this vain world are come."
We have outlived those day-dreams of the mind
Those flattering phantoms, which so many bind.
All man-made creeds ("your faith's sustaining lever,")
We have forsaken, and have left forever !
To plainly tell the truth, we do not rue,
The sober, godly course that we pursue ;
But 'tis not we who live the dronish lives,
But those who have their husbands or their wives !
But if by drones you mean, they 're lazy men —
Charlotte Cushman, take it back again ;
For one with half an eye, or half a mind,
Can there see industry and wealth combined.
Your visit must have been exceeding short,
Or else your brain is of the shallow sort.
If camps and councils — soldiers, "fields of fame,"
Or yet, a people's praise or a people's blame,
Is all that gives the sage or bard his name —
We can " forego the strife, nor own our shame."
What great temptations you hold up to view
For men of sense or reason to pursue !
The praise of mortals ! — what can it avail,
When all their boasted language has to fail ? .
" And sorrow has not scored with demon hand,
Nor o'er our hopes passed Treachery's burning brand ; "
But where the sorrows and where treachery are,
I think may easily be made appear :
In " bridal scenes," in "banquets and in bowers" ! —
'Mid revelry and variegated flowers,
Is where our mother Eve first felt their powers.
The "bridal scene," you say, we'd " grace right well " ! !
" Lang syne " there our first parents blindly fell ! —
The bridal scene ! — Is this your end or aim ? "
And can you this pursue "nor own your shame ? "
If so, *weak*, pithy, superficial thing,
Drink, silent drink, the sick Hymenial spring.
The bridal scene ! the banquet or the bowers,
Or " woman's [bed of thorns, or] path of flowers,"
Can't all persuade our souls to turn aside

To live in filthy lust or cruel pride
Alas ! Your path of flowers will disappear,
Even now a thousand thorns are pointing near ,
Ah, here you find base " treachery's burning brand,"
And sorrows score the heart, nor spare the hand
But here " Beauty 's sovereign," so say you,
A thing that in one hour may lose its hue,
It lies upon the surface of the skin —
Aye, Beauty's self was never worth a pin ,
But still it suits the superficial mind —
The slight observer of the human kind ,
The airy, fleety, vain, and hollow thing,
That only feeds on wily flattering
" Man owns its powers ? '— and what will man *not* own
To gain his end, to captivate, dethrone ?
The truth is this, whatever he may feign,
You'll find your greatest loss his greatest gain ,
For like the bee he will improve the hour,
And all day long he 'll buzz from flower to flower,
And when he sips the sweetness all away,
For aught he cares the flowers may all decay
But here each other's virtues we partake,
Where men and women all those ills forsake ,
True virtue spreads her bright Angelic wing,
While saints and seraphs praise the Almighty King
And when the matter 's rightly understood,
You 'll find we labor for each other s good ,
And this, Charlotte Cushman, is our aim,
" Can you forego this strife, nor own your shame ? '
Now if you would receive a modest hint,
You'd keep your *name*, at least, from public print —
Nor have it hoisted, handled round and round,
And echoed o'er the earth from mound to mound —
As the great advocate of (O, the name !)
Now can you think of this, nor " own your shame ? "
But Charlotte, learn to take a deeper view
Of what your neighbors say, or neighbors do
And when some flattering knaves around you tread
Just think of what a SHAKER GIRL has said